21世纪信息传播专业英语系列教材

ENGLISH FOR EDUCATIONAL TECHNOLOGY

# 教育技术学专业英语

吴军其 严 莉 /主 编
熊桂枝 李 莎 刘玉梅 庄文杰 /副主编

图书在版编目(CIP)数据

教育技术学专业英语/吴军其,严莉主编.—北京:北京大学出版社,2009.11
(21世纪信息传播专业英语系列教材)
ISBN 978-7-301-15852-4

Ⅰ.教… Ⅱ.①吴… ②严… Ⅲ.教育技术学-英语-高等学校-教材 Ⅳ.H31

中国版本图书馆 CIP 数据核字(2009)第167714号

| | |
|---|---|
| 书　　　　名 | 教育技术学专业英语 |
| 著作责任者 | 吴军其　严　莉　主编 |
| 丛 书 策 划 | 周志刚 |
| 责 任 编 辑 | 周志刚 |
| 标 准 书 号 | ISBN 978-7-301-15852-4/G·2676 |
| 出 版 发 行 | 北京大学出版社 |
| 地　　　　址 | 北京市海淀区成府路205号　100871 |
| 网　　　　址 | http://www.jycb.org　http://www.pup.cn |
| 电　　　　话 | 邮购部 62752015　发行部 62750672　编辑部 62767346　出版部 62754962 |
| 电 子 邮 箱 | zly@pup.pku.edu.cn |
| 印 刷 者 | 涿州市星河印刷有限公司 |
| 经 销 者 | 新华书店 |
| | 787毫米×1092毫米　16 开　18.75 印张　427 千字 |
| | 2009年11月第1版　2021年1月第5次印刷 |
| 定　　　　价 | 45.00 元 |

未经许可,不得以任何方式复制或抄袭本书之部分或全部内容。
版权所有,侵权必究
举报电话:010-62752024　电子邮箱:fd@pup.pku.edu.cn

# 内 容 简 介

　　本书的主要目的是使学生掌握教育技术学专业英语术语及用法，培养和提高学生阅读和翻译专业英语文献资料以及用英语进行学术交流的能力。全书包括专业英语基础篇与应用篇两部分，其中基础篇由 20 个单元组成，涵盖教育技术领域的主要分支和实践领域，主要内容包括：教育技术学、教育技术学的历史和理论基础、传播理论、系统理论、信息与传播技术、教学系统设计、开发学习资源、远程教育、教学评价等内容，都是精选国外的经典文献。每个单元由知识目标、专业词汇、2～4 篇课文、新单词、课文注释、其中一篇课文的参考翻译及练习这七个部分组成。同时为了方便教学，应用篇系统地介绍了科技论文的结构、写作与投稿等问题，归纳了中国学生撰写英文科技论文中常见的错误，最后总结了常用应用文写作的要求与规范，并给出了一些实际的范例。

　　本书可作为教育技术学专业本科生和研究生的专业英语、文献研究、双语课程的教材，也可供从事相关专业的人员参考使用。

# 前　　言

教育技术学的飞速发展正在影响着教育的各个领域，并成为教育深化改革的突破口和制高点，它与素质教育、教育信息化、教育创新、创新人才培养、促进终身学习体系的建立等重大问题紧密相关，因此，从业人员必须通过不断学习专业英语，来迅速掌握教育技术学的新理论知识与新技术。为进一步提高教育技术学本科生和研究生的专业英语能力，促进人才的高层次培养，我们撰写了这本教材。选材的原则如下：

（1）语言的规范性与纯正性。本书中的课文选自国外的经典文献，包括国际权威网站和经典论文。

（2）专业知识的广泛性与先进性。选材综合选取了信息与传播技术、教学系统设计、开发学习资源、在线学习、远程教育、教学评价等内容，使读者在学习科技英语的同时也了解教育技术学的最新发展动态。

（3）专业知识的全面性。本书不仅重点强调了科技文献的"读"，也对"写"与口头表达作了尝试，同时还系统地阐述了科技论文的写作、投稿与应用文写作。

（4）专业知识的扩展性。教育技术学是一门知识更新极快的专业，因此学生必须了解本专业的最权威期刊，掌握科技文献的查阅方法。

此外，本书还针对同类型教材的不足，结合作者多年来的实际工作经验与学术交流的体会，补充了Internet上常用的教育技术文献资源。

学生学习本书后，能熟悉和掌握大量教育技术学专业英语的常用词汇和术语，提高阅读和理解原始的专业英语文献的能力，了解本专业里的一些新的理论知识与技术，从而增强国际交流能力。

由于经验不足，加之作者水平有限，书中的疏漏之处在所难免，敬请读者批评指正，以便进一步改进和充实我们的工作。

编者
2009年8月

# 目 录

**Part 1　The Outline of Educational Technology** ……… (1)
　Unit 1　The Basic Concepts of Educational Technology ……… (1)
　　Text A　What is Educational Technology? ……… (2)
　　Text B　Perspectives and Meaning of Educational Technology ……… (2)
　　Text C　Research Methods of Educational Technology ……… (4)
　　专业英语简介 ……… (9)
　Unit 2　The History of Educational Technology ……… (11)
　　Text A　History of Educational Technology ……… (11)
　　Text B　A Critical Period of Educational Technology: 1950—1970 ……… (13)
　　Text C　Current Status of Educational Technology ……… (15)
　　专业英语的词汇特征 ……… (17)
　Unit 3　The Practice and Future of Education Technology ……… (19)
　　Text A　Four Perspectives on Educational Technology ……… (20)
　　Text B　The Professionalization of the Field ……… (22)
　　Text C　Future Trends in Educational Technology ……… (23)
　　Text D　Your Future in the Field ……… (24)
　　专业英语常见的语法现象 ……… (28)

**Part 2　The Theoretical Foundation of Educational Technology** ……… (31)
　Unit 4　Learning Theories ……… (31)
　　Text A　The Importance of Learning Theory to Education Technology ……… (32)
　　Text B　The Behaviorist Orientation to Learning ……… (33)
　　Text C　Cognitivism and Gagne's Model of Learning ……… (34)
　　Text D　Constructivism ……… (35)
　　专业英语翻译的标准 ……… (40)
　Unit 5　Communication Theories ……… (42)
　　Text A　Defining Communication ……… (43)
　　Text B　Communication System ……… (44)
　　Text C　Communication Theory ……… (45)
　　Text D　Two Typical Models of Communication Theory ……… (46)

　　　　从句的翻译（Ⅰ）……………………………………………………… (51)
　Unit 6　Instructional Theories ………………………………………… (54)
　　　Text A　A Brief Introduction to Instructional Theory ……………… (54)
　　　Text B　Taxonomy of Educational Objectives …………………… (55)
　　　Text C　Gagne's Theory of Instruction …………………………… (57)
　　　Text D　Elaboration Theory ……………………………………… (59)
　　　　从句的翻译（Ⅱ）……………………………………………………… (63)
　Unit 7　Systems Theory ………………………………………………… (64)
　　　Text A　The Systems View ……………………………………… (65)
　　　Text B　What is Systems Theory ………………………………… (66)
　　　Text C　The Functions of Systems Theory ……………………… (67)
　　　Text D　General Systems Theory ………………………………… (68)
　　　　被动句的翻译 …………………………………………………… (73)

Part 3　Media, Technology and Learning ……………………………… (76)
　Unit 8　Brief Introduction to Several Media and Technologies ……… (76)
　　　Text A　Multimedia ……………………………………………… (76)
　　　Text B　Hypermedia ……………………………………………… (78)
　　　Text C　Interactive Media ………………………………………… (80)
　　　Text D　Virtual Reality …………………………………………… (81)
　　　Text E　Expert Systems …………………………………………… (82)
　　　　长句的翻译 ……………………………………………………… (86)
　Unit 9　Information Technology and Education ……………………… (89)
　　　Text A　The Information Age …………………………………… (89)
　　　Text B　ICTs and Globalization ………………………………… (90)
　　　Text C　Information Technology and Education ………………… (92)
　　　Text D　Basic IT Skills and Personal Qualifications …………… (93)
　　　　英汉语序的对比与翻译 ………………………………………… (97)
　Unit 10　The Development Trends of Media and Technologies ……… (99)
　　　Text A　Continuing Use of Traditional Media …………………… (99)
　　　Text B　Advancing Telecommunications and Interactive Technologies …… (100)
　　　Text C　Predictions of Technology Trends ……………………… (101)
　　　Text D　Electronic Learning ……………………………………… (103)
　　　　文献检索简介 …………………………………………………… (106)

Part 4　Instructional Systems Design …………………………………… (109)
　Unit 11　Instructional Systems and Instructional Systems Design ……… (109)
　　　Text A　Instructional Systems …………………………………… (109)

  Text B Instructional Design ……………………………………… (112)

  文献检索方法简介 ……………………………………………………… (116)

 Unit 12 Instructional Systems Design Models ………………………… (118)

  Text A Instructional System Design (ISD): Using the ADDIE Model …… (119)

  Text B The ASSURE Model ……………………………………… (121)

  Text C Dick and Carey Model …………………………………… (124)

  Text D Rapid Prototyping ………………………………………… (126)

  Internet 上常用的教育技术文献资源 …………………………………… (133)

 Unit 13 Automating Instructional Design ……………………………… (134)

  Text A Automating Instructional Design ………………………… (135)

  Text B Four Types of Automated Instructional Design Tools ……… (136)

  Text C Current Trends in Automated Tools ……………………… (138)

  教育技术期刊——Your Guide to Educational Technology

   Journals on the Web(Ⅰ) …………………………………………… (143)

## Part 5 Developing Learning Resources ……………………………… (146)

 Unit 14 Audio ………………………………………………………… (146)

  Text A Audio Formats …………………………………………… (146)

  Text B Produce Materials on Cassette Tapes …………………… (151)

  Text C Using Audio Files in Multimedia ………………………… (153)

  教育技术期刊——Your Guide to Educational Technology

   Journals on the Web(Ⅱ) ………………………………………… (160)

 Unit 15 Video ………………………………………………………… (163)

  Text A Video Formats …………………………………………… (163)

  Text B Selecting Video …………………………………………… (167)

  Text C Producing Video ………………………………………… (168)

  科技论文的结构与写作初步(Ⅰ) ……………………………………… (176)

 Unit 16 Developing Online Courses …………………………………… (178)

  Text A Creating a Web Page …………………………………… (178)

  科技论文的结构与写作初步(Ⅱ) ……………………………………… (186)

## Part 6 Network Education …………………………………………… (197)

 Unit 17 Distance Education …………………………………………… (197)

  Text A Distance Education: An Overview ………………………… (198)

  Text B Distance Education, Face to Face Teaching and Technology …… (202)

  Text C Distance Learning Technologies …………………………… (205)

  Text D Summary and Recommendations for the Future of

     Distance Education …………………………………… (209)

　　　　投稿指南（Ⅰ） ········································································ (216)
　Unit 18　Online Learning ································································ (221)
　　　　Text A　A Brief Introduction of Online Learning ···················· (222)
　　　　Text B　Educational Benefits of Online Learning ···················· (224)
　　　　Text C　Evaluating Online Learning ······································ (229)
　　　　投稿指南（Ⅱ） ········································································ (242)

**Part 7　The Evaluation of Educational Technology** ···················· (247)
　Unit 19　The Evaluation of Learning Source and Learning Process ········ (247)
　　　　Text A　The History and Context of Evaluation ···················· (247)
　　　　Text B　Three Basic Methods of Learning Evaluation ············ (248)
　　　　Text C　Evaluation for Distance Education ·························· (250)
　　　　应用文写作之一——信函 ···························································· (257)
　Unit 20　Educational Evaluation ······················································ (263)
　　　　Text A　Educational Evaluation ············································ (264)
　　　　Text B　Evaluating Web-based Learning-A Clustered Study of
　　　　　　　　Two Online Projects ················································ (265)
　　　　Text C　Computer-assisted Assessment（CAA） ···················· (269)
　　　　应用文写作之二——简历和求职信 ················································ (276)

注：本书各单元习题参考答案见教育出版网（www.jycb.org）。

# Part 1　The Outline of Educational Technology

## Unit 1　The Basic Concepts of Educational Technology

▲ **Knowledge Objectives**

When you have completed this unit, you will be able to:
- Define educational technology
- Identify the differences and similarities of the two versions of the definition
- State the perspectives and meaning of educational technology
- List the types of research methods and approaches

▲ **Professional Terms**

| | |
|---|---|
| educational technology | 教育技术 |
| instructional technology | 教学技术 |
| instructional systems design | 教学系统设计 |
| audiovisual technology | 视听技术 |
| human performance technology | 人类绩效技术 |
| cognitive psychology | 认知心理学 |
| formative evaluation | 形成性评价 |
| summative evaluation | 总结性评价 |
| AECT | 教育传播与技术协会 |
| design | 设计 |
| development | 开发 |
| utilization | 运用 |
| management | 管理 |
| evaluation | 评价 |
| quantitative | 定量的 |
| qualitative | 定性的 |

## Text A

### What is Educational Technology?[①]

"Educational technology" is a term widely used in the field of education (and other areas), but it is often used with different meanings. The word "technology" is used by some to mean "hardware"—the devices that deliver information and serve as tools to accomplish a task, but those working in the field use "technology" to refer to a systematic process of solving problems by scientific means (Figure 1-1).[1]

Figure 1-1 Educational technology means not only hardware, but also educators' thoughts, experience techniques, etc.

In 1994, the definition of the field has been published by the Association for Educational Communications and Technology (AECT): "Instructional Technology is the theory and practice of design, development, utilization, management and evaluation of processes and resources for learning." (Seels & Richey)

The 1994 definition is built upon five separate areas of concern to instructional technologists: Design, Development, Utilization, Management, and Evaluation, which are five areas of study and practice within the field. In the book, *Instructional Technology: The Domains and Definitions of the Field*, the authors present the domains and sub-domains of the field (Figure 1-2).

With the development of educational technology, the definition continues to evolve. In 2004, AECT defines educational technology as follows: "Educational technology is the study and ethical practice of facilitating learning and improving performance by creating, using and managing appropriate technological processes and resources." The term educational technology is often associated with, and encompasses, instructional theory and learning theory. While instructional technology covers the processes and systems of learning and instruction, educational technology also includes other systems used in the process of developing human capability.

## Text B

### Perspectives and Meaning of Educational Technology[②]

Educational technology is most simply and comfortably defined as an array of tools that might prove helpful in advancing student learning.[2] Educational technology relies on a broad definition of the word "technology" (Figure 1-3). Technology can refer to material objects of

---

① http://www.ifets.info/journals/8_3/10.pdf
② http://en.wikipedia.org/wiki/Educational_technology

Part 1 The Outline of Educational Technology 3

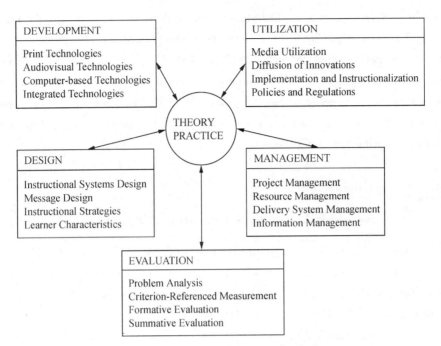

Figure 1-2 The domains of instructional technology

use to humanity, such as machines, hardware or utensils, but it can also encompass broader themes, including systems, methods of organization, and techniques. Those who employ educational technologies to explore ideas and communicate means are learners or teachers.

Consider the Handbook of Human Performance Technology. The word technology for the sister fields of Educational and Human Performance Technology means "applied science". In other words, any valid and reliable process or procedure that is derived from basic research using the "scientific method" is considered a "technology".[3] Educational or Human Performance Technology may be based purely on algorithmic or heuristic processes, but neither necessarily implies physical technology. The word technology comes from the Greek "Techne" which means craft or art. Another word "technique", with the same origin, also may be used when considering the field Educational technology. So educational technology may be extended to include the techniques of the educator. A classic example of an Educational Technology is Bloom's 1956 book, *Taxonomy of Educational Objectives*.

Figure 1-3 Educational technology is widely used in all kinds of fields.

According to some, an Educational Technologist is someone who transforms basic educational and psychological research into an evidence-based applied science (or a technology) of learning or instruction.[4]

But the term seems very stuffy and almost arrogant to those who work with the tools. Educational Technologists typically have a graduate degree (Master's, Doctorate, Ph. D., or D. Phil.) in a field related to educational psychology, educational media, experimental psychology, cognitive psychology or, more purely, in the fields of Educational, Instructional or Human Performance Technology or Instructional (Systems) Design. But few of those listed above as theorists would ever use the term "educational technologist" as a term to describe themselves, preferring less stuffy terms like educator.

## Text C

## Research Methods of Educational Technology①

In research, selecting the best strategy to approach a particular research topic or question is half the battle. Research can be classified or defined in many different ways. In order to pick the appropriate techniques, it's essential to know what types and methods are available.

### Types of Research: From Basic to Applied

Research can be classified by the degree of direct applicability of the research to educational practice or settings. It can range from basic research (focused on developing or enhancing theory) to applied research (conducted to solve current educational problems) (Figure 1-4).

Figure 1-4  Types of research spectrum

### Research Methods: Quantitative and Qualitative

There are two basic research methods: quantitative and qualitative. Each method approaches a research topic differently and each consists of multiple approaches.

Quantitative research is very traditional and is adopted from the natural sciences. It relies on the belief or assumption that our world and the claims about it are not considered meaningful unless they can be verified through direct observation.[5]

Qualitative research, on the other hand, is fairly new and is based on different beliefs. In qualitative research, all meaning is tied to perspective or context, so there is typically never one right answer. The table which follows tabulates the many differences between the two methods of inquiry (Table 1).

---

① http://coe.sdsu.edu/eet/articles/methodsofinq/index.htm

Part 1　The Outline of Educational Technology

Table 1　Characteristics of the Research Methods

| Characteristics | Quantitative Research | Qualitative Research |
| --- | --- | --- |
| Purpose | To generalize about or control phenomena | To provide in-depth descriptions of settings and people |
| Reasoning Method | Primarily Deductive: Specific predictions based on general observations, principles, or experiences | Primarily Inductive: Generalization based on specific observations and experiences |
| Hypothesis | Identified prior to research, purpose of research is to test it | Begins with guiding research questions, which will be refined during data collection and analysis |
| Nature | More narrowly focused and outcome oriented | Holistic and process oriented |
| Design | Clear, well-ordered sequence of steps | Flexible and changeable during research |
| Interaction with Context | Tries to eliminate the influence of contextual variables | Tries to capture the richness of the context of the subjects and their perspectives |
| Data Collection | Primarily numerical data gathered through paper-and-pencil, non-interactive instruments (can also include narrative data) | Primarily narrative data, collected from fieldwork (can also include numerical data) |

## Research Approaches: Complementary vs. Oppositional

Choosing the most appropriate strategy or strategies allows the researcher to design the most effective framework to better understand his/her research topic or question. Approaches fall under one of the two methods described above.

Quantitative methods tend to gather numerical data, while qualitative methods tend to gather narrative, non-numerical data. Although these methods sound oppositional, they are in fact complementary (Figure 1-5), and the approaches or strategies from each can be used together in order to better explore a research topic.

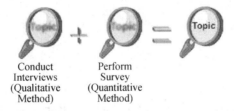

Conduct Interviews (Qualitative Method)　　Perform Survey (Quantitative Method)

Figure 1-5　The effects of quantitative and qualitative are shown in the equation.

## The (Interactive) Research Tree

The types of, methods of, and approaches to research are represented below (Figure 1-6):

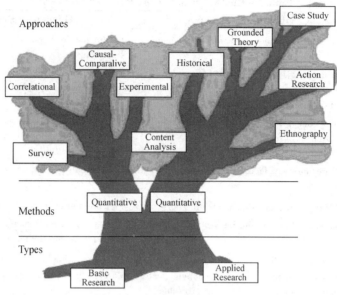

Figure 1-6　Interactive research tree

## New Words

systematic　*adj.* 系统的,体系的
evolve　*vt.*, *vi.* (使)发展,(使)进展,(使)进化
ethical　*adj.* 1. 伦理的;道德的 2. 合乎道德的
encompass　*vt.* 围绕;包围
stuffy　*adj.* 1. 空气不好的,通风不好的,闷热的 2. (观点、举止)陈腐的,呆板的,拘谨的
arrogant　*adj.* 傲慢的,自大的
oppositional　*adj.* 反对的,对抗的
complementary　*adj.* 互补的

## Notes

[1] The word "technology" is used by some to mean "hardware"—the devices that deliver information and serve as tools to accomplish a task—but those working in the field use "technology" to refer to a systematic process of solving problems by scientific means.

译文：一些人运用"技术"这个单词来表示"硬件"——一种传递信息的设备并作为完成一项任务的工具,但那些教育技术行内人运用"技术"来指代通过科学手段来解决问题的系统过程。

- The devices that deliver information and serve as tools to accomplish a task 作为 hardware 的同位语从句,其中的 that 从句又作为 devices 的定语从句,用来解释说明 devices。
- Working in the field 是现在分词做定语,修饰限定 those。
- refer to 查阅,提到,谈到,打听,涉及,认为与……有关,认为……起源于……,参考

[2] Educational technology is most simply and comfortably defined as an array of tools that might prove helpful in advancing student learning.

译文:教育技术可以最简便而充分地被定义为一系列能够在促进学生学习方面起作用的工具。

- That might prove helpful in advancing student learning 是定语从句,修饰先行词。
- an array of 一排,一群,一批

[3] In other words, any valid and reliable process or procedure that is derived from basic research using the "scientific method" is considered a "technology."

译文:换而言之,任何有根据的、可靠的过程或程序,即源自使用"科学方法"的基础研究的过程或程序,被称做"技术"。

- That is derived from basic research using the "scientific method" 作定语从句,修饰先行词 process or procedure,其中 using the "scientific method" 是现在分词作后置定语,修饰 basic research。
- be derived from 源自

[4] According to some, an Educational Technologist is someone who transforms basic educational and psychological research into an evidence-based applied science (or a technology) of learning or instruction.

译文:根据一些人的说法,一个教育技术家是将基本的教育、心理研究转换成以事实为基础的有关学习或教学的应用科学(或技术)。

- Who transforms basic educational and psychological research into an evidence-based applied science (or a technology) of learning or instruction 整个句子作定语从句,修饰先行词 someone。
- According to 根据
- Transform...into 转换成……

[5] It relies on the belief or assumption that our world and the claims about it are not considered meaningful unless they can be verified through direct observation.

译文:定量研究建立在这样的信念或假设之上:除非我们的世界和对世界的看法能通过直接的观察来验证,否则它们并不是有意义的。

- That our world and the claims about it are not considered meaningful unless they can be verified through direct observation 是同位语从句,修饰先行词 the belief or assumption。
- unless 除非
- rely on v. 依赖,依靠

## Selected Translation

### Text A

<h3 style="text-align:center">教育技术是什么</h3>

"教育技术"这个术语在教育领域(还有其他领域)被广泛运用,但通常被理解成不

同的含义。一些人运用"技术"这个单词来表示"硬件"——一种传递信息的设备并作为完成一项任务的工具,但那些教育技术行内人运用"技术"来指代通过科学手段来解决问题的系统过程。

在1994年,美国教育传播与技术协会发表了该领域的定义:"教育技术是设计、开发、运用、管理和评价学习过程、学习资源的理论与实践。"

1994定义建立在教学技术专家所关心的五个独立的专门领域——设计、开发、运用、管理与评价——之上。在《教育技术:领域的定义与范畴》中,作者给出了这个领域的范畴及其子范畴。(见图1)

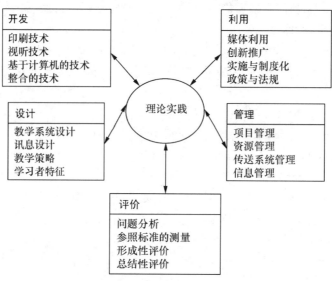

图1 教学技术的范畴

随着教育技术的发展,其定义继续演化。在2004年,美国教育传播与技术协会将教育技术定义如下:教育技术是通过创建、使用、管理合适的技术过程和资源来促进学习、提高绩效的理论和合乎伦理道德的实践。教育技术这个术语通常与教学理论和学习理论相联系,并包括了教学理论和学习理论。教学技术涉及的是学习和教学的过程和系统,而教育技术则包括在发展人类能力的过程中所使用的其他系统。

## Exercises

**1. Please Explain the Following Professional Terms:**

(1) audiovisual technology

(2) Human Performance Technology (HPT)

(3) Instructional Systems Design (ISD)

(4) AECT

(5) cognitive psychology

**2. Short Answers:**

(1) In the AECT's definition in 1994, what domains does educational technology include?

Part 1　The Outline of Educational Technology

（2）Can educational technology be extended to include the techniques of the educator?

（3）What are the differences between the quantitative research and qualitative research?

# 专业英语简介

信息技术的飞速发展,给社会带来了重大的变革,各国之间的交流也愈益广泛,各种国际学术会议也不断举行。但是,教育学、心理学以及教育技术学等等的文献和会议,大部分都是使用英文。所以,掌握好专业英语的阅读、翻译和书写的方法对我们了解最新的技术动态、吸收先进的科技成果是至关重要的。教育技术专业英语是教育技术专业学生学好教育技术课程的一个重要工具,也是一门必修课,同时它与公共英语密切相关。作为教育技术专业的学生,他们既有教育技术的基础知识,也有不错的公共英语基础,但一看到教育技术专业的英文文献、英文资料、英文会议还是有些不知所措。如何在较短的时间里掌握好专业英语呢?首先要了解教育技术专业英语的三大特点。

## 一、专业性

专业英语的专业性体现在它的特殊专业内容和特殊专业词汇上。词汇是构成句子的基本元素,对词汇含义不能确定,就很难理解句子内容,甚至可能得出可笑的、相反的结果。很多公共英语,如:communication（传播）,elaboration（细化）,development（开发）等,在专业领域内被赋予了专业含义,这就要求我们熟悉所学专业。

新词汇层出不穷,有的是随着本专业发展应运而生的,有的是借用公共英语中的词汇,有的是借用外来语词汇,有的则是人为构造成的词汇。有些专业词汇并不好懂,我们只有对专业知识有相当的了解之后才会明白它们的意思。如:

programmed instruction　　　　程序教学
audiovisual communication　　　视听传播
stimulus-response theory　　　　刺激—反应理论
Information Processing Theory　信息加工理论
affective domain　　　　　　　　情感领域
artificial intelligence　　　　　　人工智能
virtual reality　　　　　　　　　虚拟现实

## 二、灵活性

专业英语一般讲述的是基本理论、教学媒体的开发与应用等等,这就决定了专业英语的客观性和灵活性。在学习过程中,尤其是在阅读专业文章时,必须尊重客观内容,不能主观想象。为了表示公允性和客观性,专业英语往往在句子结构和词性的使用上比较灵活。如:

1. Regardless of the quality and sophistication of computer hardware and software, the success of technology often depends on the support and encouragement that students and teach-

ers receive in using it.

不管计算机硬件和软件的质量和复杂性存在怎么样的差别,技术在学校的成功更多地取决于我们如何支持和鼓励学生和教师使用各类技术。

2. What's more, by means of information technology, education can thus be made available outside of working hours, at the weekend, during working hours in co-operation between companies and educational institutions, as well as in a completely different part of the country from that in which the teaching is taking place.

另外,在工作时间之外,在周末,在公司和教育机构合作的工作时间里,或者是在与上课地点完全不同的地方,学习者也可以通过信息技术接受教育。

### 三、简明性

为求精炼,专业英语中常希望能够用尽可能少的单词来清晰地表达原意。这就导致了非限定动词、名词化单词或词组,以及其他简化形式的广泛使用。

1. 动名词短语可用来取代时间从句或简化时间陈述句,如:

Before being executed, the program should be loaded into main memory.

2. 过去分词短语可以取代被动语态关系从句,现在分词可以取代主动语态关系从句,如:

In Britain electricity energy generated in power station is fed to the national Grid.

The number of people working in the field of educational technology can be larger in the future.

3. 不定式短语用以替换表示目的、功能的从句,如:

The best way to introduce this theory is through Gagne's model.

总的说来,与普通英语相比,专业英语很注重客观事实和真理,并且要求逻辑性强,条理规范,表达准确、精练、正式。专业英语有如下显著特点:

- 长句多
- 被动语态使用频繁
- 用虚拟语气表达假设或建议
- 在说明书、手册中广泛使用祈使语句
- 名词性词组多
- 非限定动词(尤其是分词)使用频率高
- 介词短语多
- 常用 It... 句型结构
- 单个动词比动词词组用得频繁
- 常使用动词或名词演化而成的形容词
- 希腊词根和拉丁词根比例大
- 专业术语多
- 缩略词经常出现
- 半技术词汇多

- 缩写使用频繁
- 插图、插画、表格、公式、数字所占比例大
- 合成新词多

# Unit 2　The History of Educational Technology

## ▲ Knowledge Objectives

When you have completed this unit, you will be able to:
- State the history of educational technology
- Describe the important theories or ideas of educational technology during the period 1950s to 1970s
- Recognize the current status of educational technology

## ▲ Professional Terms

| | |
|---|---|
| visual instruction | 视觉教学 |
| audiovisual instruction | 视听教学 |
| programmed instruction | 程序教学 |
| task analysis | 任务分析 |
| cognitive psychology | 认知心理学 |
| Dick and Carey Model | 迪克—克雷模式 |
| general system theory | 一般系统论 |
| audiovisual communication | 视听传播 |
| Human Performance Technology(HPT) | 人类绩效技术 |

## Text A

### History of Educational Technology[①]

The first use of educational technology cannot be attributed to a specific person or time. Many histories of educational technology start in the early 1900s, while others go back to the 1600s. This depends on the definition of educational technology. Definitions that focus on a systems approach tend to reach further back in history, while those definitions focused on sensory devices are relatively more recent.

Here is a brief outline of educational technology:

The time prior to 1920 was known as the Visual Instruction Movement in education. At this time, film making became an important part of American culture and the first educational

---

① http://en.wikipedia.org/wiki/Educational_technology
　http://hbohn.wordpress.com/2007/09/04/history-of-educational-technology/

Figure 2-1　In the early days, film was an effective tool for teaching and training.

films were used in the classroom (Figure 2-1). Thomas Edison then predicted that we would no longer see or need books in schools.

The movement in the 1920s and 30s paved the way for where we are today in the world of Educational Technology. "Technological advances in such areas as radio broadcasting, sound recordings, and sound motion pictures led to increased interest in educational media." This movement became known as the "audiovisual instruction movement". The great depression couldn't keep this fast moving technological advance from spreading rapidly. The limitations were unknown as people kept stretching this rapidly growing phenomenon farther and farther.

In the 1940s, educational technology shifted from the classroom to the military training needs of the country. Because of World War II, hundreds of films were developed and used to train military troops. These films provided a consistent and quick way to train people from diverse backgrounds.

With the invention of the television in the 1950s, the TV became the new wave of educational technology in schools (Figure 2-2). It was viewed as a tool for "educational broadcasting" because it was quick and inexpensive. Unfortunately it was mainly used for showing a teacher present a lecture and its use for this purpose was phased out by the early 1960s. The Soviet launch of Sputnik forced Americans to see the importance of incorporating science and technology into our educational system.

In the late 1980s, the 90s, and up to the present time, computers have been viewed as the next wave of technology integration in educational use (Figure 2-3). Personal computers have been made affordable and have been showing up in households and schools at an astonishing rate. The World Wide Web was developed and has changed how we access information and communicate with others.

Figure 2-2　Teachers sometimes use TV to help them deliver teaching materials.

Figure 2-3　Computers are very popular media in school education nowadays, especially in universities.

# Text B

## A Critical Period of Educational Technology: 1950—1970[①]

1950 through 1970 witnessed great changes in the field. At this stage, television and other media were widely used. Programmed instruction and task analysis appeared and applied. The theory of communications, general systems and cognitive psychology were introduced into the field. The issue of professionalization of the field was proposed by the professionals. Educational system design (ESD) originated. Based on all the above mentioned, the terminology of the field changed and the field shifted from Audiovisual Instruction to Educational Technology.

The first teaching machine was invented by Sydney L. Pressey, but it was not until 1950s that practical methods of programming were developed. In 1954, programmed instruction was reintroduced by B. F. Skinner, a behavioral psychologist of Harvard University, who became famous for his work operant conditioning and reinforcement using his "Skinner Box" (Figure 2-4).[1] In his 1954 article, The Science of Learning and the Art of Teaching, Skinner advocated for the Teaching Machine as an educational tool that reinforced students learning.

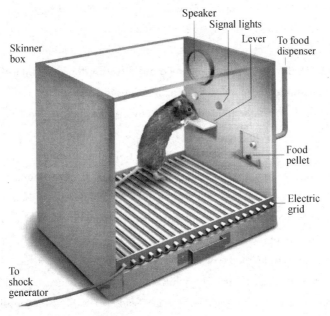

Figure 2-4  Experimenting with his "Skinner Box", Skinner elicited a famous conclusion called "stimulate and response".

Programmed instruction is a method of presenting new subject matter to students in a graded sequence of controlled steps. Students work through the programmed material by themselves at their speed and after each step test their comprehension by answering an examination question or filling in a diagram. They are immediately shown the correct answer or given addi-

---

① Jiao jianli and Ye lihan, *Professional English for Educational Technology*, 2005.

tional information.

Figure 2-5  Computer-assisted instruction provokes students' thoughts and creativity.

Although there has been considerable controversy regarding the merits of programmed instruction as the sole method of teaching, many educators agreed that they can contribute to more efficient classroom procedure supplement the conventional teaching methods.[2] And the roots of computer-assisted instruction (CAI) (Figure 2-5) can be traced back to programmed instruction.

In 1962, Robert Glaser employed the educational system and discussed its components. In 1965, Robert M. Gagne published *the Conditions of Learning* which elaborates the analysis of learning objectives and relates different classes of learning objectives to appropriate educational designs. Activities of the 1970s were a logical outgrowth of the path-breaking ideas proposed in 1960s. In 1970s, numbers of educational design models emerged, including the Dick and Carey Model, and educational design approached to maturation. Later in 1974, with L. J. Briggs, Gagne published another book, *Principles of Educational Design*. As milestones, the two books set the ground for educational design.

From 1950s to 1970s, another important trend affecting the evolution of the field was the theories of communications and general system was introduced into the field.

In 1949, Claude E. Shannon and Warren Weaver published the book, *Mathematical Theory of Communication*, and proposed a model in this book. Almost each model which has been used in relation to educational technology is derived from this model. At about the same time, Harold Lasswell proposed the "five W's model". From the idea of Shannon and Weaver and Lasswell, Wilbur Schramm developed his approach to communications. Schramm developed his approach of communication. Schramm developed several communication models and identified six ways to categorize the delivery systems.

When the general system theory was introduced into the field, Charles Hoban, Jr. and James. Finn were regarded as the two most influential contributors. In his 1956 presentation, Hoban first recognized that the field was a system. And in 1960s, Finn published his series of articles in Audiovisual Communication Review. Finn reviewed systems as the necessary characteristics of automation and technology and applied systems concepts to educational planning and delivery emphasized the man-machine systems of instruction.

Based on the theories, the professionals in the field offered a focus on the process and on the systematic organization of diverse elements in educational settings.

While these changes were taking place, leaders among education professionals who had considered themselves primarily as media specialists began to lobby actively to broaden the field of audiovisual instruction to embrace the larger concept of educational technology.[3] Finn, Arthur Lumsdaine, and other leaders talked about the proper name for the field. In 1970, DAI (Department of Audiovisual Instruction) Board of Director changed the organization name from the Department of Audiovisual Instruction to the Association for Educational Communications and Technology(AECT). And more and more professionals preferred instructional technology or educational technology to audiovisual instruction when they referred to the field.

## Text C

### Current Status of Educational Technology[①]

Educational technology is a growing field of study which uses technology as a means to solve educational challenges, both in the classroom and in distance learning environments.

While educational technology promises solutions to many educational problems, resistance from faculty and administrators to the use of technology in the classroom is not unusual. This reaction can arise from the belief—or fear—that the ultimate aim of educational technology is to reduce or even remove the human element of instruction. However, most educational technologists would counter that education will always require human intervention from instructors or facilitators.

Many graduate programs are producing educational designers, who increasingly are being employed by industry and universities to create materials for distance education programs. These professionals often employ e-learning tools, which provide distance learners the opportunity to interact with instructors and experts in the field, even if they are not located physically close to each other. More recently a new form of educational technology known as Human Performance Technology (HPT) has evolved. HPT focuses on performance problems and deals primarily with corporate entities.

## New Words

  phase *n.* 阶段，状态，相，相位 *v.* 定相
  sputnik *n.* （苏联）人造地球卫星
  terminology *n.* 术语学
  incorporate *adj.* 合并的，结社的，一体化的 *vt.* 合并，使组成公司 *vi.* 合并，混合，组成公司 *vt.* ［律］结社，使成为法人组织
  operant *n.* 发生作用之人或物，工作之人或物 *adj.* 动作的
  outgrowth *n.* 长出，派出，结果，副产物
  lobby *n.* 大厅，休息室，〈美〉游说议员者 *vi.* 游说议员，经常出入休息室
  corporate *adj.* 团体的；法人组织的；团结的；组合的；具体的；共同的；自治的

---

① http://en.wikipedia.org/wiki/Educational_technology

**Notes**

[1] In 1954, programmed instruction was reintroduced by B. F. Skinner, a behavioral psychologist of Harvard University, who became famous for his work operant conditioning and reinforcement using his "Skinner Box".

译文：1954年，B.F.斯金纳再次提出了程序教学，斯金纳是哈佛大学的一位行为心理学家，他因用"斯金纳箱"在操作性条件反射和强化方面的贡献而出名。

- a behavioral psychologist of Harvard University 是同位语
- who became famous for his work operant conditioning and reinforcement using his "Skinner Box"是非限制性定语从句，修饰先行词 B. F. Skinner。
- be famous for 因……而出名

[2] Although there has been considerable controversy regarding the merits of programmed instruction as the sole method of teaching, many educators agreed that they can contribute to more efficient classroom procedure supplement the conventional teaching methods.

译文：虽然把程序教学看做是教学的唯一方法的观点受到了相当大的争议，但是许多教育家赞同这样的观点：程序教学能提供更有效的教学程序来弥补传统的教学方法。

- regarding the merits of programmed instruction as the sole method of teaching 是分词短语做状语
- that they can contribute to more efficient classroom procedure supplement the conventional teaching methods 是宾语从句
- regard...as... 把……视为；认为……是

[3] While these changes were taking place, leaders among education professionals who had considered themselves primarily as media specialists began to lobby actively to broaden the field of audiovisual instruction to embrace the larger concept of educational technology.

译文：当这些变化正在发生的时候，曾经自认为是媒体专家的教育专业人员的领导们开始主动游说以扩大视听教学的领域，使其包括教育技术的更大的概念。

- who had considered themselves primarily as media specialists 是定语从句，修饰先行词 education professionals。
- while 当……的时候
- take place 产生，发生

**Selected Translation**

**Text C**

### 教育技术的现状

教育技术是一种日益增长的研究领域，它利用技术作为一种手段来解决教育——无论是在课堂还是远程学习环境中的教育——所面临的挑战。

教育技术提供了解决许多教育问题的方案，但与此同时，教师和管理员拒绝在课堂上使用技术也并不少见。这种反应可以从这样的信仰或恐惧中产生:教育技术的最终目的是减少或甚至消除教学的人为因素。然而,大多数的教育技术人员将反驳:教育将永远需要教师或引导者的人为干预。

许多研究生教育课程体系正在培养教学设计师,他们也逐渐被工业和大学聘用来为远程教育课程开发资源。这些专业人士往往采用电子学习工具。这些学习工具给远程学习者提供了与该领域内的教师和专家互动的机会,即使远程学习者在空间上不能与他们接触。最近,一种被称为人类绩效技术的教育技术新形式形成了。人类绩效技术侧重于绩效问题并主要涉及公司实体。

## Exercises

**1. Translate the Following Professional Terms into English:**
(1) 视觉教学
(2) 视听教学
(3) 视听传播
(4) 一般系统论
(5) 程序教学
(6) 人类绩效技术

**2. Short Answers:**
(1) What movement paved the way of educational technology? And why?
(2) Why was the period 1950 to 1970 a critical period to educational technology?
(3) What are the contributions of programmed instruction?
(4) Why do many people refuse to use technology in the classroom? What are the responses of educational technologists?

# 专业英语的词汇特征

## 一、词汇构成

专业英语词汇有其自身的特点,一般来说,可以分为以下几类:

1. 专业词汇

这类词的意义狭窄,一般只使用在各自的专业范围内,因而专业性很强。

　　qualitative　　定性的　　audiovisual　　　　　视听的
　　constructivism　建构主义　programmed instruction　程序教学

2. 次专业词汇

次专业词汇是指不受上下文限制的、在各专业中出现频率都很高的词。这类词往往在不同的专业中具有不同的含义。如:

　　communication　elaboration

其中,communication 常用含义是"交流,沟通",但是在专业英语指"传播,通讯";elaboration 常指"苦心经营,苦心经营的结果,详尽的细节",但在专业英语里指"细化",如 Elaboration theory。

3. 特用词

在日常英语中,为使语言生动活泼,常使用一些短小的词或词组。而在专业英语中,表达同样的意义时,为了准确、正式、严谨以及不引起歧义,却往往选用一些较长的特用词。这些词在非专业英语中极少使用但属于非专业英语。

日常生活中常用下列句子:This kind of measure is not accurate.

在专业英语中,却表示为:This kind of measure is qualitative.

这是由于 qualitative 词义单一准确,可以避免歧义。而 accurate 不仅可以表示"精确的",而且还可以表示其他意义,如:

He gave an accurate(正确的) answer to the question.

类似对应的特用词还有:

go down—depress     upside down—invert
keep—maintain       enough—sufficient
take away—remove    at once—immediately
push in—insert      a lot of—appreciable
use up—consume      find out—determine

4. 功能词

它包括介词、连词、冠词、代词等。功能词为词在句中的结构关系提供了十分重要的结构信号,对于理解专业内容十分重要,而且出现频率极高。研究表明,在专业英语中,出现频率很高的十个词都是功能词,其顺序为:the, of, in, and, to, is, that, for, are, be。

## 二、构词法

英语的构词法主要有四种:前缀法、后缀法、合成和转化。前缀法和后缀法也叫派生法(derivation),专业英语词汇大部分都是用派生法构成的,即通过各种前缀和后缀来构成新词。有专家作过统计,以 semi-构成的词有 230 个以上,以 auto-构成的词有 260 个以上,以 micro-构成的词有 300 个以上,以 thermo-构成的词有 130 个以上。仅这四个前缀构成的词就达近千个,而常用的前缀和后缀也多达上百个,可见派生法的构词能力非常强。

1. 常用的前缀

inter-: intersection interface
counter-: counterpart
sub-: subway submarine
through-: throughput
hyper-: hyperons hyperplane
tele-: telescope
photo-: photosphere
super-: superheated
in-: inadequate insufficient

im-: impossible
re-: reuse recharge
over-: overwork overload
under-: underpay
dis-: discharge dissatisfy
ab-: abstract
con-: confound
ex-: exit
trans-: transformer

2. 常用的后缀
-ist: scientist artist
-logy: anthropology
-ism: mechanism
-able: noticeable stable
-ive: reactive effective
-ic: electronic metallic
-ous: synchronous porous
-proof: waterproof acid-proof
-en: weaken harden shorten

3. 常用的合成（composition）方法
名词+名词形式,如:discovery learning（发现学习）,motor skill（动作技能）
形容词+名词,如:affective domain（情感领域）,cognitive psychology（认知心理学）
动词+名词,如:feedback（反馈）,learning theory（学习理论）
名词+动词,如:input（输入）,output（输出）
介词+名词,如:outside（在外边）,outgrowth（长出,滋生,结果,副产物）

## Unit 3　The Practice and Future of Education Technology

▲ Knowledge Objectives

When you have completed this unit, you will be able to:
• Describe the four perspectives on educational technology
• State the practices of educational technology
• State the future trends of educational technology
• Recognize your future in the field of educational technology

## Professional Terms

| | |
|---|---|
| audiovisual communication | 视听传播 |
| slide | 幻灯片 |
| instructional systems | 教学系统 |
| interactive media | 交互媒体 |
| computer-assisted-design (CAD) | 计算机辅助设计 |

## Text A

### Four Perspectives on Educational Technology[①]
—Media, Instructional Systems, Vocational Training and computers

Figure 3-1  All kinds of media are indispensable to educational technology, and they are playing an important part in education and other fields.

If educational technology is viewed as both process and tools, it is important to begin to examine four different historical perspectives on these processes and tools, all of which have helped shape the current practices in the field.[1]

**Technology in education as media and audiovisual communication (Figure 3-1).** The earliest view of educational technology is one that continues today: technology as media. According to Saettler, this view grew out of the audiovisual movement: ways of delivering information used as alternatives to lectures and books. Beginning in 1930s, some higher education instructors proposed that media such as slides and films delivered information in more concrete, and therefore more effective, ways. This perspective later became the audiovisual communications, "the branch of educational theory and practice concerned primarily with the design and use of messages which control the learning process." However, the view of technology as media continued to dominate areas of education and the communications industry. Saettler reports that as late as 1986, the National Task Force on Educational Technology used a definition that equated educational technology with media, treating computer as another medium.

**Technology in education as instructional system.** The instructional design or instructional systems movement took shape in 1960s and 1970s, adding another dimension to the media-and-communications view of technology in education. Systems approaches to solving educational problems originated in military and industry training but later emerged in university research and development projects. Practices began to reflect systems approaches when university personnel began advocating them in their work with schools. These approaches were based

---

① M. D. Roblyer, *Integrating Educational Technology into Teaching*, Third Edition.

on the belief that both human and nonhuman resources (teachers and media, respectively) could be parts of a system for addressing an instruction need (Figure 3-2). From this viewpoint, educational technology was not seen just as a medium for communicating instructional information, but as a systematic approach to designing, developing, and delivering instruction matched to carefully indentified needs. Resources for delivering instruction were indentified only after detailed analysis of learning tasks and objectives and the kinds of instructional strategies required to teach them.

Figure 3-2  Instructional system includes teacher, students, media, and materials.

From the 1960s through the 1980s, applications of systems approaches to instruction were influenced and shaped by learning theories from educational psychology. Behaviorists held sway initially and cognitive theories gained influence later. Views of instructional systems in 1990s were also influenced by popular learning theories. However, these theories criticized systems approaches as too rigid to foster some kinds of learning, particularly the higher order ones. Thus, the current view of educational technology as instructional systems seems to be changing once again.

Figure 3-3  Technologies are often used as vocation training tools, and they can help enhance training in specific skills.

**Technology in education as vocation training tool (Figure 3-3).** Another popular view of technology in education has developed from the perspectives of technology as tools used in business and industry. Generally referred to as technology education, this view originated with industry trainers and vocational educators in the 1980s and reflects their need for technology to enhance training in specific skills. This perspective is based on two promises. First, it holds that one important function of school learning is to prepare students for the world of work. Therefore students need to learn about and use technology that they will encounter after graduation. For example, the educators believe that all students should learn word processing to help them to perform in many jobs or professions. Second, technology educators believe that vocation training can be a practical means of teaching all content areas such as math, science, and language. Technology education also includes other topics such as robotics, manufacturing systems, and computer-assisted-design (CAD) systems.

**Technology in education as computer and computer-based system.** The advent of computers in the 1950s created yet another view of educational technology. Business, industry,

Figure 3-4  Computer and computer-based system have become pervasive in business, military, education, and they greatly influence the life of people.

and military trainers, as well as educators in higher education, recognized the instructional potential of computers (Figure 3-4). Many of these trainer and educators predicted that computer technology would quickly transform education and become the most important component of educational technology. Although the instructional application of computers did not produce the anticipated overnight success, they inspired the development of another branch of educational technology. From the time that computers came into classrooms in the 1960s until about 1990, this perspective was known as educational computing and encompassed both instructional and support applications of computers.

Educational computing applications originally were influenced by technical personnel such as programmers and systems analysts. By the 1970s, however, many of the same educators involved with media, audiovisual communications, and instructional systems were directing the course of research and development in educational computing. By the 1990s, these educators began to see computers as part of a combination of technology resources, including media, instructional systems, and computer-based support systems. At that point, educational computing became known as educational technology.

## Text B

## The Professionalization of the Field[①]

In the first issue of the first volume of *AV (Audio-Visual) Communication Review*, perhaps the best scholarly journal in the field, the late James D. Finn wrote "Professionalizing the Audio-Visual Field." His contention—and it is still true—is that the audio-visual is not yet a profession.

Most people in the audio-visual field are still guided by a theory which is fragmentary; theory as now guiding the field (the generalization held by many of the workers) is not even inclusive of the notions contained in the audio-visual literature.

By any test theory, the audio-visual field does not meet professional standards. Its workers are craftsmen, not professionals, in the majority of instances because they are operating in Whitehead's word, on "customary activities modified by the trial and error of individual practice."

These added and shifting emphases within the field that is known as instructional or edu-

---

① Jiao jianli and Ye lihan, *Professional English for Educational Technology*, 2005.

cational technology seem to indicate that the field does not qualify for status as a discipline.[2] But this fact should not diminish the importance of the field or the contributions that it makes in the improvement of learning. As Donald Ely has suggested, on the way to the future, technology offers the best organizing concept for the development of the field and its evolution into a discipline.

## Text C

## Future Trends in Educational Technology[①]

The development of the personal computer and the Internet has "enabled man to transcend the barriers of physical distance." People no longer limit their learning to an educational setting such as a school or university. Learning can take place at home or at the office, by online distance learning (Figure 3-5). The future of technology will enable people to be life-long learners. Learning will continue into the work place where there is a "need to keep up with current information."

Figure 3-5 Learning can be very convenient by online distance learning.

Learners do not have to depend on their memories. They can store information on their personal computers and be able to retrieve it at all times. The concept of knowledge has changed from having information in the brain to having access to information about a particular topic and knowing how to use it. Teachers' roles will ultimately change since they will no longer be providers of information. They will be facilitators who concentrate on the teaching of social skills rather than academic or technical expertise. However, teacher-mediated classrooms do not foster computer-mediated learning. Technology requires changes in the way humans work, yet schools are adding computers to a traditional, authoritarian, classroom-centered setting. It won't work. As General Electric CEO Jack Welch has said, "If the rate of change inside an institution is less than the rate of change outside, the end is in sight." Technology is developing at a very fast pace. If education fails to keep up with the current trends, will it keep up with those of the future?

Aureo Castro and David Thornburg are educational futurists who have looked at future trends in technology and their impacts on education. Aureo Castro predicts, "increasing in web enabled courses, more home schoolers, new roles for teachers, a paradigm shift in primary education, new roles for schools and centralization of curriculum and instructional development" are the main trends. And he focuses on the Internet (Figure 3-6) and distance education as trends of educational technology, which will become even more popular in the future.

---

① http://www.nelliemuller.com/Future_Trends_in_Educational_%20Technology.html

Figure 3-6 People can have easier access to information and resources through internet, and internet has been changing people's thoughts and values.

However, David Thornburg predicts that, "rapid increase in the growth of information, the collapse of the information float, increasingly global marketplace, computers continue to increase in power while dropping in cost, the computer chips continue to follow Moore's Law, bandwidth is becoming free and finally network power continues to obey Metcalfe's Law as future trends that will have implications for education." David Thornburg focuses on another trend for the future of schools. He claims that once technologies become commonplace with all students, the tools for lifelong learning will be in place, adding that the notion of lifelong learning is a survival skill.

Technology can improve students' learning and make teachers' work much easier, and educational technology will become more powerful, which can make learning more engaging and knowledge more accessible. Educators must work in partnership to break down the barriers of time, space, content and form so learners can collaborate, communicate, and share ideas.

## Text D

## Your Future in the Field[①]

You are entering this field at an exciting time as a teacher, trainer, or media/technology professional. Unlike some educational areas, educational technology is becoming more and more pervasive in formal and informal education each year. Correspondingly, ever-larger numbers of people are being employed in this specialty.

The fastest-growing specialty is school technology coordinator (Figure 3-7). Regardless of the quality and sophistication of computer hardware and software, the success of technology often depends on the support and encouragement that students and teachers receive in using it.[3] Technology coordinators can assist with planning, selecting software and hardware, consulting on purchases, implementing, and supervising maintenance and repair.

Figure 3-7 School technology coordinators serve many roles in school, such as planning, selecting hardware and software and repairing, etc.

Some schools and corporations have even divided the technology coordinator position into two specialties. A software specialist orders, catalogs, distributes, and consults with teachers on implementing

---

① Sharon E. Smaldino, James D. Russell, Robert Henich and Michael Molenda, *Instructional Technology and Media for Learning*, Eighth Edition.

software. A hardware consultant serves a similar role with hardware. In other schools, a software specialist and a hardware consultant report to the technology coordinator.

At school, district, regional, and state levels, media professionals are employed to run programs and, depending on the size of the organization, produce materials for use in schools. As school districts and regional media centers have built up their collections of audiovisual materials for distribution, they have employed instructional media professionals to select these materials. Another career area at all education levels is in professional management of media collections, including classification, storage, and distribution.

Instructional product design—developing valid and reliable instructional materials—has been an important specialty in the field of instructional technology for some time. Publishers and producers of instructional materials, along with school districts, community colleges, and colleges and universities, employ specialist trained in product design skills. Computer-assisted instruction, interactive media, and other emerging forms of individualized instruction (Figure 3-8) constitute an important growth area within this field.

Figure 3-8 Individualized instruction can help students, especially those having difficulties in learning, learn better.

Organizations other than schools also require specialists in educational technology. Healthcare institutions, for example, are heavily involved in instructional technology and have been employing an increasing number of professionals to help develop the instruction used in those programs.

Training programs rely heavily on instructional technology and media. Consequently, specialists in instructional technology are in demand in these programs. These specialties include the following:
- Trainer. Presents information, leads discussions, and manages learning experiences.
- Instructional designers. Assesses training needs, translates training needs into training programs, determines media to be used, and designs course materials.
- Training manager. Plans and organizes training programs, hires staff, prepares and manages budgets.

Hardware and software developments are occurring so rapidly that our expectation increasingly lags behind reality. In previous generations our vision extended beyond our capabilities. Now it struggles to keep up with what is available. Wireless telephone communication, for example, is now widely used. Not too long ago, it was science fiction. Hand-held computers and Internet-enabled cellular telephones are common among professionals who need quick and easy access to data—including color photos and even video. The combination of wireless, cellular, and miniaturized technologies allows people literally to access the Internet in the palm of their hand. All these developments and trends make this an exciting and challenging time for professionals engaged in education and training. Make the most of it!

## New Words

sway　　*v.* 摇摆，摇动
vocation　　*n.* 召唤，号召，天命，天职，特殊的适应性，才能，行业，职业
robotics　　*n.* 机器人技术
advent　　*n.* （尤指不寻常的人或事）出现，到来
fragmentary　　*adj.* 由碎片组成的，断断续续的
transcend　　*vt.* 超越，胜过
bandwidth　　*n.* 带宽
pervasive　　*adj.* 蔓延的，遍布的，弥漫的，渗透的
catalog　　*n.* 目录，目录册 *v.* 编目录
cellular　　*adj.* 细胞的
miniaturize　　*vt.* 使小型化
palm　　*n.* 手掌，棕榈，（象征胜利的）棕榈叶 *vt.* 与……握手，藏……于掌中，蒙混

## Notes

[1] If educational technology is viewed as both process and tools, it is important to begin to examine four different historical perspectives on these processes and tools, all of which have helped shape the current practices in the field.

译文：如果教育技术被看成既是过程又是工具的话，那么从关于这些过程和工具的四个不同的历史观点开始审视就是非常重要的。这些过程和工具帮助形成了这个领域目前的实践。

• If educational technology is viewed as both process and tools 是条件状语从句。

• it is important to begin to examine four different historical perspectives on these processes and tools 中的 it 是形式主语，不定式 to begin to examine four different historical perspectives on these processes and tools 作真正的主语。

• all of which have helped shape the current practices in the field 是非限制性定语从句，修饰先行词 processes and tools。

[2] These added and shifting emphases within the field that is known as instructional or educational technology seem to indicate that the field does not qualify for status as a discipline.

译文：这个被称作教学技术或教育技术的领域中的这些附加的、多变的言论似乎表明：这个领域还没有学科地位。

• that is known as instructional or educational technology 作定语从句，修饰先行词 the field。

• that the field does not qualify for status as a discipline 是宾语从句。

• be known as 被认为是

- qualify for 使合格，有……的资格，(使)有资格充任……

[3] Regardless of the quality and sophistication of computer hardware and software, the success of technology often depends on the support and encouragement that students and teachers receive in using it.

**译文**：不管计算机硬件和软件的质量和复杂性存在什么样的差别，技术在学校的成功更多地取决于我们如何支持和鼓励学生和教师使用各类技术。

- that students and teachers receive in using it 是 the support and encouragement 的同位语从句。
- regardless of 不管，不顾
- depend on 依靠，依赖

## Selected Translation

## Text D

### 教育技术从业者的未来

无论作为教师、培训者，还是作为媒体/技术专家，你正在一个激动人心的时刻进入教育技术领域。和其他教育领域不同，教育技术正变得越来越普及，在正规教育和非正规教育领域都是如此。相信会有更多的人进入这个领域。

增长最快的专业人员是学校的教育技术协调人。不管计算机硬件和软件的质量和复杂性存在怎么样的差别，技术在学校的成功更多地取决于我们如何支持和鼓励学生和教师使用各类技术。技术负责人可以帮助制订计划，选择软件和硬件，在设备购买和安装过程中提供咨询并且监督设备的维护和维修。

有的学校和企业把技术协调人的职位分为两个角色。一个是软件专家，他负责对软件进行订购、编目、发放，以及为教师提供应用咨询。一个是硬件专家，在硬件方面承担相应的责任。另外还有一些学校，有三个人负责教育技术方面的工作，其中，软件专家和硬件专家都要向技术负责人汇报工作。

在学校、学区、区域和国家层次上，媒体专家都被雇佣来运作教育技术相关项目，并根据组织规模的大小制作学校所需要的教学材料。学区和地区性的媒体中心已经收集了一定的教学视听材料，这些媒体中心也雇佣教学媒体专家来负责选择教学材料。在各级教育机构中，另外一个常见的教育技术职位是媒体资源管理员，这些人负责对多种媒体资源进行分类、保存和分发。

教学产品设计(开发有效的和可靠的教学材料)已经成为教育技术领域中的一个重要的专业。教育材料的发行者和生产者，还有学区、社区学院、学院和大学，都雇佣了很多接受过产品设计技能培训的专业人员。计算机辅助教学、交互媒体、新出现的个别化教学产品，构成了教育技术最重要的增长点。

学校以外的其他组织，也需要教育技术专家。例如，健康保健机构就大量采用了教学技术，该行业雇佣了越来越多的教育技术专业人员，开发健康保健方面的教学节目。

培训课程也极大地依赖教学技术和教学媒体。结果，这些课程都需要教育技术专业

人员的加盟。他们包括：
- 培训师：演示信息、引导讨论、管理学习过程。
- 教学设计师：分析培训需求、把培训需求转化为培训内容、确定培训媒体、设计课程材料。
- 培训管理者：计划和管理培训项目、雇佣员工、准备和控制预算。

硬件和软件的发展如此迅速，以至于我们的预测远远落后于现实。前面几代技术兴起的时候，我们对教育技术的憧憬超过了我们的能力。现在，我们只有奋力追赶，才能跟上技术发展的步伐。例如，不久之前，无线电通信还是一个科学幻想，现在已经普遍使用。在那些需要快捷、迅速地获取数据（包括彩色图片和视频）的专业人士中，手持电脑和网络支持的移动电话也已经普及。无线技术、移动技术和小型化技术的结合，理论上让人们都能够通过掌上设备访问因特网。对于教育技术和培训领域的专业人员来说，所有的这些发展趋势为我们营造了一个令人激动的、富有挑战的时代。努力工作吧，不要辜负这个时代！

## Exercises

**Short Answers：**

1. What are the four perspectives of educational technology?
2. Why was the audiovisual field not qualified for status of a discipline?
3. What are the focuses of the two educational futurists—Aureo Castro and David Thornburg as to the trends of educational technology?
4. What can you do after graduation in the field of educational technology?

# 专业英语常见的语法现象

专业英语的语法特点可以归纳为客观、准确和精练，所以在专业英语中经常出现如下的语法现象。

### 一、动名词

动名词的作用相当于名词，它在句子中可作主语和宾语。它可以取代时间从句或简化时间从句。例如：

1. Reading is a good habit. 动名词在句中做主语。
2. I enjoy working with you. 动名词在句中做动词宾语。
3. I am interested in reading. 动名词在句中做介词宾语。

在专业英语中，动名词的应用相当普遍。它可以令句子精练。例如：通常的表达形式为：

4. Before it is executed, the program should be loaded into main memory.
5. When you use the mouse to click a button, you can select an option from a list.

相应地用动名词来表示的精练形式为：

Before being executed, the program should be loaded into main memory.

By using the mouse to click a button, you can select an option from a list.

**二、分词短语**

使用过去分词可以取代被动语态的关系从句，使用现在分词可以取代主动语态的关系从句。

1. 现在分词短语一般做形容词用，可修饰动作的发出者，有主动的意义。可译成"……的……"，此时多做定语，在意思上和一个定语从句差不多。如：

The word "technology" is used by some to mean "hardware"—the devices that deliver information and serve as tools to accomplish a task—but those working in the field use "technology" to refer to a systematic process of solving problems by scientific means.

2. 现在分词短语还可以作状语，用来表示方式、目的、条件、结果和背景等等；有时可以表示伴随状态。如：

He emphasized that real systems are open to, and interact with, their environments, and that they can acquire qualitatively new properties through emergence, resulting in continual evolution. 此句中现在分词作状语，表示结果。

3. 过去分词短语一般做形容词用，可修饰动作的对象。如：

The effectiveness of human communication, Weaver asserted, may be measured by "the success with which the meaning conveyed to the receiver leads to the desired conduct on his part."

**三、不定式**

在专业英语中，不定式短语可以大量地用作状语或定语。当然，它也可以替换表示目的、功能的状态从句。如：

What is the task of the educational system in general? It qualifies the individual for work and for life in general. 可以简化为：The task of the educational system is to qualify the individual for work and for life in general. 又如：

The best way to introduce this theory is through Gagne's model which describes the set of factors that influence learning and that collectively may be called the conditions of learning.

**四、被动语态**

被动语态在专业英语中用得非常频繁，这主要有两个原因：一是专业文章在描写行为或状态本身时注重客观事实或道理，所以由谁或由什么行为或状态作为主体就显得不那么重要了。例如：

The information is held in short-term memory for about 20—30 seconds (unless rehearsed) and then the information to be acquired is transformed by a process known as semantic encoding to a form that enters long-term memory. 又如：

Each of the objectives must be stated in performance terms using one of the standard verbs (i. e. states, discriminates, classifies, etc.) associated with the particular learning outcome.

被动语态使用频繁的另外一个原因是便于向后扩展句子,构成更长的句子,以便于对问题做出更精确的描述,但又不至于把句子弄得头重脚轻。例如:

Elaboration theory is an instructional design theory that argues that content to be learned should be organized from simple to complex order, while providing a meaningful context in which subsequent ideas can be integrated.

### 五、其他现象

在专业英语中,一些其他的常用短语也经常出现。

1. 在专业英语中,要对概念或术语下定义时,我们常用以下短语。

be defined as,如:Learning is defined as "persisting change in human performance or performance potential"。

be called,如:Educational technology is also called instructional technology sometimes。

refer to,如:The word "technology" is used to refer to a systematic process of solving problems by scientific means。

be regarded as,如:Computer is regarded as multimedia。

2. 专业英语中,"主语 + be 形容词 + to 名词"的结构是很常见的。它用于对某一事物、概念或论点加以定论、叙述。

be necessary to,如:It is necessary to examine the efficiency of the new design。

be adaptable to,如:A living thing is adapted to a special environment。

# Part 2　The Theoretical Foundation of Educational Technology

## Unit 4　Learning Theories

▲ **Knowledge Objectives**

When you have completed this unit, you will be able to:
- State the importance of learning theory to educational technology
- Describe behaviorism, cognitivism and constructivism
- State the information-processing theory
- Compare and contrast behaviorism, cognitivism and constructivism
- Name some important learning theorists

▲ **Professional Terms**

| | |
|---|---|
| learning theory | 学习理论 |
| behaviorism | 行为主义 |
| discovery learning | 发现学习 |
| motivation | 动机 |
| cognitive science | 认知科学 |
| schema theory | 图式理论 |
| elaboration theory | 细化理论 |
| stimulus-response theory | 刺激—反应理论 |
| reinforcement | 强化 |
| cognitivism | 认知主义 |
| information processing theory | 信息处理理论 |
| sensory register | 感觉登记器 |
| short-term memory | 短时记忆 |
| semantic encoding | 语义编码 |
| long-term memory | 长时记忆 |
| response generator | 反应发生器 |
| constructivism | 建构主义 |

## Text A

## The Importance of Learning Theory to Education Technology[1]

Figure 6-1  After learning, people can know the reason why apples fall from the tree.

Most people have an intuitive notion of what it means to learn: They can do something they could not do before or they know something that they did not know before (Figure 6-1). In most psychology theories, learning is defined as "persisting change in human performance or performance potential," however, the major concepts and principles of learning vary with learning theories.

Regardless of the differences among psychological perspectives on learning, a solid foundation in various learning theories is the undoubtedly the essential element in the preparation of ISD professionals. They must be familiar with the theory and research on learning and must be able to apply them to actual practice. For example, a designer working on the early childhood education project will find insight into children's behavior and the value of a rich learning environment in the work of Piaget. Designers familiar with social learning theory of Bandura will not ignore the environment factors that significantly affect instructional programs, nor overlook the power of informal learning channels (e.g., observational learning).[1] Bruner's rich philosophical insight of discovery learning and problem solving (Figure 6-2), Keller's work on motivation, Knowles' emphasis on the factors that facilitate adult learning, and the work of others contribute to a designer's overall understanding of learning process and skills in designing instructional strategies. Cognitive science (Klatzky, Anderson, Gagne, Wildman and Burton) is making a major contribution to our understanding of how humans perceive, process, store and retrieve information. Schema theory, elaboration, metacognition, automaticity, expert/novice studies, and transfer are only a few of the constructs studied by cognitive psychologist that have important implications for design of instruction.

Figure 6-2  Through problem solving, students can understand the knowledge deeply and utilize it well, and therefore become more creative.

Without a broad foundation in learning theory, the practice of ISD becomes narrowly forces on means (the steps in systems model) rather than on the rightful end (learning).

---

[1] Jiao jianli and Ye lihan, *Professional English for Educational Technology*, 2005.

Part 2   The Theoretical Foundation of Educational Technology

# Text B

## The Behaviorist Orientation to Learning[①]

The behaviorist movement in psychology has looked to the use of experimental procedures to study behavior in relation to the environment.

John B. Watson, who is generally credited as the first behaviorist, argued that the inner experiences that were the focus of psychology could not be properly studied as they were not observable.[2] Instead he turned to laboratory experimentation. The result was the generation of the stimulus-response model. In this model, the environment is seen as providing stimuli to which individuals develop responses.

In essence three key assumptions underpin this view:

• Observable behavior rather than internal thought processes are the focus of study. In particular, learning is manifested by a change in behavior.

• The environment shapes one's behavior; what one learns is determined by the elements in the environment, not by the individual learner.

• The principles of contiguity (how close in time two events must be for a bond to be formed) and reinforcement (any means of increasing the likelihood that an event will be repeated) are central to explaining the learning process.

Researchers like Edward L. Thorndike build upon these foundations and, in particular, developed an S-R (stimulus-response) theory of learning (Figure 6-3). He noted that that responses (or behaviors) were strengthened or weakened by the consequences of behavior. This notion was refined by Skinner and is perhaps better known as operant conditioning—reinforcing what you want people to do again, ignoring or punishing what you want people to stop doing.

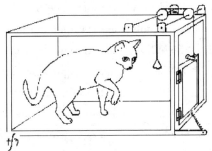

Figure 6-3   With his experiment of cat, Thorndike developed the stimulus-response theory of learning.

In terms of learning, according to James Hartley four key principles come to the fore:

• Activity is important. Learning is better when the learner is active rather than passive. ("Learning by doing" is to be applauded.)

• Repetition, generalization and discrimination are important notions. Frequent practice—and practice in varied contexts—is necessary for learning to take place. Skills are not acquired without frequent practice.

• Reinforcement is the cardinal motivator. Positive reinforcers like rewards and successes are preferable to negative events like punishments and failures.

---

① http://www.infed.org/biblio/learning-behavourist.htm

- Learning is helped when objectives are clear. Those who look to behaviorism in teaching will generally frame their activities by behavioral objectives e. g. "By the end of this session participants will be able to...". With this comes a concern with competencies and product approaches to curriculum.

## Text C

## Cognitivism and Gagne's Model of Learning[①]

Cognitivism has its roots in cognitive psychology and Information Processing Theory. Information Processing Theory emphasizes the identification of the internal processes of learning and concentrates on how the learner comes to know rather than respond in an instructional situation.[3] This theory was a landmark in the field of instructional design since it represented a major paradigm shift from Skinner's behaviorist approach to learning. The behaviorist approach did not investigate the internal states of the learner claiming that such states cannot be directly observed and instead focused on stimulus-response strategies (Pavlov's Classical Conditioning Theory and Thorndike's Laws of Effect) by reinforcing the desired learning behavior through reward and/or punishment. The learner was a reactive rather than a proactive agent of instruction and learning.

The best way to introduce this theory is through Gagne's model which describes the set of factors that influence learning and that collectively may be called the conditions of learning.[4] They include internal as well as external conditions that shape the learning processes. The figure below is a widely accepted framework that incorporates the ideas of Information Processing Theory by modeling the process of how a learner comes to know (Figure 6-4).

A learner's environment activates the receptors (senses) and information is then transmitted through the sensory registers to short-term memory in selected and recognizable patterns (7 + or -2 chunks of information). The information is held in short-term memory for about 20—30 seconds (unless rehearsed) and then the information to be acquired is transformed by a process known as semantic encoding to a form that enters long-term memory. This information now becomes meaningful because it is related to existing information and it takes the form of a schema or a collection of related propositions which can be later retrieved into working memory (another way of referring to short-term memory) when needed. Finally information passes through a response generator which activates the necessary effectors that transform the information into action. Executive control and expectancies are structures that govern this flow of information and how it will be stored and retrieved by the learner. It represents the learner's use of cognitive strategies that are affected by external cues in the learning environment. The way that

---

① http://www.coe.uh.edu/courses/cuin6373/idhistory/cognitivism.html
http://www.personal.psu.edu/users/w/x/wxh139/cognitive_1.htm#major

## Part 2 The Theoretical Foundation of Educational Technology

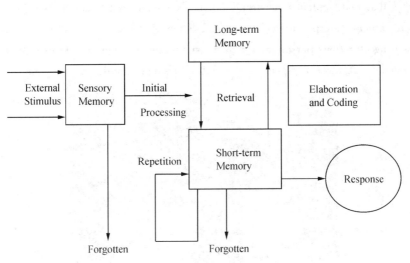

Figure 6-4 Information processing theory

the learner uses those cognitive strategies will determine how the information is encoded and later retrieved.

The central issues that interest cognitive psychologists include the internal mechanism of human thought and the processes of knowing. Cognitive psychologists have attempted to find out the answers to mental structures, such as what is stored and how it is stored, and to mental processes concerning how the integration and retrieval of information is operated. The theoretical assumptions in cognitive psychology lend instructional systems a hand in the design of efficient processing strategies for the learners to acquire knowledge, e. g. mnemonic devices to reduce the workload of the short-term memory, rehearsal strategies to maintain information, and the use of metaphors and analogies to relate meaning of the new information to prior knowledge.

## Text D

## Constructivism[①]

Constructivism is an epistemology, a metatheory, a theory of knowledge, the generic definitions of which are centered on the active participation of the subject in construing reality, rather than on reflecting or representing reality.[5] In the view of constructivist, learning is a constructive process in which the learner is building an internal illustration of knowledge, a personal interpretation of experience (Figure 6-5). This representation is continually open to modification, its structure and linkages forming the ground to which other knowledge structures are attached. Learning is an active process in which meaning is accomplished on the basis of experience. This view of knowledge does not necessarily reject the existence of the real world,

---

① http://starfsfolk.khi.is/solrunb/construc.htm

and it agrees that reality places constrains on the concepts, but contends that all we know of the world are human interpretations of our experience of the world. Conceptual growth comes from the sharing of various perspectives and the simultaneous changing of our internal representations in response to those perspectives as well as through cumulative experience.

Figure 6-5  Through interact, people construct their own internal illustration of knowledge on the basis of their experience.

The fundamental challenge of constructivism is in its changing the locus of control over learning from the teacher to the student. Educational technologists, with their foundations in behavioural psychology, have sought to design programs in such a way that students would be enticed to achieve prespecified objectives. Constructivists have said that this violates both what we know now about the nature of learning (situated, interactive) and about the nature of knowledge (perspectival, conventional, tentative, evolutionary). They have claimed that objectives should be negotiated with students based on their own felt needs, that programmed activities should emerge from within the contexts of their lived worlds, that students should work together with peers in the social construction of personally significant meaning, and that evaluation should be a personalized, ongoing and shared analysis of progress.

Agreeing with this view of knowledge, learning must be placed in a rich context, reflective of real world context, for this constructive process happens and transfers to environments beyond the school or training classroom. Learning through cognitive apprenticeship, mirroring the collaboration of real world problem solving, and using the tools available in problem solving situations, are key. How effectual the learner's knowledge structure is in facilitating thinking in the content field is the measure of learning.

## New Words

  operant *n.* 发生作用之人或物，工作之人或物 *adj.* 动作的
  orientation *n.* 方向，方位，定位，倾向性，向东方
  generalization *n.* 一般化，普遍化，概括，广义性
  discrimination *n.* 辨别，区别，识别力，辨别力，歧视
  cardinal *n.* 枢机主教，红衣主教 *adj.* 主要的，最重要的

paradigm　　*n.* 范例
mechanism　　*n.* 机械装置,机构,机制
mnemonic　　*adj.* 记忆的,记忆术的
rehearsal　　*n.* 排演,演习,预演,试演
metaphor　　*n.* [修辞]隐喻,暗喻
metatheory　　*n.* 元理论(用以阐明某一理论或某类理论的理论)
epistemology　　*n.* [哲]认识论
cumulative　　*adj.* 累积的
generic　　*adj.* [生物]属的,类的,一般的,普通的,非特殊的
tentative　　*n.* 试验,假设 *adj.* 试验性的,试探的,尝试的,暂定的

## Notes

[1] Designers familiar with social learning theory of Bandura will not ignore the environment factors that significantly affect instructional programs, nor overlook the power of informal learning channels(e.g., observational learning).

译文:熟悉班杜拉的社会性学习理论的设计者不会忽视极大影响教学程序的环境因素,也不会忽略非正式学习途径的作用(例如观察学习)。

• familiar with social learning theory of Bandura 作定语,修饰 designers。
• be familiar with 熟悉
• that significantly affect instructional programs 是定语从句,修饰先行词 the environment factors。

[2] John B. Watson, who is generally credited as the first behaviorist, argued that the inner experiences that were the focus of psychology could not be properly studied as they were not observable.

译文:约翰·华生通常被认为是第一位行为主义学家,他认为作为心理学研究重点的内心活动无法得到正确的研究,因为它们是不可观察的。

• who is generally credited as the first behaviorist 是非限制性定语从句,修饰先行词 John B. Watson。
• that were the focus of psychology 是限制性定语从句,修饰先行词 inner experiences。
• as they were not observable 是原因状语从句,用来解释说明原因。

[3] Information Processing Theory emphasizes the identification of the internal processes of learning and concentrates on how the learner comes to know rather than respond in an instructional situation.

译文:信息处理理论强调对学习内在过程的识别,并关注学习者如何学习,而不是对教学情况作出反应。

• how the learner comes to know rather than respond in an instructional situation 是宾语从句。
• come to *v.* 达到,继承,复苏,停止,想起,共计

* rather than 胜于，而不是

[4] The best way to introduce this theory is through Gagne's model which describes the set of factors that influence learning and that collectively may be called the conditions of learning.

译文：介绍认知主义的最好的方式就是通过加涅的信息加工理论模型，这个模型描述了一系列影响学习以及那些可以被称为学习条件的要素。

* 不定式 to introduce this theory 做定语，修饰 The best way。
* which describes the set of factors 是定语从句，修饰先行词 Gagne's model。
* that influence learning and that collectively may be called the conditions of learning 是两个定语从句，修饰先行词 the set of factors。
* a set of 一组，一套

[5] Constructivism is an epistemology, a metatheory, a theory of knowledge, the generic definitions of which are centered on the active participation of the subject in construing reality, rather than on reflecting or representing reality.

译文：建构主义是一种认识论，一种元理论，一种关于知识的理论，它通用的定义是以主体积极参与构建现实为中心，而不是以反映或代表现实为中心。

* the generic definitions of which are centered on the active participation of the subject in construing reality, rather than on reflecting or representing reality 是非限制性定语从句，修饰先行词 Constructivism。
* be centered on 以……为中心，围绕

## Selected Translation

## Text D

### 建 构 主 义

建构主义是一种认识论，一种元理论，一种关于知识的理论，它通用的定义是以主体积极参与构建现实为中心，而不是以反映或代表现实为中心。建构主义学家认为，学习是学习者对知识进行内化处理和对经验进行个性化解释的过程。这个代表性的定义不断地被修改，其结构和联系成了其他知识结构参照的基础。学习是一个在经验的基础上完成意义建构的积极的过程。这一关于知识的观点并不一定拒绝现实世界的存在，并且这种观点也认为现实世界会对学习中所产生的概念加以限制，但它认为我们所有对世界的认识是人类对自身经验的解释。概念的增长既来自于我们对各种观点的分享，同时也来自于在我们对这些观点作出反应以及积累经验的过程中我们内在表征的改变。

建构主义根本性的挑战在于其将学习控制的核心从老师转换到了学生。以行为主义心理学为学科基础的教育技术学家力求通过引导学生达到预定目标的方式来设计方案。建构主义学家曾经说过，这违背了我们现在所了解的学习的本质（情境的，互动的）和知识的性质（观察的，常规的，实验性的，进化的）。他们声称：应该根据学生的自我需要通过商议来确定目标；为课程所设计的活动应该来自他们生活世界的背景中；学生应与同龄人携手合作，对个人认为重要的意义进行社会性构建；并且，评价应该是对进展给

予个性化的、渐进的、共享性的分析。

一经认同这种知识观,学习就必须放置在一个能够反映真实世界的丰富背景下,因为这种建构性的过程将发生于和转移到学校或培训课堂以外的环境中。通过认知学徒制来学习,借鉴现实世界中解决问题的合作,并在解决问题的情境中使用那些可获取的工具,是很关键的。学习者的知识结构如何能有效地促进相关领域的思考是对学习的衡量。

## Exercises

**1. Translate the Following Terms into English:**

(1) 行为主义

(2) 认知主义

(3) 刺激—反应理论

(4) 长时记忆

(5) 发现学习

(6) 语义编码

(7) 信息加工理论

(8) 建构主义

**2. Choose the One that Best Suits the Sentence According to the Text.**

(1) _____ argues that "what one learns is determined by the elements in the environment, not by the individual learner."

   A. Cognitivism             B. Constructivism

   C. Behaviorism

(2) Which theory was a landmark in the field of instructional design?

   A. cognitivism             B. behaviorism

   C. constructivism

(3) How many recognizable patterns can be stored in short-term memory?

   A. 7 or 9                  B. 5 or 9

   C. 9 or 11

(4) Which model describes the set of factors that influence learning and that collectively may be called the conditions of learning?

   A. Gagne's information-processing model

   B. Dick and Carey Model

   C. Berlo's Model

(5) According to Constructivism, which one is the most important?

   A. the external stimulus

   B. the active participation of the subject in construing reality

   C. reflect or represent reality

# 专业英语翻译的标准

翻译是一种语言表达法,是译者用本国语言表达原作者的思想。这就要求译者必须确切地理解和掌握原著的内容和意思,丝毫不可以离开它而主观地发挥译者个人的想法和推测。在确切理解的基础上,译者必须很好地运用本国语言把原文通顺而流畅地表达出来。

随着国际学术交流的日益广泛,专业英语已经受到普遍的重视,因此,掌握一些专业英语的翻译技巧是非常必要的。专业英语作为一种重要的英语文体,与非专业英语文体相比,具有词义多、长句多、被动句多、词性转换多、非谓语动词多、专业性强等特点,这些特点都是由专业文献的内容所决定的。因此,专业英语的翻译也有别于其他英语文体的翻译。

### 一、翻译人员必须了解相关专业领域的知识

在专业翻译中,要达到融会贯通,必须了解相关的专业知识,熟练掌握同一事物的中英文表达方式。单纯靠对语言的把握也能传达双方的语言信息,但运用语言的灵活性特别是选词的准确性会受到很大的限制。要解决这个问题,翻译人员就要积极主动地熟悉本专业领域的相关翻译知识。比如,要翻译"conductor"这个词,仅仅把字面意思翻译出来还远远不够。"conductor"在日常生活中的意思是"售票员和乐队指挥",但在电学中却表示导体的意思。因此,了解了专业领域,在翻译过程中就会大大提高理解能力和翻译质量。

### 二、专业英语翻译标准

关于翻译的标准,历来提法很多。有的主张"信、达、雅",有的主张"信、顺",有的主张"等值"等等,并曾多次展开过广泛的争论和探讨。从他们的争论中可以看出,有一点是共同的,即一切译文都应包括原文思想内容和译文语言形式这两个方面。简单地说,符合规范的译文语言、确切忠实地表达原作的风格,这就是英语翻译的共同标准。为此,笔者认为,在进行英语翻译时要坚持两条标准:

1. 忠实

译文应忠实于原文,准确、完整、科学地表达原文的内容,包括思想、精神与风格。译者不得歪曲、增删、遗漏和篡改原文内容。

2. 通顺

译文语言必须通顺、符合规范。用词造句应符合本民族语言的习惯,要用民族的、科学的、大众的语言,以求通顺易懂。不应有文理不通、逐词死译和生硬晦涩等现象。

### 三、专业英语翻译过程中要体现中文的语言特色

1. 大量使用名词化结构

大量使用名词化结构(Nominalization)是专业英语的特点之一。因为专业文体要求行文简洁、表达客观、内容确切、信息量大,强调存在的事实,而非强调某一行为。如:

A. Archimedes first discovered **the principle that water is displaced** by solid bodies.

B. Archimedes first discovered **the principle of displacement of water** by solid bodies.

**译文**:阿基米德最先发展固体排水的原理。

前者显然有一个同位语从句。这样的结构出现在一般的英语文章中。但是在专业文章里,你需要将上述结构转换成名词结构。句中 of displacement of water by solid bodies 系名词化结构,一方面简化了同位语从句,另一方强调 displacement 这一事实。

2. 广泛使用被动语句

专业英语中的谓语至少 1/3 是被动态。这是因为专业文章侧重叙事推理,强调客观准确。第一、二人称使用过多,会造成主观臆断的印象。因此尽量使用第三人称叙述,采用被动语态,如:

A. **You must state each of the objectives** using one of the standard verbs (i.e. states, discriminates, classifies, etc.) associated with the particular learning outcome.

B. **Each of the objectives must be stated** using one of the standard verbs (i.e. states, discriminates, classifies, etc.) associated with the particular learning outcome.

**译文**:应当使用与特定的学习结果有关的标准动词来陈述每一个目标。

在一般英文作文中经常使用主动句,但是在专业文章中,以被描述的事物充当主语更为常见。但在翻译成中文时应将其还原成主动句,句子的主语一般不译出。

3. 非限定动词的应用和大量使用后置定语

专业文章要求行文简练、结构紧凑,因此,往往使用分词短语代替定语从句或状语从句,使用分词独立结构代替状语从句或并列分句,使用不定式短语代替各种从句,使用介词+动名词短语代替定语从句或状语从句。这样既可缩短句子,又比较醒目。如:

Designers **familiar with social learning theory of Bandura** will not ignore the environment factors that significantly affect instructional programs, nor overlook the power of informal learning channels(e.g, observational learning).

**译文**:熟悉班杜拉的社会性学习理论的设计者不会忽视极大影响教学程序的环境因素,也不会忽略非正式学习途径的作用(例如观察学习)。

短语 **familiar with social learning theory of Bandura** 代替了定语从句,使句子简洁紧凑。

又如:

Systems analysis, **developed independently of systems theory**, applies systems principles to aid a decision-maker with problems of identifying, reconstructing, optimizing, and controlling a system (usually a socio-technical organization), while taking into account multiple objectives, constraints and resources.

**译文**:系统分析是系统理论中独立发展的一种理论,它在考虑多重目标、约束和资源的同时,应用系统原则来帮助决策者鉴别问题,改造、优化和控制系统(通常是社会技术组织)等。

过去分词结构 developed independently of systems theory 做定语,避免了使用定语从句的麻烦,使句子变得简洁。

4. 大量使用常用句型

科技文章中经常使用若干特定的句型,这些特定的句型因而成了科技文体区别于其他文体的标志。例如 It—that 结构句型、被动态结构句型、结构句型、分词短语结构句型、省略句结构句型等。如:

It is evident that a well lubricated bearing turns more easily than a dry one。

**译文**:显然,润滑好的轴承,比不润滑的轴承容易转动。

5. 为了描叙事物精确,多使用长句

为了表述一个复杂概念,使之逻辑严密、结构紧凑,科技文章多用长句。有的长句多达七八十个词。如:

The term knowledge engineers has been coined to describe the people who work with experts in a field to assemble or organize a body of knowledge and then design the software package that makes it possible to train someone to become skilled in the area or to enable anyone to call on the skills of experts to solve a problem.

这确实是一个很长的句子,但是在对句子进行分析之后,问题就迎刃而解了。**译文**:知识工程师这个词描述那些与领域专家共同工作、负责收集和组织知识,然后设计软件的人。知识工程师开发的专家系统可以帮助一些人掌握相关领域的知识,也可以帮助各类人员利用系统中的专家知识来解决面临的问题。

6. 大量使用复合词与缩略词

大量使用复合词与缩略词是科技文章的特点之一,如:full-enclosed 全封闭的(双词合成形容词)。复合词从过去的双词组合发展到多词组合。缩略词趋向于任意构词,例如某一篇论文的作者可以就仅在该文中使用的术语组成缩略词,这给翻译工作带来一定的困难。

# Unit 5   Communication Theories

▲ Knowledge Objectives

When you have completed this unit, you will be able to:

• Define the term communication

• State the components of communication system and their meanings

• State the relationship of communication theory and other disciplines

• Identify advantages and disadvantages of Shannon-Weaver Model and Berlo's S-M-C-R Model

# Part 2  The Theoretical Foundation of Educational Technology

* Compare and contrast the two different models of communication theory

▲ **Professional Terms**

communication theory　传播理论
medium　媒体
feedback　反馈
information theory　信息理论
encoder　编码
channel　信道
decoder　译码

## Text A

### Defining Communication[①]

There is much discussion in the academic world of communication (Figure 5-1) as to what actually constitutes communication. Currently, many definitions of communication are used in order to conceptualize the processes by which people navigate and assign meaning.

Frank Dance took a major step toward clarifying this muddy concept by outlining a number of elements to distinguish communication. He found three points of "critical conceptual differentiation" that form the basic dimensions of communication. The first dimension is the level of observation, or abstractness. Some definitions are broad and inclusive, others are restrictive. For example, the definition of communication as "the process that links discontinuous parts of the living word to one another" is general. On the other, communication as "the means of sending military messages, orders, etc., as by telephone, telegraph, radio, couriers" is restrictive.

Figure 5-1  Communication is very important for transmitting information.

The second distinction is intention. Some definitions include only purposeful message sending and receiving; other do not impose this limitation. The following is an example of definition that includes intention: "Those situations in which a source transmits a message to a receiver with conscious intent to affect the latter's behaviors." Here is a definition that does not require intent: "It is a process that makes common to two or several what was the monopoly of one or some."

The third dimension is normative judgment. Some definitions include a statement of

---

① http://en.wikibooks.org/wiki/Communication_Theory
Little john, S W, *Theories of Human Communication*(7th Edition), 清华大学出版社, 2003。

success or accuracy; other definitions do not contain such implicit judgments. The following definition, for example, presumes that communication is successful: "Communication is the verbal interchange of a though or idea." The assumption in this definition is that a thought or idea is successfully exchanged. Another definition, on the other hand, does not judge whether the outcome is successful or not: "Communication is the transmission of information." Here information is transmitted, but it is not necessarily received or understood.

We might say that communication consists of transmitting information. In fact, many scholars of communication take this as a working definition, and use Lasswell's maxim ("who says what to whom") as a means of circumscribing the field of communication. Others stress the importance of clearly characterizing the historical, economic and social context. The field of communication theory can benefit from a conceptualization of communication that is widely shared.

## Text B

### Communication System[①]

In general, for any message system—from computers linked by modems to tin cans connected by string—we can identify and evaluate its basic components. The components of a typical communication system, and the relationships between those components, are depicted graphically in the following illustration (Figure 5-2):

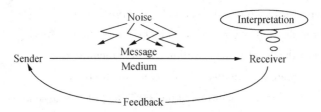

Figure 5-2　Communication system

**Sender (or Encoder)**: An information source; a person or device that originates a message.

**Receiver (or Decoder)**: The audience for a message. Also known as the addressee.

**Message**: The actual information or signal sent from a sender to a receiver. The "content" of a communique.

**Medium (or Channel)**: The method used to transmit a message (e.g., print, speech, telephone, smoke signals, etc.).

**Noise**: Technical or semantic obstacles; that is, anything that interferes with the clear transmission of a message (e.g., low visibility, poor ink quality, static electricity).

---

① http://collaboratory.nunet.net/dsimpson/comtheory.html

**Interpretation**: All operations that a receiver performs in order to decode and understand a message.

**Feedback**: Information about a message that a receiver sends back to the sender; the receiver's reaction or response to a communique.

# Text C

## Communication Theory[①]

Communication is intertwined with all of human life (Figure 5-3), and any study of human life must touch on this subject. Some scholars treat communication as central while others see it is as more peripheral, but it is always there. Communication stands so deeply rooted in human behaviors and the structures of society that scholars have difficulty thinking of it while excluding social or behavioral events. Because communication theory remains a relatively young field of inquiry and integrates itself with other disciplines such as philosophy, psychology, and sociology, one probably cannot yet expect a consensus conceptualization of communication across disciplines. The Communication Theory attempts to document types of communication, and to optimize communications for the benefit of all.

Figure 5-3  Students learn something from the teacher through communication, which is informal and comfortable.

It is well accepted that communication theories have developed through the realms of psychology and sociology over the past 100 years. Modern Communication Theory is based on mathematical theorems developed by Claude Shannon, an engineer and researcher at Bell Laboratories, in 1948. Shannon's original theory (also known as "information theory") was later elaborated and given a more popular, non-mathematical formulation by Warren Weaver, a media specialist with the Rockefeller Foundation. In effect, Weaver extended Shannon's insights about electronic signal transmission and the quantitative measurement of information flows into a broad theoretical model of human communication, which he defined as "all of the ways by which one mind may affect another."

The effectiveness of human communication, Weaver asserted, may be measured by "the

---

① http://en.wikipedia.org/wiki/Communication_theory
   http://collaboratory.nunet.net/dsimpson/comtheory.html

success with which the meaning conveyed to the receiver leads to the desired conduct on his part."[1] He thus introduced concepts of human purpose and reaction into what had originally been a set of highly technical equations for analyzing and evaluating the transmission of messages.

## Text D

## Two Typical Models of Communication Theory①

### Shannon-Weaver Model

Claude Shannon, a telecommunications engineer at Bell Telephone Laboratories, synthesized the early work in information. His book with Warren Weaver, *The Mathematical Theory of Communication*, is now a classic. The Shannon-Weaver model is typical of what are often referred to as transmission models of communication (Figure 5-4).

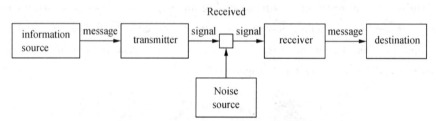

Figure 5-4 Shannon-Weaver Model

This is now known as the Shannon-Weaver Model. Although they were principally concerned with communication technology, their model has become one which is frequently introduced to students of human communication early in their study. However, despite the fact that it is frequently used early in the study of human communication, it's worth bearing in mind that information theory, or statistical communication theory was initially developed to separate noise from information-carrying signals.[2] That involved breaking down an information system into sub-systems so as to evaluate the efficiency of various communication channels and codes. The Shannon-Weaver Model (1947) proposes that all communication must include six elements:

- a source
- an encoder
- a message
- a channel
- a decoder
- a receiver

---

① http://www.cultsock.ndirect.co.uk/MUHome/cshtml/introductory/sw.html
　http://www.peoi.org/Courses/Coursesen/mass/mass2.html
　http://www.uri.edu/artsci/lsc/Faculty/Carson/508/03Website/Hayden/berlo.html

These six elements are shown graphically in the model. As Shannon was researching in the field of information theory, his model was initially very technology-oriented. The emphasis here is very much on the transmission and reception of information. This model is often referred to as an "information model" of communication. Apart from its obvious technological bias, a drawback from our point of view is the model's obvious linearity. It looks at communication as a one-way process. That is remedied by the addition of the feedback loop which you can see in the developed version of the mode 1 (Figure 5-5):

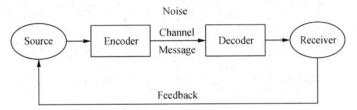

Figure 5-5 The developed Shannon-Weaver Model with the feedback loop

A further drawback with this kind of model is that the message is seen as relatively unproblematic. It's fine for discussing the transformation of "information", but when we try to apply the model to communication, problems arise with the assumption that meanings are somehow contained within the message. However, both mathematical and diagrammatic in character, the Shannon-Weaver model measures the efficiency and flexibility of a communication system. Harold Lasswell, a communications expert famous for his invention of content analysis and his research on propaganda techniques, probably provided the best characterization of the Shannon-Weaver model when he defined communication as essentially a matter of "who says what in which channel to whom and with what effects?"[3]

**Berlo's S-M-C-R Model**

Berlo's SMCR (source, message, channel, and receiver) Model (Figure 5-6) focuses on the individual characteristics of communication and stresses the role of the relationship between the source and the receiver as an important variable in the communication process. The more highly developed the communication skills of the source and the receiver, the more effectively the message will be encoded and decoded.

Berlo's model represents a communication process that occurs as a source drafts messages based on one's communication skills, attitudes, knowledge, and social and cultural system.[4] These messages are transmitted along channels, which can include sight, hearing, touch, smell, and taste. A receiver interprets messages based on the individual's communication skills, attitudes, knowledge, and social and cultural system. The limitations of the model are its lack of feedback.

The Berlo S-M-R-C Model accounts for a variety of variables that are present in person-to-person communication. When one is attempting to convey an emotionally complex message, the Berlo Model may be the more appropriate choice. For the transmission of a straightforward

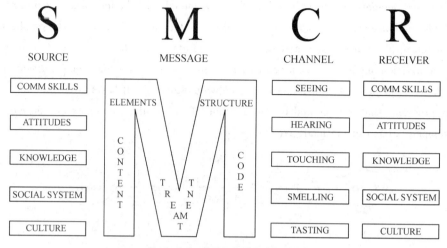

Figure 5-6  Berlo's S-M-R-C Model

message where both parties have a similar knowledge base, the Shannon-Weaver Model, although often thought of as simplistic, can be more effective than the Berlo Model.[5]

## New Words

  component *n.* 成分 *adj.* 组成的，构成的
  graphical *adj.* 绘成图画的，绘画的
  intertwine *v.* （使）纠缠，（使）缠绕
  peripheral *adj.* 外围的 *n.* 外围设备
  inquiry *n.* 质询，调查
  consensus *n.* 一致同意，多数人的意见，舆论
  document *n.* 公文，文件，文档，档案，文献 *v.* 证明
  realm *n.* 领域
  elaborate *adj.* 精心制作的，详细阐述的，精细 *vt.* 精心制作，详细阐述
  technical *adj.* 技术的，技术上的，技巧方面的
  synthesize *v.* 综合，合成
  transmission *n.* 播送，发射，传动，传送，传输，转播
  principal *n.* 负责人，首长，校长，主犯，本金 *adj.* 主要的，首要的
  drawback *n.* 缺点，障碍，退还的关税
  linearity *n.* 线性，直线性
  diagrammatic *adj.* 图表的，概略的
  efficiency *n.* 效率，功效
  flexibility *n.* 弹性，适应性，机动性，柔韧性
  propaganda *n.* 宣传
  interpret *v.* 解释，说明，口译，通译，认为是……的意思
  straightforward *adj.* 正直的，坦率的，简单的，易懂的，直截了当的 *adv.* 坦率地

Part 2　The Theoretical Foundation of Educational Technology

## Notes

[1]　The effectiveness of human communication, Weaver asserted, may be measured by "the success with which the meaning conveyed to the receiver leads to the desired conduct on his part."

**译文:** 韦弗宣称,人类交流的有效性可用这样的结果来衡量,即,传达给接受者的意义会使得接受者做出相应的行为。

- Weaver asserted 在此处是插入语。
- with which the meaning conveyed to the receiver leads to the desired conduct on his part 作定语从句,修饰先行词 the success。
- conveyed to the receiver 过去分词短语作定语,修饰 the meaning。
- lead to 导致,通向
- on one's part 在……方面,就……来说,由……所做出的

[2]　However, despite the fact that it is frequently used early in the study of human communication, it's worth bearing in mind that information theory, or statistical communication theory was initially developed to separate noise from information-carrying signals.

**译文:** 然而,尽管香农—韦弗模型早期经常用在研究人类交流上,值得记住的是,信息理论或统计学传播理论最初形成时是为了把噪音与承载信息的信号分离开来的。

- that it is frequently used early in the study of human communication 是同位语从句,先行词是 the fact。
- that information theory, or statistical communication theory was initially developed to separate noise from information-carrying signals. 是主语从句,其前的 it 是形式主语。
- bear in mind 记住

[3]　Harold Lasswell, a communications expert famous for his invention of content analysis and his research on propaganda techniques, probably provided the best characterization of the Shannon-Weaver model when he defined communication as essentially a matter of "who says what in which channel to whom and with what effects?"

**译文:** 哈罗德·拉斯韦尔是传播专家,因内容分析方面的创造和在宣传技术方面的研究而出名。他把传播定义为从本质上说是这样的问题:谁,说什么,通过什么渠道,对谁以及产生什么效果?由此他可能给出了香农—韦弗模型最好的表征。

- a communications expert famous for his invention of content analysis and his research on propaganda techniques 是同位语,详细说明 Harold Lasswell。
- be famous for 因……而著名

[4]　Berlo's model represents a communication process that occurs as a source drafts messages based on one's communication skills, attitudes, knowledge, and social and cultural system.

**译文:** 贝罗的模型代表了传播过程。当信源基于个人的交流技能、态度、知识以及社会和文化发出信息时,这个过程就发生了。

    • that occurs as a source drafts messages based on one's communication skills, attitudes, knowledge, and social and cultural system 是定语从句,修饰先行词 communication process。

    • base on 基于

[5] For the transmission of a straightforward message where both parties have a similar knowledge base, the Shannon-Weaver Model, although often thought of as simplistic, can be more effective than the Berlo Mode。

**译文**:虽然香农—韦弗模型通常被认为是过分简化的,但是对于具有相似知识背景的收发双方之间的信息直接传播来说,这个模型就比贝罗的模型更有效。

    • where both parties have a similar knowledge base 作定语从句,修饰先行词 a straightforward message。

    • although often thought of as simplistic 是插入语,解释说明 the Shannon-Weaver Model。

## Selected Translation

### Text A

### 给传播下定义

在传播的学术界,有很多关于传播到底是由什么组成的讨论。最近,为了将传播过程概念化,人们使用了许多有关传播的定义。

弗兰克·丹斯在澄清这个模糊的概念上向前迈进了一大步,他通过列举许多要素来对传播进行界定。他发现了构成传播的基本维度的三个"关键的概念性差异"。第一维度是观察的层面,或抽象的层面。基于该层面的定义有的内容广泛而且具有包容性,有的则是限制性的。例如,将传播定义为"把现存世界中不相关联的部分相互连接起来的过程"就是概括性的。另一方面,将传播解释为"通过诸如电话、电报、无线电、信使等发送军事情报、命令等内容的方式"则是限制性的定义。

第二个区别是意图。有的定义只强调有目的地发送和接收的信息,有的则没有这个限制。接下来的这个定义的例子强调目的性:"信源为了有意识地影响受者的行为而向受者传递信息的那些情境。"这里也有一个定义并不强调意图:"传播是将一个使某些人独占的信息为两个人或几个人所共有的过程。"

第三个维度是标准化判断。有的定义含有对传播成功或精确性的表述;有的定义则不包括这种隐含的判断。例如,在接下来的这个定义中,传播被假设为成功的:"传播是对思想或观念进行的语言交互。"这个定义中就假设了该思想或观点得到了成功的交换。另一方面,另一个定义则没有对传播结果的成功与否进行判断:"传播是信息的传送。"这里信息被传送了,但并不一定会被接收或被理解。

我们可以说传播是由传递信息构成的。事实上,许多传播学的学者将其作为一个起作用的定义,并用拉斯韦尔的最大化理论(谁对谁说什么)作为限制传播理论的一种方式。其他学者强调明确地描述历史、经济和社会背景的特征的重要性。传播理论的领域能从达成共识的"传播"概念中受益。

Part 2  The Theoretical Foundation of Educational Technology

## Exercises

**1. Please Choose the Right Explanation for Each Word:**

(1) Sender (or Encoder)

(2) Receiver (or Decoder)

(3) Message

(4) Media

(5) Noise

(6) Interpretation

(7) Feedback

A. The actual information or signal sent from a sender to a receiver. The "content" of a communique.

B. Technical or semantic obstacles; that is, anything that interferes with the clear transmission of a message (e.g., low visibility, poor ink quality, static electricity).

C. Information about a message that a receiver sends back to the sender; the receiver's reaction or response to a communique.

D. An information source; a person or device that originates a message.

E. The method used to transmit a message (e.g., print, speech, telephone, smoke signals, etc.).

F. All operations that a receiver performs in order to decode and understand a message.

G. The audience for a message. Also known as the addressee.

**2. Short Answers:**

(1) According to Frank Dance, what are "the critical conceptual differentiation" that form the basic the dimensions of communication?

(2) In general, how many components are included in a communication system? And what are they?

(3) How can we choose one of the two models—the Shannon-Weaver Model and the Berlo Model—when transmitting a message in person-to-person communication?

# 从句的翻译（Ⅰ）

英语中的从句有定语从句、状语从句、主语从句、表语从句、宾语从句以及同位语从句。翻译英语从句时，应弄清原文的句法结构，根据汉语的特点和表达方式，正确地译出原文的意思。下面根据不同的从句结构，来讨论它们的译法。

## 一、定语从句翻译法

定语从句的翻译方法较多，一般有三种方法：一是将从句翻译成前置定语，二是将从句单独翻译成一句话。三是将定语从句译成状语分句。对每一种方法的解释及说明都是针对本部分的定语从句的翻译而言的。一般来说,限制性定语从句一般采用第一种译法,非限制性定语从句采用第二种译法。以下是几种典型的方法:

1. 合译法:合译法通常用于句式较短的情况,主要以限制性定语从句为主。翻译时,可采用前置法,把定语从句译成带"的"的定语词组,放在被修饰词之前,从而将复合句译成汉语单句。如:

(1) Educational technology is most simply and comfortably defined as an array of tools that might prove helpful in advancing student learning.

教育技术可以最简便地定义为一系列能够在促进学生学习方面起作用的工具。

(2) The best way to introduce this theory is through Gagne's model which describes the set of factors that influence learning and that collectively may be called the conditions of learning.

介绍认知主义的最好的方式就是通过加涅的信息加工理论模型,该模型描述了一系列影响学习以及那些可以被称作学习条件的要素。

2. 分译法:分译法是指将主句和从句分开翻译的一种方法,主要用于较长的非限制性定语从句里。采用这种方法可避免句子的冗长和累赘。翻译时,将从句从句子中抽出来单独组成分句,放在主句后面。如:

(1) Hypermedia refers to computer software that uses elements of text, graphics, video, and audio connected in such a way that the user can easily move within the information.

超媒体是指一种计算机软件,它使用文本、图形、视频及音频等信息元素建立了特别的链接方式,使用户可以方便地在各种媒体间跳转。

(2) A similar effect is commonly observed in western movies, where the wheels of a stagecoach appear to be rotating more slowly than would be consistent with the coach's forward motion, and sometimes in the wrong direction.

一个类似的效果也常在西部电影中观察到,在这些电影中,马车的轮子看上去转得比马车实际向前运动的速度要慢,偶尔还会向相反的方向转动。

(3) Charles Reigeluth of Indiana University posited Elaboration Theory, an instructional design model that aims to help select and sequence content in a way that will optimize attainment of learning goals.

印第安纳大学的查尔斯·瑞格卢斯提出了细化理论,该理论是一种教学设计模式,它的目标是用一种能优化实现学习目标的方式来选择和编排学习内容。

3. 转译法:有些非限制性定语从句,从形式上看它们是定语从句,但它们并不表示先行词的特征和属性,而起状语的作用,这时可根据具体情况,采用转译法,把定语从句译成目的、结果、原因、条件、让步等状语从句。如:

(1) The strike would prevent the docking of ocean steamships, which require assistance of tugboats.

罢工会使远洋航船不能靠岸,因为他们需要拖船的帮助。(翻译成原因状语从句。)

(2) He wishes to write an article, which will attract public attention to the matter.

他想写一篇文章,以便能引起公众对这件事的关注。(翻译成目的状语从句。)

综上所述,定语从句一般要视其含义,与先行词关系的密切程度、长度的不同而采取不同的翻译方法,一般可以将其译成前置定语、独立成分,与先行词等融合在一起,甚至将其译成各种状语分句。

**二、状语从句翻译法**

在复合句中状语从句通常由连词或起连词作用的词引导,用来修饰主句中的动词、形容词或副词。状语从句一般情况下应按正常语序翻译。如:

(1) Although there has been considerable controversy regarding the merits of programmed instruction as the sole method of teaching, many educators agreed that they can contribute to more efficient classroom procedure supplement the conventional teaching methods.

虽然在把程序教学看做是教学唯一方式的优点方面一直有很多的争议,但是许多教育家赞同这样的观点:程序教学能提供更有效的教学程序来弥补传统教学方法。(由 although 引导让步状语从句。)

(2) If the hi-fi system has tone controls, we can change the tonal quality of the reproduced signal.

如果高保真的系统具有音调控制功能的话,那么我们就可以改变被录制信号的音调质量。(由 if 引导的条件状语从句。)

(3) John B. Watson, who is generally credited as the first behaviorist, argued that the inner experiences that were the focus of psychology could not be properly studied as they were not observable.

约翰·华生通常被认为是第一位行为主义学家,他认为作为心理学研究重点的内心活动无法得到正确的研究,因为它们是不可观察的。(由 as 引导原因状语从句。)

(4) When instruction is delivered at a distance, additional challenges result because students are often separated from others sharing their backgrounds and interests, have few if any opportunities to interact with teachers outside of class, and must rely on technical linkages to bridge the gap separating class participants.

教学被远程传送将导致额外的挑战,因为学生通常并没有共享他们的背景和兴趣,很少有机会在课外与老师交流,而且必须依赖技术来连接分散的课程参与者之间的距离。(由 when 引导时间状语从句。)

(5) I could understand his point of view, in that I'd been in a similar position.

我能理解他的观点,因为我也有过类似的处境。(In that = because)

(6) For all that he seems so bad-tempered, I still think he has a very kind nature.

尽管他好像脾气很坏,我仍然认为他心地善良。(for all that 引导让步状语从句,翻译为"尽管……""虽然……"。)

(7) Electricity is such an important energy that modern industry couldn't develop without it.

电是一种非常重要的能量,没有它,现代化工业就不能发展。(由 such...that... 引导的结果状语从句,译为并列句。)

# Unit 6  Instructional Theories

▲ **Knowledge Objectives**

When you have completed this unit, you will be able to:
- State the functions and categories of instructional theories
- State the Taxonomy of Educational Objectives and describe its cognitive domain
- Compare and contrast the Bloom's Taxonomy with Gagne's taxonomy
- Describe the nine events of instruction
- Outline the procedure of instruction according to Elaboration Theory

▲ **Professional Terms**

| | |
|---|---|
| instructional theory | 教学理论 |
| educational objective | 教育目标 |
| learning objective | 学习目标 |
| cognitive domain | 认知领域 |
| affective domain | 情感领域 |
| verbal information | 言语信息 |
| intellectual skills | 智力技能 |
| cognitive strategies | 认知策略 |
| attitudes | 态度 |
| motor skills | 动作技能 |
| evaluation | 评价 |
| learning outcome | 学习结果 |
| Elaboration Theory | 细化理论 |

## Text A

### A Brief Introduction to Instructional Theory[①]

Instructional theory is a discipline that focuses on how to structure material for promoting the education of humans, particularly youth (Figure 7-1). Originating in the United States in the late 1970s, instructional theory is typically divided into two categories: the cognitive and behaviorist schools of thought. Instructional theory was spawned off the 1956 work of Benjamin Bloom, a University of Chicago professor, and the results of his Taxonomy of Education Objectives—one of the first modern codifications of the learning process. One of the first instructional

---

① http://www.k12academics.com/instructional_theory.htm

theorists was Robert M. Gagne, who in 1965 published *Conditions of Learning* for the Florida State University's Department of Educational Research.

Figure 7-1  The teacher is transmitting knowledge to his students under the guidance of instructional theory.

Renowned psychologist B. F. Skinner's theories of behavior were highly influential on instructional theorists because their hypotheses can be tested fairly easily with the scientific process. It is more difficult to demonstrate cognitive learning results. Paulo Freire's *Pedagogy of the Oppressed*—first published in English in 1968—had a broad influence over a generation of American educators with his critique of various "banking" models of education and analysis of the teacher-student relationship.

In the context of e-learning (Figure 7-2), a major discussion in instructional theory is the potential of learning objects to structure and deliver content. A standalone educational animation is an example of a learning object that can be re-used as the basis for different learning experiences. There are currently many groups trying to set standards for the development and implementation of learning objects. At the forefront of the standards groups is the Department of Defense's Advanced Distributed Learning initiative with its SCORM standards. (SCORM stands for Shareable Content Object Reference Model)

Figure 7-2  E-learning is becoming more and more popular, especially for the adults.

## Text B

## Taxonomy of Educational Objectives[①]

The Taxonomy of Educational Objectives, often called Bloom's Taxonomy, is a classification of the different objectives and skills that educators set for students (learning objectives). The taxonomy was proposed in 1956 by Benjamin Bloom, an educational psychologist at the University of Chicago. Bloom's Taxonomy divides educational objectives into three "domains":

---

① http://en.wikipedia.org/wiki/Taxonomy_of_Educational_Objectives
　　http://jem-thematic.net/en/node/346

Figure 7-3  Teaching should not only focus on the cognitive aspect of students, but also concern the affective and psychomotor aspects of them.

Affective, Psychomotor, and Cognitive (figure 7-3). Like other taxonomies, Bloom's is hierarchical, meaning that learning at the higher levels is dependent on having attained prerequisite knowledge and skills at lower levels. A goal of Bloom's Taxonomy is to motivate educators to focus on all three domains, creating a more holistic form of education.

According to Bloom, one may classify a limited number of activities that affect the cognitive domain and involve knowledge and the development of intellectual skills. The cognitive domain is the one most relevant for the mathematics and scientific study areas since it includes the recall or recognition of specific facts (definitions and theorems abound in math), procedural patterns (algorithms and solving strategies), and concepts that serve in the development of intellectual abilities and skills (abstraction).[1] There are six major competence categories, which are listed in order below, starting from the simplest behavior to the most complex. These categories can also be thought of as degrees of difficulties and may be used to classify learning objects. Notice that, if a learning module tackles more of them, then the first ones must be mastered before the next ones can take place. Each competence is described by the math skills demonstrated by it and by some keywords that are likely to appear in the learning module.

1. Knowledge—Recall a definition or a theorem, basic knowledge of e.g. rules of derivation, trigonometric equivalences, terminology and major results in a certain area. Question cues: list, define, tell, describe, state, match, select, identify, show, label, collect, examine, tabulate, quote, name, what, etc.

2. Comprehension—Understand the meaning, translation, interpolation, and interpretation of instructions and problems. State a problem in one's own words. Understand a definition or a theorem and how they depend on other definitions, grasp the meaning of a certain symbolic expression, use abstract knowledge in concrete examples, derive and predict consequences of assumptions on mathematical objects e.g. given this function, describe its first and second derivative or write an algorithm to compute the greatest common divisor of two polynomials. Question cues: summarize, describe, interpret, contrast, predict, associate, distinguish, estimate, differentiate, discuss, extend, give examples, give counter-example.

3. Application—Use a theorem or more theorems to show properties of a mathematical object. Describe a concrete example in abstract terms. Apply a solving strategy to solve an exercise in a new domain. Question cues: apply, demonstrate, calculate, complete, illustrate, show, solve, examine, modify, relate, change, classify, experiment, discover.

4. Analysis—Separates definitions and axioms and from theorems. Understands logical

structures of proofs and complex mathematical domains. Recognizes hidden consequences following by initial assumptions and components of mathematical objects. Ability to classify abstract structures and objects, e.g. classify a conic. Question cues: analyze, separate, order, explain, connect, classify, arrange, divide, compare, select, explain, infer.

5. Synthesis—Define a new structure from known elements and derive its properties. Generalize a theorem or prove a new theorem. Relate the results in a certain area to results in a different area. Question cues: formulate, generalize, rewrite, combine, integrate, modify, rearrange, substitute, invent, compose.

6. Evaluation (Figure 7-4)—Compare and discriminate between ideas, assess value of theories, presentations and research. Be able to make hypotheses based on mathematical facts. Verify validity of mathematical claims. Judge usefulness of results. Question cues: assess, decide, rank, grade, test, measure, recommend, convince, select, judge, explain, discriminate, support, conclude, compare, summarize.

Figure 7-4 Having a test is the most common way to evaluate the knowledge students have learned in school.

## Text C

### Gagne's Theory of Instruction[①]

Figure 7-5 Instructional designers commonly design materials and strategies of instruction for teachers.

Robert Gagne's theory of instruction has provided a great number of valuable ideas to instructional designers (Figure 7-5), trainers, and teachers. Gagne's theory can be broken into three major areas—the taxonomy of learning outcomes, the conditions of learning, and the events of instruction.

Gagne's taxonomy of learning outcomes is somewhat similar to Bloom's taxonomies of cognitive, affective, and psychomotor outcomes. Both Bloom and Gagne believed that it was important to break down humans' learned capabilities into categories. Gagne's taxonomy consists of five categories of learning outcomes—verbal information, intellectual skills, cognitive strategies, attitudes, and motor skills. Gagne and Briggs explained that each of the categories leads to a

---

① http://home.gwu.edu/~mcorry/corry1.htm
   http://web.syr.edu/~jlbirkla/kb/c_instru.html

different class of human performance.

Essential to Gagne's ideas of instruction are what he calls "conditions of learning". He breaks these down into internal and external conditions. The internal conditions deal with previously learned capabilities of the learner, or in other words, what the learner knows prior to the instruction. The external conditions deal with the stimuli (a purely behaviorist term) that is presented externally to the learner.

To tie his theory of instruction together, Gagne formulated nine events of instruction. His events of instruction are based on the cognitive information processing learning theory. When followed, these events are intended to promote the transfer of knowledge or information. The steps he proposed do not have to occur in order, although good instruction should contain all of the steps:

1. Gaining attention: a stimulus change to alert the learner and focus attention on desired features.

2. Informing learners of the objective: a statement or demonstration to form an expectation in the learner as to the goals of instruction.

3. Stimulating recall of prior learning: a question or activity to remind the learner of prerequisite knowledge.

4. Presenting the stimulus: an activity or information that presents the content of what is to be learned.

5. Providing learning guidance: a cue or strategy to promote encoding.

6. Eliciting performance: an opportunity to practice or otherwise perform what is being learned.

7. Providing feedback: information of a corrective nature that will help learners to improve their performance.

8. Assessing performance: an opportunity to demonstrate what has been learned.

9. Enhancing retention and transfer: examples or activities that promote the learners to go beyond the immediate context of instruction.

The way Gagne's theory is put into practice is as follows. First of all, the instructor determines the objectives of the instruction. These objectives must then be categorized into one of the five domains of learning outcomes. Each of the objectives must be stated in performance terms using one of the standard verbs (i.e. states, discriminates, classifies, etc.) associated with the particular learning outcome. The instructor then uses the conditions of learning for the particular learning outcome to determine the conditions necessary for learning. And finally, the events of instruction necessary to promote the internal process of learning are chosen and put into the lesson plan. The events in essence become the framework for the lesson plan or steps of instruction.

# Text D

## Elaboration Theory[①]

Elaboration theory is an instructional design theory that argues that content to be learned should be organized from simple to complex order, while providing a meaningful context in which subsequent ideas can be integrated. [2]

The paradigm shift from teacher-centric instruction to learner-centered instruction has caused "new needs for ways to sequence instruction." Charles Reigeluth of Indiana University posited Elaboration Theory, an instructional design model that aims to help select and sequence content in a way that will optimize attainment of learning goals. [3] Proponents feel the use of motivators, analogies, summaries and syntheses leads to effective learning (Figure 7-6). While the theory does not address primarily affective content, it is intended for medium to complex kinds of cognitive and psychomotor learning.

Figure 7-6  Well organized teaching as well as good strategies will lead to effective learning.

According to Reigeluth, Elaboration Theory has the following values:

• It values a sequence of instruction that is as holistic as possible, to foster meaning-making and motivation

• It allows learners to make many scope and sequence decisions on their own during the learning process

• It is an approach that facilitates rapid prototyping in the instructional development process

• It integrates viable approaches to scope and sequence into a coherent design theory

There are three major approaches: (1) Conceptual Elaboration Sequence (used when there are many related concepts to be learned), (2) Theoretical Elaboration Sequence (used when there are many related principles to be learned), and (3) Simplifying Conditions Sequence (used when a task of at least moderate complexity is to be learned).

The simplest version of the concept, principle or task should be taught first. Teach broader, more inclusive concepts, principles, or tasks before the narrower, more detailed ones that elaborate upon them. One should use either a topical or a spiral approach to this elaboration. Teach "supporting" content such as principles, procedures, information, higher-order thinking skills, or attitudes together with the concepts to which they are most closely related. Group concepts, principles, or steps and their supporting content into "learning episodes" of a useful

---

① http://www.learning-theories.com/elaboration-theory-reigeluth.html

size (not too small or large). Finally, allow students to choose which concepts, principles, or versions of the task to elaborate upon or learn first (or next).

Some scholars have offered various criticisms of Elaboration Theory. For example, there is no prescription for providing "authentic" or "situated" learning. Also, the use of three primary structures (i.e. conceptual, procedural, and theoretical) is a design constraint. As conceptual structures are sequenced from the most general category down to the most detailed subcategory, elaboration theory does not accommodate learners' prior knowledge.

## New Words

  taxonomy *n.* 分类法，分类学
  codification *n.* 法规汇编，编号，译成代码
  renowned *adj.* 有名的，有声誉的
  hierarchical *adj.* 分等级的
  symbolic *adj.* 象征的，符号的
  algorithm *n.* [数]运算法则
  polynomial *adj.* [数]多项式的 *n.* 多项式，由两个以上的词组成的学名
  theorem *n.* [数]定理，法则
  substitute *n.* 代用品，代替者，替代品 *v.* 代替，替换，替代
  scaffolding *n.* 脚手架
  authentic *adj.* 可信的

## Notes

[1] This domain is the one most relevant for the mathematics and scientific study areas since it includes the recall or recognition of specific facts (definitions and theorems abound in math), procedural patterns (algorithms and solving strategies), and concepts that serve in the development of intellectual abilities and skills (abstraction).

译文：认知领域是与数学和科学研究最相关的，因为它包括回忆和识别具体事实（数学中大量的定义和理论）、程序模式（运算法则和解题策略），以及在发展智力能力和技能方面起作用的概念（抽象概念）。

• since it includes the recall or recognition of specific facts (definitions and theorems abound in math), procedural patterns (algorithms and solving strategies), and concepts that serve in the development of intellectual abilities and skills (abstraction)作原因状语从句，其中 that serve in the development of intellectual abilities and skills 是定语从句，修饰先行词 concepts。

[2] Elaboration theory is an instructional design theory that argues that content to be learned should be organized from simple to complex order, while providing a meaningful context in which subsequent ideas can be integrated.

译文：细化理论是一种教学设计理论，它认为，要学习的内容应该按照从简单到复杂

的顺序组织,同时还需提供能整合并发理论的有意义的背景。

• that argues that content to be learned should be organized from simple to complex order 作定语从句,修饰先行词 an instructional design theory,其中的 that content to be learned should be organized from simple to complex order 作 argue 的宾语从句。

• while providing a meaningful context in which subsequent ideas can be integrated 作伴随状语,其中的 in which subsequent ideas can be integrated 作定语从句,修饰先行词 a meaningful context。

[3] Charles Reigeluth of Indiana University posited Elaboration Theory, an instructional design model that aims to help select and sequence content in a way that will optimize attainment of learning goals.

**译文:** 印第安纳大学的查尔斯·瑞格卢斯提出了细化理论,细化理论是一种教学设计模式,它的目标是用一种能优化实现学习目标的方式来选择和编排学习内容。

• that aims to help select and sequence content in a way that will optimize attainment of learning goals 作定语从句,修饰先行词 an instructional design model,其中 that will optimize attainment of learning goals 作定语从句,修饰先行词 way。

## Selected Translation
## Text C

### 加涅的教学理论

罗伯特·加涅的教学理论给教学设计者、培训人员和教师提供了大量有价值的思路。加涅的理论能分为为三个主要领域——学习结果分类、学习条件,以及教学事件。

加涅的学习结果分类,有些类似布卢姆有关认知领域、情感领域和精神领域的分类。布卢姆和加涅都认为对人类的学习能力进行分类是很重要的。加涅把学习结果分为五类:言语信息、智力技能、认知策略、态度和运动技能。加涅和布里格斯解释说,每一类别都指向不同类别的人类行为。

对加涅的教学理念非常重要的是他所谓的"学习条件"。他把学习条件分为内部条件和外部条件。内部条件涉及学习者以前的学习能力,换句话说,涉及学习者在教学前所知道的事情。外部条件涉及外部呈现给学习者的刺激(一个纯粹的行为主义术语)。

为使他的教学理论成为一个整体,加涅制定了九大教学事件。他的教学事件是建立在认知信息加工学习理论基础上的。如果遵循这九大教学事件的话,这些事件能够促进知识或信息的迁移。虽然良好的教学应包含所有的步骤,但是他建议的这些步骤不一定按照顺序来做:

1. 引起注意:通过刺激变化来引起学习者的注意,使其将注意力集中到所期望的事情上。
2. 告知学习者目标:通过陈述或展示以使学习者形成对教学目标的期望。
3. 刺激回忆先前知识:通过问题或活动向学习者提示先决知识。
4. 呈现刺激材料:用活动或信息来呈现将要学习的内容。

5. 提供学习指导:采用一种线索或策略来促进编码。
6. 诱导学习行为:提供机会来实践或展示所学的内容。
7. 提供反馈:(反馈回来的)正确信息将会帮助学习者提高绩效。
8. 评价行为:提供证明所学知识的机会。
9. 促进保持和迁移:通过案例或活动来促进学习者对当前教学内容进行迁移。

将加涅的理论付诸实践的方式如下:首先,教师确定教学目标。这些目标必须能纳入学习结果的五大范畴之一。每个目标必须用与特定的学习结果相关的标准动词(如:陈述、鉴别、分类,等等)在行为术语里表述出来。然后,为了达到特定的学习结果,教师运用该结果的学习条件来确定学习中的一些必要的影响。最后,选择那些能促进内在学习历程的教学事件并制订教案。这些教学事件实际上就成了教案或教学步骤的基本框架。

## Exercises

**1. Match Each Objective Below with the Level of Bloom's Taxonomy that It Describes.**

   a. Knowledge
   b. Comprehension
   c. Application
   d. Analysis
   e. Synthesis
   f. Evaluation

(1) _____ The student should be able to list in order the levels of Bloom's Taxonomy.

(2) _____ Given a general educational goal, the student should be able to state it as an objective at the appropriate level of Bloom's Taxonomy.

(3) _____ The student should be able to explain the meaning of each of the levels of Bloom's Taxonomy.

(4) _____ The student should be able to write lessons plans that state clear objectives, contain appropriate activities for attaining these objectives, and include methods for evaluating student performance.

(5) _____ Given a teacher's lesson plan, the student should be able to identify the principles of instructional design that the teacher incorporated into that lesson and ways in which these principles contribute to the effectiveness of the lesson.

(6) _____ Given a teacher's well-constructed lesson plan, the student should be able to determine how effective the lesson is likely to be by identifying the principles of instructional design employed in the lesson and how well they are likely to contribute to attaining the stated objectives.

**2. Short Answers:**

(1) According to the texts, what are Bloom's taxonomy of educational objectives and

Gagne's taxonomy of learning outcomes?

(2) What are the Gagne's nine events of instruction?

(3) How can an instructor teach his lesson according to Reigeluth's elaboration theory?

# 从句的翻译(Ⅱ)

## 一、主语从句翻译法

1. "主—谓—宾"结构:以 what, how, whether, that, where, when 引导的主语从句,可以译成"主—谓—宾"结构,从句本身做句子的主语,其余部分按原文顺序译出。如:

(1) What someone chooses to observe and the way one observes it must, after all, in part be a reflection of experience and of ideas as to what is significant.

某人选择观察的事物和他观察事物的方式在某种程度上必然会部分地反映这个人的经历和他关于什么是有意义的看法。(what 引导的主语从句,译成名词"……的事"。)

(2) When we will begin to work has not been decided yet.

什么时候开始工作还没决定呢。(when 引导的主语从句,直接翻译成"……时候"。)

2. 分译法:把原来的主语从句从整体结构中分离出来,译成另一个相对独立的单句。如:

(1) It has been rightly stated that this situation is a threat to international security.

这个局势对国际安全是个威胁,这样的说法是完全正确的。(It 是形式主语,that this situation is a threat to international security 是真正的主语。)

(2) It is my duty that I must teach English well.

我必须教好英语,这是我的职责。

## 二、表语从句翻译法

大部分情况下可以采用顺译法,间或也可以用逆译法。如:

(1) That was how they were defeated.

他们就是这样被打败的。(顺译法)

(2) His view of the press was that the reporters were either for him or against him.

他对新闻界的看法是,记者们不是支持他,就是反对他。(顺译法)

(3) Water and food is what the people in the area badly need.

该地区的人们最需要的是水和食品。(逆译法)

## 三、宾语从句翻译法

宾语从句一般可遵照原句的顺序进行翻译。当句中有 it 作形式宾语时,it 一般省略不译。如:

(1) Lagrange argued that trigonometric series were of very limited use.

拉格伦日认为三角级数的应用是非常有限的。

(2) I don't believe he has seen the film.

我相信他没看过这部电影。

(3) I took it for granted that he would sign the document.

我认为他当然会在文件上签字。

### 四、同位语从句翻译法

同位语从句是用来进一步说明从句前面一个名词的具体内容。常见的带同位语从句的名词有：fact, news, promise, truth, belief, idea, answer, information, knowledge, doubt, hope, law, opinion, plan, suggestion, question 等。同位语从句较短时，翻译时可考虑将其前置；如果较长，则可考虑后置。如：

(1) The question whether we need it has not yet been considered.

我们是否需要它，这个问题还没有考虑。（从句前置）

(2) This is a universally accepted principle of international law that the territory sovereignty does not admit of infringement.

一个国家的领土不容侵犯，这是国际法中尽人皆知的准则。（从句前置）

(3) In this case, the sampling process corresponds to the fact that moving pictures are a sequence of individual frames with a rate (usually between 18 and 24 frames per second) corresponding to the sampling frequency.

在这种情况下，抽样过程与这样一个事实相符：活动图像是一串单个的画面，帧频（通常每秒18到24帧）相当于抽样频率。（顺译法）

(4) His criticism was based on his own belief that it was impossible to represent signals with corners using trigonometric series.

他批评的论据是基于自己的信念，即不可能用三角函数级数来表示具有间断点的信号。（从句后置）

(5) It relies on the belief or assumption that our world and the claims about it are not considered meaningful unless they can be verified through direct observation.

定量研究建立在这样的信念或假设之上：除非我们的世界和对世界的看法能通过直接的观察来验证，否则它们并不是有意义的。（从句后置）

# Unit 7　Systems Theory

▲ Knowledge Objectives

When you have completed this unit, you will be able to:

- Know the basement of the systems view
- State the concept of system
- Recognize the relationships between systems theory and the diverse subjects

## Part 2  The Theoretical Foundation of Educational Technology

- State the functions of systems theory
- List the elements of General systems theory
- Explain the function of each element of General systems theory

▲ **Professional Terms**

| | |
|---|---|
| systems theory | 系统理论 |
| cybernetics | 控制论 |
| thermodynamics | 热力学 |
| artificial intelligence | 人工智能 |
| closed system | 封闭系统 |
| open system | 开放系统 |
| feedback | 反馈 |

# Text A

## The Systems View[①]

The systems view is a world-view that is based on the discipline of Systems Inquiry. Central to systems inquiry is the concept of System. In the most general sense, system means a configuration of parts connected and joined together by a web of relationships. The Primer group defines system as a family of relationships among the members acting as a whole. Bertalanffy defined system as elements in standing relationship.

The systems view was based on several fundamental ideas. First, all phenomena can be viewed as a web of relationships among elements, or a system. Second, all systems, whether electrical, biological, or social, have common patterns, behaviors, and properties that can be understood and used to develop greater insight into the behavior of complex phenomena and to move closer toward a unity of science. System philosophy, methodology and application are complementary to this science. By 1956, the Society for General Systems Research was established, renamed the International Society for Systems Science in 1988. The Cold War had its affects upon the research project for systems theory in ways that sorely disappointed many of the seminal theorists. Some began to recognize theories defined in association with systems theory had deviated from the initial General Systems Theory (GST) view. The economist Kenneth Boulding, an early researcher in systems theory, had concerns over the manipulation of systems concepts. Boulding concluded from the effects of the Cold War that abuses of power always prove consequential and that systems theory might address such issues since the end of the Cold War, there has been a renewed interest in systems theory with efforts to strengthen an ethical view.

---

① http://en.wikipedia.org/wiki/Systems_theory

## Text B

## What is Systems Theory[①]

Systems theory was proposed in the 1940s by the biologist Ludwig von Bertalanffy (Figure 4-1), and furthered by Ross Ashby (*Introduction to Cybernetics*, 1956). Ludwig von Bertalanffy was both reacting against reductionism and attempting to revive the unity of science. He emphasized that real systems are open to, and interact with, their environments, and that they can acquire qualitatively new properties through emergency, resulting in continual evolution.[1]

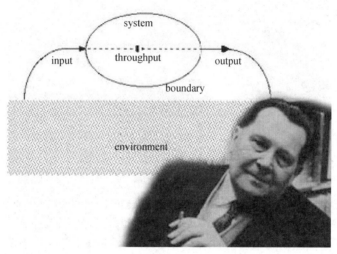

Figure 4-1　Ludwig von Bertalanffy is a famous biologist, and he contributes a lot to the general system theory.

Rather than reducing an entity (e.g. the human body) to the properties of its parts or elements (e.g. organs or cells), systems theory focuses on the arrangement of any relations between the parts which connect them into a whole.[2] This particular organization determines a system, which is independent of the concrete substance of the elements (e.g. particles, cells, transistors, people, etc.). Thus, the same concepts and principles of organization underlie the different disciplines (physics, biology, technology, sociology, etc.), providing a basis for their unification. Systems concepts include: system-environment boundary, input, output, process, state, hierarchy, goal-directedness, and information.

The developments of systems theory are diverse, including conceptual foundations and philosophy (e.g. the philosophies of Bunge, Bahm and Laszlo); mathematical modeling and information theory (e.g. the work of Mesarovic and Klir); and practical applications. Mathematical systems theory arose from the development of isomorphism between the models of electrical circuits and other systems. Applications include engineering, computing, ecology,

---

① http://pespmc1.vub.ac.be/SYSTHEOR.html

management, and family psychotherapy. Systems analysis, developed independently of systems theory, applies systems principles to aid a decision-maker with problems of identifying, reconstructing, optimizing, and controlling a system (usually a socio-technical organization), while taking into account multiple objectives, constraints and resources.[3] It aims to specify possible courses of action, together with their risks, costs and benefits. Systems theory is closely connected to cybernetics, and also to system dynamics, and its related ideas are used in the emerging "sciences of complexity", studying self-organization and associated domains such as far-from-equilibrium thermodynamics, chaotic dynamics, artificial intelligence, neural networks, and computer modeling and simulation, etc.

## Text C

## The Functions of Systems Theory[①]

Systems theory is an interdisciplinary field of science and the study of the nature of complex systems in nature, society, and science. More specifically, it is a framework by which one can analyze and/or describe any group of objects that work in concert to produce some result.[4] This could be a single organism, any organization or society, or any electro-mechanical or informational artifact. Systems theory first originated in biology in the 1920s out of the need to explain the interrelatedness of organisms in ecosystems. As a technical and general academic area of study, it predominantly refers to the science of systems that resulted from Bertalanffy's General System Theory (GST), among others, in initiating what became a project of systems research and practice. It was Margaret Mead and Gregory Bateson who developed interdisciplinary perspectives in systems theory (such as positive and negative feedback in the social sciences).

Ideas from systems theory have grown with diversified areas, exemplified by the work of Béla H. Bánáthy, ecological systems with Howard T. Odum, Eugene Odum and Fritjof Capra, organizational theory and management with individuals such as Peter Senge, interdisciplinary study with areas like Human Resource Development from the work of Richard A. Swanson, and insights from educators such as Debora Hammond. As a transdisciplinary, interdisciplinary and multiperspectival domain, the area brings together principles and concepts from ontology, philosophy of science, physics, computer science, biology, and engineering as well as geography, sociology, political science, psychotherapy (within family systems therapy) and economics among others. Systems theory thus serves as a bridge for interdisciplinary dialogue between autonomous areas of study as well as within the area of systems science itself.

In this respect, with the possibility of misinterpretations, Bertalanffy believed a general theory of systems "should be an important regulative device in science," to guard against superficial

---

① http://en.wikipedia.org/wiki/Systems_theory

analogies that are useless in science and harmful in their practical consequences. Others remain closer to the direct systems concepts developed by the original theorists. For example, Ilya Prigogine, of the Center for Complex Quantum Systems at the University of Texas, Austin, has studied emergent properties, suggesting that they offer analogues for living systems. The theories of autopoiesis of Francisco Varela and Humberto Maturana are a further development in this field.

Systems theory provides an internally consistent framework for classifying and evaluating the world. There are clearly many useful definitions and concepts in systems theory. In many situations it provides a scholarly method of evaluating a situation. An even more important characteristic, however, is that it provides a universal approach to all sciences. As von Bertalanffy points out, "there are many instances where identical principles were discovered several times because the workers in one field were unaware that the theoretical structure required was already well developed in some other field. General systems theory will go a long way towards avoiding such unnecessary duplication of labor."

## Text D

### General Systems Theory[①]

General systems theory was originally proposed by biologist Ludwig von Bertalanffy in 1928 (Figure 4-2). Since Descartes, the "scientific method" had progressed under two related assumptions. A system could be broken down into its individual components so that each component could be analyzed as an independent entity, and the components could be added in a linear fashion to describe the totality of the system.[5] Von Bertalanffy proposed that both assumptions were wrong. On the contrary, a system is characterized by the interactions of its components and the nonlinearity of those interactions.

One common element of all systems is described by Kuhn. Knowing one part of a system enables us to know something about another part. The information content of a "piece of information" is proportional to the amount of information that can be inferred from the information. Systems can be either controlled (cybernetic) or uncontrolled. In controlled systems, information is sensed, and changes are effected in response to the information. Kuhn refers to this as the detector, selector, and effector functions of the system. The detector is concerned with the communication of information between systems. The selector is defined by the rules that the system uses to make decisions, and the effector is the means by which transactions are made between systems. Communication

Figure 4-2 General systems theory was originally proposed by biologist Ludwig von Bertalanffy.

---

① http://www.survey-software-solutions.com/walonick/systems-theory.htm

and transaction are the only intersystem interactions. Communication is the exchange of information, while transaction involves the exchange of matter-energy. All organizational and social interactions involve communication and/or transaction.

The study of systems can follow two general approaches. A cross-sectional approach deals with the interaction between two systems, while a developmental approach deals with the changes in a system over time. There are three general approaches for evaluating subsystems. A holist approach is to examine the system as a complete functioning unit. A reductionist approach looks downward and examines the subsystems within the system. The functionalist approach looks upward from the system to examine the role it plays in the larger system. All three approaches recognize the existence of subsystems operating within a larger system.

Kuhn's model stresses that the role of decision is to move a system towards equilibrium. Communication and transaction provide the vehicle for a system to achieve equilibrium. "Culture is communicated, learned patterns... and society is a collectively of people having a common body and process of culture." Kuhn's terminology is interlocking and mutually consistent. The following summarizes his basic system definitions:

A system variable is any element in an acting system that can take on at least two different states. Some system variables are dichotomous, and can be one of two values—the rat lives, or the rat dies. System variables can also be continuous. The condition of a variable in a system is known as the system state. The boundaries of a system are defined by the set of its interacting components. Kuhn recognizes that it is the investigator, not nature, that bounds the particular system being investigated.

A controlled (cybernetic) system maintains at least one system variable within some specified range, or if the variable goes outside the range, the system moves to bring the variable back into the range. This control is internal to the system. The field of cybernetics is the discipline of maintaining order in systems.

A system's input is defined as the movement of information or matter-energy from the environment into the system. Output is the movement of information or matter-energy from the system to the environment. Both input and output involve crossing the boundaries that define the system. When all forces in a system are balanced to the point where no change is occurring, the system is said to be in a state of static equilibrium. Dynamic (steady state) equilibrium exists when the system components are in a state of change, but at least one variable stays within a specified range. Homeostasis is the condition of dynamic equilibrium between at least two system variables. Kuhn states that all systems tend toward equilibrium, and that a prerequisite for the continuance of a system is its ability to maintain a steady state or steadily oscillating state.

Negative equilibrating feedback operates within a system to restore a variable to an initial value. It is also known as deviation-correcting feedback. Positive equilibrating feedback operates within a system to drive a variable future from its initial value. It is also known as

Figure 4-3  Both Positive feedback and negative feedback are important to systems.

deviation-amplifying feedback. Equilibrium in a system can be achieved either through negative or positive feedback (Figure 4-3). In negative feedback, the system operates to maintain its present state. In positive feedback, equilibrium is achieved when the variable being amplified reaches a maximum asymptotic limit. Systems operate through differentiation and coordination among its components. "Characteristic of organization, whether of a living organism or a society, are notions like those of wholeness, growth, differentiation, hierarchical order, dominance, control, and competition."

A closed system is one where interactions occur only among the system components and not with the environment. An open system is one that receives input from the environment and/or releases output to the environment. The basic characteristic of an open system is the dynamic interaction of its components, while the basis of a cybernetic model is the feedback cycle. Open systems can tend toward higher levels of organization (negative entropy), while closed systems can only maintain or decrease in organization.

A system parameter is any trait of a system that is relevant to an investigation, but that does not change during the duration of study. An environmental parameter is any trait of a system's environment that is relevant to an investigation, but that does not change during the duration of study.

## New Words

configuration  *n.* 构造，结构，配置，外形
seminal  *adj.* 种子的，精液的，生殖的
interdisciplinary  *adj.* 各学科间的
exemplify  *vt.* 例证，例示，作为……例子
nonlinearity  非(直)线性(特性)
equilibrium  *n.* 平衡，平静，均衡，保持平衡的能力，沉着，安静
hierarchical  *adj.* 分等级的
parameter  *n.* 参数，参量

## Notes

[1] He emphasized that real systems are open to, and interact with, their environments, and that they can acquire qualitatively new properties through emergency, resulting in continual evolution.

译文：他强调，真正的系统是对环境开放的，并与环境互动，而且通过紧急情况它们能获得新的特性，从而导致持续演变。

Part 2  The Theoretical Foundation of Educational Technology

* That real systems are open to, and interact with, their environments 和 that they can acquire qualitatively new properties through emergence 都是 emphasized 的宾语从句。
* resulting in continual evolution 现在分词短语作状语。
* be open to 对……开放
* interact with 与……相互作用, 与……相互影响
* result in 导致

[2] Rather than reducing an entity (e.g. the human body) to the properties of its parts or elements (e.g. organs or cells), systems theory focuses on the arrangement of any relations between the parts which connect them into a whole.

译文：系统理论关注的是排列各部分之间的联系使之成为一个整体，而不是将整体（如人体）归纳为它的部分或要素（如组织或细胞）的属性。

* which connect them into a whole 是定语从句，修饰先行词 arrangement 和 relations。
* Rather than 胜于, 而不是
* reduce to 使处于, 迫使, 使变为, 使变弱为, 归纳为
* focus on 集中

[3] Systems analysis, developed independently of systems theory, applies systems principles to aid a decision-maker with problems of identifying, reconstructing, optimizing, and controlling a system (usually a socio-technical organization), while taking into account multiple objectives, constraints and resources.

译文：系统分析的发展与系统理论无关，它在考虑多重目标、限制条件和资源的同时，应用系统原则来帮助决策者解决、鉴别、改造、优化和控制某个系统（通常是一个社会技术组织）等问题。

* developed independently of systems theory 过去分词作定语, 修饰 Systems analysis
* While taking into account multiple objectives, constraints and resources 作伴随状语。
* Apply...to 关系到, 牵涉到, 适用于; 运用于, 向……询问, 与……接洽
* take into account 重视, 考虑, 顾及

[4] More specifically, it is a framework by which one can analyze and/or describe any group of objects that work in concert to produce some result.

译文：更确切地说，系统理论是一种框架，借此我们能够分析和描述任何一组一同产生某种结果的目标。

* by which one can analyze and/or describe any group of objects 是定语从句, 修饰先行词 framework。
* that work in concert to produce some result 是定语从句, 修饰先行词 objects。
* in concert 异口同声地, 齐声

[5] A system could be broken down into its individual components so that each component could be analyzed as an independent entity, and the components could be added in a linear fashion to describe the totality of the system.

译文：一个系统能够被分解成独立的部分，这样每个部分都能作为一个独立的整体

来加以分析,而且这些部分还能用线性的方式加到一起来描述整个系统。
- break down 毁掉,制服,压倒,停顿,倒塌,中止,垮掉,分解
- so that 以便于,引导目的状语从句。

## Selected Translation

### Text B

系统理论是什么

系统理论是生物学家路德维希·冯·贝塔朗菲在20世纪40年代提出来的,并由罗斯·阿什比(《控制论简介》,1956)加以深化。贝塔朗菲反对简化论,并企图重振科学的统一性。他强调,真正的系统是对环境开放的,并与环境互动,而且通过紧急情况它们能获得新的特性,从而导致系统本身的持续演变。

系统理论关注的是排列各部分之间的联系使之成为一个整体,而不是将整体(如人体)归纳为它的部分或要素(如组织或细胞)的属性。系统是由这个特定的结构决定的,它与其要素(如粒子、细胞、晶体管、人等)的具体实质无关。因此,不同的学科(物理、生物、科技、社会学等)是以有机体相同的概念和原则为根据的,而这为它们的统一提供了基础。系统概念包括:系统与环境间的界限、输入、输出、过程、状态、层次、目标定向和信息。

系统理论的发展是多样化的,包括:概念的基础和哲学(如邦吉、巴姆和拉兹洛的哲学),数学建模和信息理论(如梅萨罗维奇和开利尔的著作)及实际应用。数学系统理论是从电子电路的模型和其他系统之间的同构发展中产生的,其应用范围包括工程、计算、生态、管理和家庭心理治疗。系统分析的发展与系统理论无关,它在考虑多重目标、限制条件和资源的同时,应用系统原则来帮助决策者解决、鉴别改造、优化和控制某个系统(通常是一个社会技术组织)等问题。它的目的是详细说明行为可能发生的进程以及随之产生的风险、成本和效益。系统理论与控制论及系统动力学是紧密联系的,其相关思想被应用于新兴的"复杂科学"中,用来研究自我组织及其相关的领域,如远离平衡热力学、混沌动力学、人工智能、神经网络和计算机建模与仿真等。

## Exercises

**Short Answers:**

1. What are the basements of the system view?
2. What are included in the systems concepts?
3. What are the functions of systems theory?
4. How can we study systems and subsystems?
5. What are the differences between Negative equilibrating feedback and Positive equilibrating feedback?

# 被动句的翻译

被动语态被广泛使用于英语中。当着重指出动作的承受者或不必说明谁是动作的执行者时,就用被动语态。尤其是在科技英语中,被动语态用得相当多。事物的名称常作为主语放在突出的位置上,用被动语态表述有关的动作或状态。而在汉语中被动句的使用却没有英语中频繁。因此,在翻译文章时,英语的被动语态一般都译成汉语的主动句式,只有在特别强调被动动作或特别突出被动者时才译成汉语被动句式或无主语句。很多被动的动作往往借助于主动语态或具有被动意义的单词来表达。英语被动句译为汉语主动句时,主语可以是原句的主语,可以是 by 后面的名词或代词,也可以是原句中隐藏的动作执行者。被动语态的译法主要有以下几种形式:

## 一、译成汉语被动句

英译汉时,汉语也有用被动形式来表达的情况,这时通常看重的是被动的动作。在把英语被动句译成汉语被动句时,我们常常使用"被"、"受到"、"遭到"、"得到"、"让"、"给"、"把"、"使"、"由"等措词。如:

(1) If the signal is transmitted by analog techniques, the received signal will be severely corrupted by noise.

如果用模拟技术进行信号传输,那么接收到的信号将要受到噪声的严重破坏。

(2) His many contributions—in particular, those concerned with the series and transform that carry his name—are made even more impressive by the circumstances under which he worked.

当时他进行研究所处的境遇使他的许多贡献(特别是以他的名字命名的级数和变换)给人留下了极深的印象。

## 二、译成汉语主动句

直接将原文的被动语态按主动语态译成汉语的主动句。这类句子有的在英语中属于形式上的被动句,但其意义又属于主动句;有的句子在英语中习惯于用被动语态表达,而在汉语中则习惯于用主动语态来表达。如:

(1) The machine will be repaired tomorrow.

这台机器明天修理。(不必译作:这台机器明天被修理。)

(2) The experiment will be finished in a month.

这项实验将在一个月后完成。(不必译作:这项实验将在一个月后被完成。)

(3) Elaboration theory is an instructional design theory that argues that content to be learned should be organized from simple to complex order, while providing a meaningful context in which subsequent ideas can be integrated.

细化理论是一种教学设计理论,它认为,要学习的内容应该按照从简单到复杂的顺序来组织,同时还需提供能整合后来观念的有意义的背景。

(4) A signal is called a digital signal if its time is discretized and its amplitude is quantized.

时间上离散、幅值上量化的信号称为数字信号。

(5) Signals are presented mathematically as functions of one or more independent variables.

在数学上,信号可以表示为具有一个或多个变量的函数。

(6) This reliability can further be improved by using error-detecting and error-correcting codes.

利用检错和纠错编码能进一步提高可靠性。

(7) This organ is situated at the base of the brain.

该器官位于脑底。

(8) It is well-known that paper was first made in China.

众所周知,纸最初是在中国发明的。

在"it is (has been) + p.p + that."句型中,it 引导的被动语态常有固定的用法:

It is assumed that:人们认为

It is said that:据说

It is learned that:据闻

It is supposed that:据推测

It is considered that:据估计

It is believed that:人们认为

It is reported that:据报道

It is well-known that:众所周知

It is asserted that:有人断言

It can't be denied that:不可否认

It must be admitted that:必须承认

It must be pointed that:必须指出

### 三、译成汉语的加强语句

当英语被动句不是强调被动的动作,而只是强调或肯定某一事实或行为的存在时,通常可用"是……的"或"为……所"等句式来翻译此类句子。如:

(1) These computers were made in Xinhua Company.

这些电子计算机是新华公司制造的。

(2) The project was completed last year.

这个项目是去年完成的。

(3) The cakes which have just been cooked are made of corn.

刚做好的蛋糕是玉米做的。

### 四、译成汉语的无主句

在科技英语中,在讲述什么事情时往往是强调如何去做,而不介意谁去做。对于这一类被动句的翻译,我们可以译为汉语无主句。

(1) Now the heart can be safely opened and its valves repaired.

现在可以安全地打开心脏,并对心脏瓣膜进行修复。

(2) This instrument must be handled with great care.

必须仔细操作这台仪器。

总之,在翻译英语被动语态语句时,不能固守原句,要灵活地采用多种翻译技巧,使译文既在内容上忠实于原文,又符合汉语的表达方式。

# Part 3   Media, Technology and Learning

## Unit 8   Brief Introduction to Several Media and Technologies

▲ **Knowledge Objectives**

When you have completed this unit, you will be able to:
* Describe the meaning of multimedia and its roles
* State the advantages of hypermedia
* Compare and contrast multimedia, hypermedia and interactive media
* Describe the types of virtual reality and their differences
* Recognize the development and functions of expert systems

▲ **Professional Terms**

| | |
|---|---|
| multimedia | 多媒体 |
| hypermedia | 超媒体 |
| interactive media | 交互媒体 |
| virtual reality | 虚拟现实 |
| expert systems | 专家系统 |
| artificial intelligence | 人工智能 |
| qualitative analysis | 定性分析 |
| individualized learning | 个别学习 |
| knowledge engineer | 知识工程师 |

## Text A

### Multimedia[①]

The term multimedia describes a number of diverse technologies that allow visual and audio media to be combined in new ways for the purpose of communicating. Multimedia often refers to the computer technologies. Nearly every PC built today is capable of multimedia because they include a CD ROM or DVD drive (Figure 8-1), and a good sound and video card (often built into the motherboard). But the term multimedia also describe a number of dedicate

---

① http://www.scala.com/multimedia-definition.htm

media appliances, such as digital video recorders (DVRs), interactive television, MP3 players (Figure 8-2), advance wireless device and public video displays.

Figure 8-1　DVD drive is a sort of tool which can be used to play multimedia materials.

Figure 8-2　MP3 player is a popular multimedia which is capable of displaying images and playing sounds.

The term multimedia, which was used during 1970s to describe a particular theater-based film and slide-show college experience, has now been shorted to just the word "multimedia". From the 1980s through the late 1990s, the prevalent meaning of multimedia was a category of "authoring" software that allow the designers to develop an interactive computer program without having to have advance programming skills. Examples include Apple's HyperCard, Icon Authorware, Asymetrix Toolbox, and Scala Multimedia. This category of software still exists, and is sometimes referred to as multimedia, but the term is used to more generally describe nearly hardware or software technology that displays images or plays sounds.

Frank attributes the origins of the computer-based multimedia to the development of industry standards for multimedia personal computers (MPCs) in 1991. "Two key components of the MPC system were (1) a compact Disk-Read-Only Memory (CD-ROM) that could approximately 600 megabytes of information, and (2) a sound board capable of producing high quality sound." Because these technical components were included in all personal computers, owners of multimedia computers were then able to explore different aspects of multimedia. Personal computers were not simply used for word processing but could incorporate sound and images as well.

The potential of multimedia technology as a communication technology began to transcend a variety of industries after the development of multimedia personal computers (Figure 8-3). Coorough states how multimedia has shifted away from being used as a form of entertainment, "At one time, multimedia was primarily used in entertainments and games. Though it is still used extensively in these two industries, the uses of multimedia have extended beyond the word of entertainment." Multimedia has been applied to web page development, computer-based training, electronic periodicals, references, and books, advertising and market-

Figure 8-3　Personal computer is an excellent multimedia, and it is widely used all over the world.

ing, and the entertainment industry.

Molina and villamil cassnanova further support the evolution of multimedia application in the 1990s and its potential as an educational tool, "Multimedia technology was first used in advertising. Its power to enhance communication, and its affordability found its way into marketing agencies. The same power brought the technology to the classroom. Multimedia's capability to appeal to a variety of learning makes it a powerful and exciting teaching and learning tool."

## Text B

## Hypermedia[①]

Hypermedia refers to computer software that uses elements of text, graphics, video, and audio connected in such a way that the user can easily move within the information (Figure 8-4).[1] Users choose the pathway that is unique to their own style of thinking and processing information. According to its very nature, it provides a learning environment that is interactive and exploratory (Figure 8-5).

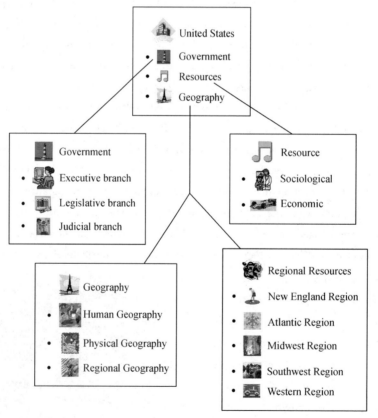

Figure 8-4　The links among the elements of hypermedia are just like what the picture depicts.

---

① Sharon E. Smaldino, James D. Russell, Robert Henich and Michael Molenda, *Instructional Technology and Media for Learning*, Eighth Edition.

Figure 8-5  Example of hypermedia environment used in the project studies

Hypermedia is based on cognitive theories of how people structure knowledge and how they learn. It is designed to resemble the way people organize information with concepts and their relationships. These relationships, or links, are associations between ideas—for example, when thinking about bicycles, one creates a link between ideas about transportation and recreation. With hypermedia, one can link asynchronous data source directly to compose and display nonsequential information that may include text, audio, and visual information. There is no continuous flow of text, as in a textbook or novel. Rather, the information is broken to small units that the author or user associates in a variety of ways. Using the bicycle example, the learner connects the word "bicycle" with a photo of a girl ding a bicycle in a field and a video clip of a Hong Kong boy carrying a duck to market on the back of a bicycle.

The Intent of hypermedia is to enable the user to move about within a particular set of information—without necessarily using a predetermined structure or sequence. The chunks of information are analogous to notes on a collection of cards. Each card contains a bit of information. Subsequent cards or sets of cards (often referred to as stacks) may contain extensions of the information from the initial card or other relevant or related information. Hypermedia programs are usually set up so that each computer screen display is equivalent to what is displayed on one of the cards.

Computer hypermedia can be used for several different purposes:

- Browsing. Users browse or navigate through the information by choosing routes that are of interest. You can explore features in details as it suits your personal learning style.
- Linking. Users can create their own special connections or links, within the information.
- Authoring. Users can author or create their own unique connections of information, adding or linking text, graphics, and audio as they wish. They can use this creation for their own individual use, or share with others, or prepare a report or presentation.

## Text C

### Interactive Media[①]

Figure 8-6　An interface of computer-based interactive media

Computer-based interactive media (Figure 8-6) creates a multimedia learning environment that capitalizes on the features of both video and computer-assisted instruction. It is an instructional delivery systems in which record visual, sound and video materials are presented under computer's control to viewers who not only see and hear the pictures and sounds but also make active responses, with those responses affecting the pace and sequence of the presentation.[2]

The video portion of interactive media is provided through CD-ROM, DVD, or the web. Because CD-ROM disc can store many types of digital information, including text, graphics, photographs, animation, and audio, they are popular in school settings, library media centers, and classroom of all sorts. Anything can be stored in computer can be stored on a CD-ROM. Multimedia CD-ROM products are commonly found in school library media centers, primarily in the form of encyclopedias or other reference data-bases. The application of multimedia and hypermedia to core curriculum is increasing with the advent of improved quality of available resources.

The images can be presented in slow motion, fast motion, or frame-by-frame (as in the slide show). The audio portion can occupy two separate audio channels, making possible two different narrations for each motion sequence.

The interactive aspect of interactive video is provided through computers, which have powerful decision making abilities. Combining computers and video allows the strengths of each to compensate for the limitations of the other to provide a rich education environment for the learners. Interactive media is a powerful and practical method for individualizing and personalizing instruction.

With the introduction of hypermedia, it has become easier to prepare teacher-developed and student-developed interactive multimedia. Students are discovering an innovative way to activate their learning through simple-to-prepare hypermedia stacks.

The heart of an interactive media is the computer, which provides the "intelligence" and interactivity required. The computer can command the system to present audio or video information, wait for the learners' response, and branch to the appropriate point in the instructional

---

① Sharon E. Smaldino, James D. Russell, Robert Henich and Michael Molenda, *Instructional Technology and Media for Learning*, Eighth Edition.

program from that response.

The learner communicates with the instructional program by responding to audio, visual or verbal stimuli displayed on the monitor. Input devices provide the means for these responses. Theses devices include such items as a keyboard, keypad, light pen, barcode reader, touch-sensitive screen, and mouse.

A monitor displays the picture and emits the sound from the video source. It can also display the output from the computer software, which may have the text, graphics, or sound effects. In most system the computer output can superimposed over the video image.

## Text D

### Virtual Reality[①]

Virtual Reality (VR) is one of the new applications of computer-based technologies. There are actually several levels of virtual reality, from complex, meaning you are completely immersed inside the environment, to augmented, or partially immersed, to desktop level, meaning you are using your computer to look into a virtual "windows".

At the complex level, virtual reality is a computer-generated, three-dimensional environment which the users can operate as an active participant (Figure 8-7). The user wears a special headpiece that contains a three-dimensional liquid crystal video display and headphones. The user participates with the three-dimensional world by manipulating a joystick or a special data glove worn on one hand. The data glove can be used to point, handle, and move objects and to direct the user's movements within the virtual world. Or the environment can be a chamber or room where the images are projected on the walls, ceiling, or floor. The "CAVE" in the university of Illinois was the first such environment where the user steps inside the chamber to experience the virtual world.

Figure 8-7　The girl is participating with three-dimensional world created by the virtual reality.

At the augmented level, the virtual world is created inside a simulated setting, such as a fighting simulator. Users interact with this type of virtual reality using the real-world artifacts such as joysticks or special equipment. This type of technology has been used by the military for many years for training.

Desktop virtual reality (desktop VR) (Figure 8-8) is most commonly found in education. The computer desktop is used to create the setting to view the virtual world without placing the

---

① Sharon E. Smaldino, James D. Russell, Robert Henich and Michael Molenda, *Instructional Technology and Media for Learning*, Eighth Edition.

users into that environment. They are free to navigate around the virtual setting using standard computer interfaces. Often what is available is a 360-degree view of an object or an environment, where the users can view it from any angle and get a perspective that would simulate seeing an actual item or setting.[3]

Figure 8-8  Desktop virtual reality creates the setting to view the virtual world without placing the users into that environment.

The essence of virtual reality is expansion of experience. Because virtual reality places the users into the virtual environment, it provide an opportunity to interact with that environment in an unique way, giving them the "ultimate" chance to grasp new ideas. For example, students can take a virtual field trip to a city without leaving their classroom.

## Text E

### Expert Systems[①]

Almost immediately after computer became a reality, scientists were intrigued by what they saw as parallels between how human brain works and how computer process information. Their experiments led to computers playing games such as checkers and chess with human experts and winning. Then they explored whether the computer could enable an amateur to play on an equal footing with an expert. It certainly could. But they reasoned why limit this to playing games? Why not see if this "artificial intelligence" could be applied to more useful problems?

This line of experimentation led to the development of the so-called expert systems (Figure 8-9). This is a software package that allows the collective wisdom of expert in a giving field to be brought to bear on a problem. One of the first such systems to be developed was MYCIN, a program that helps train doctors to make accurate diagnoses of infectious diseases on the basis of tests and patient information fed into the computer. Expert systems are rapidly making their way into education.

Scholastic Publications has developed a unique program that learns the rules of any games as it plays with

Figure 8-9  Expert system is usually very smart, and people can benefit a lot from it.

---

① Sharon E. Smaldino, James D. Russell, Robert Henich and Michael Molenda, *Instructional Technology and Media for Learning*, Eighth Edition.

human partner. The students may play the games with self-chosen rules but must identify with the computer criteria for winning the game. The computer absorbs the rules and eventually wins. Another expert system, the intelligent catalog helps a student learn to use reference tools. Any learning task that requires problem solving (e. g., qualitative analysis in chemistry) lends itself to an expert system. SCHOLAR is an expert system on the geography of South America. It is an example of "mixed-initiative" system. The student and the system can ask questions of each other, and SCHOLAR can adjust its instructional strategy according to the context of the student's inquiry.

One example that involves individualized learning is an expert system called CLASS LD. Developed at Utah State University, the program classifies learning disabilities by using an elaborate set of rules contributed by the experts. In tests, the program has proven to be at least as accurate as informed special education practitioners. The next step is to use a software package that will design an individualized education program (IEP) for children diagnosed by CLASS LD. Because many children with learning disabilities are included in regular classes, the expert system could make more manageable the classroom teacher's job of providing appropriate instruction. The school benefits from more effective and more efficient decision making.

Further down the road is an expert system that could truly individualize learning. We can imagine a system that learns all the important aptitudes and personality traits of an individual. When presented a large body of material to master, the learner would use the expert system as a guide to learn the content in the most effective manner. The program would adjust the content, instructional method, and medium to the learning styles of the student. The learner, not the experts, would be in charge of the program. When this becomes possible, we will really have individualized learning.

A new professional specialty has emerged from the development of expert systems. The term knowledge engineers has been coined to describe the people who work with experts in a field to assemble or organize a body of knowledge and then design the software package that makes it possible to train someone to become skilled in the area or to enable anyone to call on the skills of experts to solve a problem.[4] The work of knowledge engineering is similar to that done by instructional designers in task analysis and module design.

## New Words

  compact *adj.* 紧凑的, 紧密的, 简洁的 *n.* 契约, 合同, 小粉盒
  periodical *adj.* 周期的, 定期的 *n.* 期刊, 杂志
  asynchronous *adj.* 不同时的, [电] 异步的
  chunk *n.* 大(厚)块, 相当大的数量
  analogous *adj.* 类似的, 相似的, 可比拟的
  encyclopedia *n.* 百科全书
  chamber *n.* 室, 房间, 议院, 会所, (枪) 膛

augmented  *adj.* 增音的，扩张的
amateur  *n.* 业余爱好者，业余艺术家

## Notes

[1] Hypermedia refers to computer software that uses elements of text, graphics, video, and audio connected in such a way that the user can easily move within the information.

**译文**：超媒体是指一种计算机软件，它使用文本、图形、视频及音频等信息元素建立起特别的链接方式，使用户可以方便地在各种信息间跳转。

• that uses elements of text, graphics, video, and audio connected in such a way that the user can easily move within the information 是定语从句，修饰先行词 computer software，其中 that the user can easily move within the information 作 way 的同位语从句。

• refer to 查阅，提到，谈到，打听

[2] It is an instructional delivery system in which record visual, sound and video materials are presented under computer's control to viewers who not only see and hear the pictures and sounds but also make active responses, with those responses affecting the pace and sequence of the presentation.

**译文**：基于计算机的交互媒体是一种教学传输系统。在这个系统中，提前录制好的画面、声音和视频材料通过电脑的控制呈现给学习者，学习者不仅能看见画面、听到声音，而且还能进行积极的回应，学习者的回应决定了显示节奏和显示顺序。

• in which record visual, sound and video materials are presented under computer control to viewers 是定语从句，修饰先行词 instructional delivery system。

• who not only see and hear the pictures and sounds but also make active responses 是定语从句，修饰先行词 viewers。

• with those responses affecting the pace and sequence of the presentation 作伴随状语。

[3] Often what is available is a 360-degree view of an object or an environment, where the users can view it from any angle and get a perspective that would simulate seeing an actual item or setting.

**译文**：常见的桌面层次的虚拟现实是对一个物体或环境的360°视图，用户可以从任意角度进行观察，就像置身于真实环境或观察真实物体一样。

• what is available 是主语从句。

• where the users can view it from any angle and get a perspective 是定语从句，修饰先行词 360-degree view。

• that would simulate seeing an actual item or setting 是定语从句，修饰先行词 perspective。

[4] The term knowledge engineers has been coined to describe the people who work with experts in a field to assemble or organize a body of knowledge and then design the software package that makes it possible to train someone to become skilled in the area or to enable anyone to call on the skills of experts to solve a problem.

Part 3　Media, Technology and Learning

　　**译文**：知识工程师这个词描述的是那些与某个领域里的专家共同工作,负责收集或组织知识,然后设计软件包的人。知识工程师开发的软件包可以帮助一些人掌握相关领域的知识,也可以帮助各类人员利用软件包中的专家知识来解决问题。
- who work with experts in a field 是定语从句,修饰先行词 people。
- that makes it possible to train someone to become skilled in the area or to enable anyone to call on the skills of experts to solve a problem 是定语从句,修饰先行词 software package。
- call on 号召,呼吁,邀请,访问,指派,要(学生)回答问题

## Selected Translation
### Text B

超　媒　体

　　超媒体是指一种计算机软件,它使用文本、图形、视频及音频等信息元素建立起特别的链接方式,使用户可以方便地在各种信息间跳转。用户可以根据自己的思维风格和处理信息的风格,选择独特的访问路径。由于这些特点,超媒体为学习者建立一个交互性、探索性的学习环境(如图8.1)。

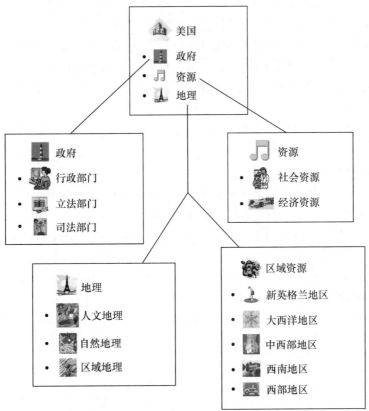

图 8.1　超媒体的元素之间的联系如此图所示

超媒体是建立在人类认知理论基础上的,认知理论致力于解释人类怎样建立自己的知识结构,怎样学习等。人类是利用概念以及概念与概念之间的关系来组织信息的,超媒体的设计类似于这样的结构。这些关系,或者说链接,表达的是思想间的联系。例如,当一个人想到自行车时,他很可能在运输和消遣这两个概念之间建立了联系。利用超媒体,人们可以直接将不同步的数据材料链接起来,经过一定的编辑处理,以非线性方式显示文本、音频信息以及视觉信息。与教科书或小说不同,超媒体不包括大段的文本叙述。相反,这里的信息被分割成很多小块。作者和读者可以采取不同的方式把这些小块信息连接起来。还是以自行车为例,学习者可以把"自行车"这个词与一幅女孩在广场上骑自行车的照片连接起来,也可以把这个词与一个香港男孩骑着自行车,往市场上送鸭子(鸭子搁在后座上)的视频片断连接起来。

超媒体的目的是使用户在一个特定的信息集合中自由浏览,而不必受到预先指定的结构和顺序的限制。这些信息块的形式类似于一组卡片。每张卡片上有一小段信息,一系列连续的卡片或者一堆卡片(通常指的是堆栈)包含有大量的信息,这些信息可能是由原始卡片提供的,也可能来自其他相关的信息。现在,计算机中一般都配置了超媒体系统,这样,每一台计算机的屏幕上都可以显示出同样的卡片信息。

计算机超媒体系统能够用于多种不同目的:

- 浏览。用户按照自己的兴趣来选择特别的路径浏览信息。学习者也可以按照自己的学习风格,详细浏览其中的某些细节。
- 链接。用户可以在信息之间创建自己定义的链接。
- 创作。用户可以创作或创建自己独特的信息集合,他们可以按照自己的想法,添加各类文本、图形以及音频材料等元素,还可以按照自己的想法,在这些元素之间创建链接。对于完成的作品,他们可以自己使用,也可以与他人分享,还可以用来准备报告或演讲。

## Exercises

**Short Answers:**

1. What does the term multimedia mean? And what are its applications?
2. What is hypermedia? And what are its advantages?
3. What is the heart of an interactive media? And what role does it play in the interactive media?
4. In general, how many levels does virtual reality have? And what environments do they create respectively?
5. According to our imagination, how can an expert system help individualize learning?

# 长句的翻译

英语习惯于用长句来表达比较复杂的概念,而汉语则不同,常常使用若干短句并列

地表达思想。长句在科技英语文章中出现得极为频繁。一般来说,造成长句的原因有三方面:

1. 修饰语过多;
2. 并列成分多;
3. 语言结构层次多。

在翻译长句时,首先不要因为句子太长而产生畏惧心理,因为无论是多么复杂的句子,它都是由一些基本的成分组成的。其次要弄清英语原文的句法结构,找出整个句子的中心内容及其各层意思,然后分析几层意思之间的相互逻辑关系,再按照汉语的特点和表达方式正确、灵活地译出原文的意思,而不必拘泥于原文的形式。

分析长句的结构应考虑以下几个方面:

1. 找出全句的主语、谓语和宾语,从整体上把握句子的结构。
2. 找出句中从句的引导词,分析从句的功能。例如,是否为主语从句、宾语从句、表语从句等;若是状语,那它是表示原因、结果,还是表示条件,等等。
3. 分析词、短语和从句之间的相互关系,例如,定语从句所修饰的先行词是哪一个。
4. 注意插入语等其他成分。
5. 注意分析句子中是否有固定词组或固定搭配。

在翻译英语长句的时候,要特别注意英语和汉语之间的差异,并恰当地将长句断成长度适中、合乎汉语习惯的句子。长句的翻译是难点也是重点,关键是首先找出句子的骨架,即主、谓、宾语,然后再将其他修饰成分嵌入框架。如果英文句子内容符合汉语规则,则可自前而后依序译出;如果句子内容顺序不符合汉语规则,可根据逻辑关系从后往前译出;如果不便用一句话表达,可将句子重新组织,按逻辑关系分成两个或数个短句。只要能完整准确地传达原意,即使与原文结构不相吻合,也算是正确的译法。下面不妨举例说明。

(1) When instruction is delivered at a distance, additional challenges result because students are often separated from others sharing their backgrounds and interests, have few if any opportunities to interact with teachers outside of class, and must rely on technical linkages to bridge the gap separating class participants.

**结构分析**:弄清该句的句法结构是翻译此句的关键。根据句子结构和语意分析,这个句子中有由 when 引导的时间状语从句,由 because 引导的原因状语从句,由 if 引导的条件状语从句,sharing 现在分词做后置定语修饰 others。找出句子的主干后,就可以根据中文习惯来进行翻译。

**参考译文**:当教学被远程传送时,将导致额外的挑战。因为,学生通常并没有共享他们的背景和兴趣,极少有机会在课外与老师交流,而且必须依赖技术来连接分散的课程参与者之间的距离。

(2) Formative-assessments which assist learning by giving feedback which indicates how the student is progressing in terms of knowledge, skills and understanding of a subject.

**结构分析**:翻译此句的关键是必须清楚从句的引导词 which(2 个)与 how,以此来分析从句的功能。

**参考译文**:形成性评价通过给予反馈来帮助学习,其中这些反馈表明了学生在知识、技能和对课题的理解等方面的进展如何。

（3）Summative evaluations judge merit and worth: the extent to which desired goals have been attained; whether measured outcomes can be attributed to observed interventions; and the conditions under which goals were attained that would affect generalizability and therefore intervention dissemination.

**结构分析**：本句含有多个由介词与which引导的定语从句，并且还有由whether引导的主语从句。

**参考译文**：总结性评价判断优点和价值：制定的目标所达到的程度，测量的结果是否可以归因于观察干预，以及达到预期目标并且能够影响普遍性进而消除干涉因素的条件。

（4）The property described in the preceding paragraph would not be particularly useful, unless it were true that a large class of interesting functions could be represented by linear combinations of complex exponentials.

**结构分析**：此句unless意为"如果不，除非"。根据汉语的表达习惯，译文的表达顺序与原文正好相反。

**参考译文**：除非很多有用信号都能用复指数函数的线性组合来表示，否则上面所讨论的性质就不是特别有用。

（5）Although sometimes disregarded, reactions are important because, if students react negatively to your courses, they are less likely to transfer what they learned to their work and more likely to give bad reports to their peers, leading in turn to lower student numbers.

**结构分析**：此句中disregarded是过去分词作后置定语，leading是现在分词作后置定语，if引导的是条件状语从句，what引导的是宾语从句。另外，此句中还有很多短语，如react to，be likely to，transfer to和lead to。

**参考译文**：虽然有时学习者的反应被忽视，但是这种反应其实是很重要的。因为如果学生对你的课程反应消极的话，他们不大可能将所学的东西运用到工作中去，并且更可能对他们周围的人给予坏的报道，而这又将导致更少的学生数量。

（6）After several other attempts to have his work accepted and published by the Institute de France, Fourier undertook the writing of another version of his work, which appeared as the text "The Analytical Theory of Heat".

**结构分析**：根据句子结构和语意分析，这个句子可分成4段：状语（After...）+嵌套在状语中的后置定语（to have...）+主句（Fourier undertook...）+定语从句（which...）。从语意上讲，主句讲的是结果，从句说的是细节。根据汉语的表达习惯，译文的表达顺序与原文相同。

**参考译文**：为了使研究成果能被法兰西研究院接受并发表，在经过了几次其他的尝试之后，傅立叶把他的成果以另一种方式呈现在《热的解析理论》这本书中。

（7）Science moves forward, they say, not so much through the insights of great men of genius as because of more ordinary things like improved techniques and tools.

**结构分析**：此句中的主要结构涉及not so much...as...的固定表达，意为"与其说……不如说……"。

**参考译文**：他们说，科学的发展与其说是借助于伟大天才的真知灼见，不如说是得益于改进了的技术和工具等这类更为普通的事物。

# Unit 9　Information Technology and Education

▲ Knowledge Objectives

When you have completed this unit, you will be able to：
- State the symbols of the information age
- Define IT and ICT
- Compare and contrast IT and ICT
- State the effects of IT in education
- Describe the basic IT skills and personal qualifications

▲ Professional Terms

information and communications technology(ICT)　　信息与传播技术
information technology(IT)　　信息技术
development　　开发

## Text A

### The Information Age[①]

The information age means something different to everyone. In 1956 in the United States, researchers noticed that the number of people holding "white collar" jobs had just exceeded the number of people holding "blue collar" jobs. These researchers realized that this was an important change, as it was clear that we were leaving the Industrial Age. As the Industrial Age ended, the newer times adopted the title of "the Information Age" (Figure 9-1).

Of course, at that time relatively few jobs had much to do with computers and computer-related technology. What was occurring was a steady trend away from people holding Industrial age manufacturing jobs. An increasing number of people held jobs as clerks in stores, office workers, teachers, nurses, and etc. We were shifting into a service economy.

Figure 9-1　In information age, computer is used as an effective tool in many jobs.

---

① http://en.wikipedia.org/wiki/Information_Age

Eventually, Information and Communications Technology (ICT)—computers, computerized machinery, fiber optics, telecommunication satellites, Internet, and other ICT tools—became a significant part of our economy. Microcomputers were developed, and many business and industries were greatly changed by ICT.

Nicholas Negroponte captured the essence of these changes in his 1995 book, *Being Digital*. At the time, he was the head of the Massachusetts Institute of Technology's Media Lab. His book discusses similarities and differences between products made of atoms and products made of bits. In essence, one can very cheaply and quickly make a copy of a product made of bits, and ship it across the country or around the world both quickly and at very low cost. Parts of the *Being Digital* book as well as many of Negroponte's articles are available free on the Web.

Nowadays, most people tend to think of the Information Age in terms of cell phones, digital music, high definition television, digital cameras, email on the Internet, the Web, computer games, and other relatively new products and services that have come into widespread use. The pace of change brought on by such technology has been very rapid.

## Text B

## ICTs and Globalization[①]

Information and Communications Technology (ICT) is an umbrella term that includes all technologies for the manipulation and communication of information. The term is sometimes used in preference to Information Technology (IT), particularly in two communities: education and government.

Figure 9-2　Information communication Technology changes the way we think, and the way we do many things.

Although, in the common usage it is often assumed that ICT is synonymous with IT, ICT is not just about technologies, but more about information transfer and communication. Information and Communications Technology is basically an electronic-based system of information transmission, reception, processing and retrieval, which has drastically changed the way we think, the way we live and the environment in which we live (Figure 9-2). It must be realized that globalization is not limited to the financial markets, but encompasses the whole range of social, political, economic and cultural phenomena. Information and communications technology revolution is the central and driving force

---

①　http://southernlibrarianship.icaap.org/content/v06n01/ogunsola_l01.htm

for globalization and the dynamic change in all aspects of human existence is the key by-product of the present globalization period of ICT revolution. The world telecommunication system, the convergence of computer technology and telecommunications technology into the Information Technology, with all its components and activities, is distinctive in its extension and complexity—and is also undergoing a rapid and fundamental change. The results of this are that National boundaries between countries and continents become indistinct and the capacity to transfer and process information increases at an exceptional rate. The global information communication has been called "the world's largest machine," and it is very complex and difficult to visualize and understand in its different hardware and software subsystems. As Kofi Annan has put it, "that the Internet holds the greatest promise humanity has been known for long-distance learning (Figure 9-3) and universal access to quality education... It offers the best chance yet for developing countries to take their rightful place in the global economy... And so our mission must be to ensure access as widely as possible. If we do not, the gulf between the haves and the have-nots will be the gulf between the technology-rich and the technology-poor."

Figure 9-3 With the assistance of ICT, distance learning is very popular in many countries.

ICTs are increasingly playing an important role in organizations and in society's ability to produce, access, adapt and apply information. They are being heralded as the tools for the post-industrial age, and the foundations for a knowledge economy, due to their ability to facilitate the transfer and acquisition of knowledge. These views seem to be shared globally, irrespective of geographical location and difference in income level and wealth of the nation. ICT may not be the only cause of changes we are witnessing in today's business environment, but the rapid developments in ICT have given impetus to the current wave of globalization.

While trans-national corporations are reaping huge profits from the flexibility and opportunities offered by globalization, the level of poverty in the world is growing. Africa in particular is hit by the growth of poverty and economic crisis. The use and production of ICT plays an important role in the ability of nations to participate in global economic activities. Apart from facilitating the acquisition and absorption of knowledge, ICT could offer developing countries unprecedented opportunities to change educational systems, improve policy formulation and execution, and widen the range of opportunities for business and for the poor. It could also support the process of learning, knowledge networking, knowledge codification, and science systems. ICT could be used to access global knowledge and communication with other people. However, over major parts of developing countries ICT is available only on a very limited scale, and this raises doubts about developing countries' ability to participate in the current ICT—induced global knowledge economy. There has also been concern that this unequal distribution of ICT may in fact further contribute to the marginalization of poor countries in relation to developed countries, and to disruptions of the social fabric. Hence, one can conclude that the concept of "digital slavery" is inevitable for developing countries as far as ICT is concerned. The wide gap in the availability and use of ICT across the world, and the influences ICT exerts on globalization, raise questions about whether globalization entails homogeneity for organizations and societies in developing countries. It also raises questions about the feasibility and desirability of efforts to implement the development of ICT through the transfer of best practices from western industrialized countries to developing countries, and whether organizations can utilize ICT in accordance with the socio-cultural requirements of the contexts. Information and Communications Technology development is a global revolution. It has become a subject of great significance and concern to all mankind. Relevant studies have shown that the greatest impact of the ICT revolution will revolve around the "Digital Divide" equation. The most important aspect of the ICT challenge is the need to plan, design and implement a National Information Infrastructure (NII) as the engine of economic growth and development.

## Text C

## Information Technology and Education[①]

New knowledge based on the latest research and alternative interpretations of existing knowledge can be sent around the world in seconds by means of information technology and electronic communication. Knowledge is being changed constantly or is so quickly made obsolete that the disseminators of knowledge—the teachers—cannot always be up-to-date.

Figure 9-4  With the development of IT, the role of a teacher has changed from a Knowledge transmitter to a planner, guider, and mediator of instruction.

Knowledge is not static but dynamic and moves with lightning speed in the information society. IT opens up opportunities for a more individualized form of teaching in which pupils and students can themselves control the learning process and the teacher is not necessarily present. Teaching has to be organized in such a way that learners learn to learn and to accept responsibility for their own education. Educational courses based on IT technology can be developed to support everyone, in new and more effective ways, including specially weak learner groups in the learning of basic skills such as reading, writing and arithmetic. Therefore it is necessary to revise the traditional view of the role of the teacher. The role of the teacher as planner and mediator of teaching must be

---

① http://eng.uvm.dk/publications/9Informationtec/eng_it.htm

developed concurrently with the integration of IT into education (Figure 9-4). There will also be a growing demand for the sorting of information and for the conversion of accumulated information into usable knowledge. In the future, the teacher must also be able to work as a guide and sparring partner for pupils and students.

What's more, by means of information technology, education can thus be made available outside of working hours, at the weekend, during working hours in co-operation between companies and educational institutions, as well as in a completely different part of the country from that in which the teaching is taking place (Figure 9-5).[1] Education can, in this way, be said to be "unlimited". Meanwhile, we can also say that information technology creates an opportunity for a greater degree of internationalization of education.

Figure 9-5  Thanks to information technology, we can learn at anywhere and any time if we are convenient.

## Text D

## Basic IT Skills and Personal Qualifications①

Figure 9-6  In the IT society, people should gain basic IT skills in order to qualify themselves for work and life.

Overall, the task of the educational system is to qualify the individual for work and for life in general. The aim of the educational system is thus not merely to qualify young people and adults to gain and reproduce the knowledge which their teachers disseminate.[2] The decisive new quality of the IT society is that young people and adults can be qualified to creatively sort, choose, process and use the great amounts of information that IT makes available (Figure 9-6). In this way, the learning process and the ability constantly to develop one's own learning processes and utilize information as a raw material to be processed into relevant knowledge, are supported. The basic IT skills and personal qualifications of young people and adults are developed in order to meet the requirements of the information society.

Multimedia, the Internet and video conference systems are useful tools for the gaining of knowledge and their use will eventually be regarded as being just as much a basic skill as

---

① http://eng.uvm.dk/publications/9Informationtec/eng_it.htm

reading, writing and arithmetic. Learners must thus become qualified IT users and this includes taking greater independent responsibility for their own learning process. Therefore, the effort to give all—young people and adults—the necessary basic IT skills must be strengthened.

The precondition for an increased use of IT in teaching is, of course, that the basic skills of reading, writing and arithmetic continue to have high priority—if possible, higher than today. In addition, school subjects must be soundly based in order to counteract tendencies to confuse uncritical information-seeking with knowledge and perception.

Many IT systems are general in nature, it is up to the user to find out how a given task is to be solved. It is thus the user who has to discover a series of operational steps leading to the solution of the problem. It is here that one comes across a threshold in the use of IT systems. It is not only operational skills or professional skills that are required but skills that are peculiar to IT systems. For the sake of simplicity, they can be called IT skills.

Quite fundamentally, the users of the educational system must be helped to achieve an understanding of the tools of presentation of the technology, where text, sound, still pictures and film can be combined into an integrated whole. The user must be encouraged to gain experience in the automatic handling of information and data in digital form. It has turned out that these skills are best gained through independent use—and not with the help of text books. Therefore, it is quite important that computers, networks and software be made available as an integral part of the teaching process, depending on the needs and wishes of the various sectors.

In addition to ensuring a development of IT skills and other professional/technical qualifications, it is also important to develop a number of personal qualifications in pupils and students—both in the quite young and in adults.

Figure 9-7  Information technology can help strengthen people's personal qualifications, such as communication and cooperation.

Correctly used, information technology has new and more effective possibilities for further strengthening the development of the personal qualifications of pupils and students, such as independence and the abilities to cooperate and communicate (Figure 9-7).

The prerequisite for a sense of responsibility and social involvement is the ability of the individual to turn information into knowledge. Therefore, the ability to sort information and distinguish between important and unimportant, as well as the ability to listen and reflect, is given great weight at all levels of education. The ability to cooperate, the ability to function in various roles, to adjust to the efforts of others and to the whole, the ability to communicate and the ability to understand other cultures and ways of life are other personal qualifications which are to be supported and developed in a course of education. Finally, the educational system must have room for a great deal of initiative and inventiveness and for process-orientated work forms. It is these qualifications, among others, that strengthen in the individual the development of leadership and the desire to start new enterprises.

Only through a simultaneous development of the basic IT skills and personal qualifications can it be ensured that the individual, companies and society will reap the full benefit of information technology.[3]

## New Words

    synonymous  *adj.* 同义的
    magnetic  *adj.* 磁的；有磁性的；有吸引力的
    optical  *adj.* 眼的；视力的；光学的
    gamut  *n.* [音]音阶；全音阶；全音域 [喻]整个领域，全部
    balloon  *n.* 气球；气缸 *vi.* 乘气球上升；膨胀如气球；迅速增加 *vt.* 充气，使如气球 *adj.* 膨胀如气球的；分量轻而体积大的
    obsolete  *adj.* 荒废的；陈旧的 *n.* 废词；陈腐的人
    disseminator  *n.* 传播者；撒种者
    arithmetic  *n.* 算术；算法
    counteract  *vt.* 抵消，中和，阻碍
    threshold  *n.* 开始；开端；极限
    prerequisite  *n.* 先决条件 *adj.* 必须先具备的
    simultaneous  *adj.* 同时的；同时发生的

## Notes

[1] What's more, by means of information technology, education can thus be made available outside of working hours, at the weekend, during working hours in co-operation between companies and educational institutions, as well as in a completely different part of the country from that in which the teaching is taking place.

译文：另外，在工作时间之外，在周末，在公司和教育机构合作的工作时间里，以及在另一个完全不熟悉的地方开课的情况下，学习者也可以通过信息技术受到教育。

- in which the teaching is taking place 是定语从句，修饰先行词 part。
- What's more 另外，而且
- by means of 利用
- as well as 也，又

[2] The aim of the educational system is thus not merely to qualify young people and adults to gain and reproduce the knowledge which their teachers disseminate.

译文：因此教育体系的目的并不仅仅是使年轻人和成年人获得或复制他们老师传播的知识。

- which their teachers disseminate 是定语从句，修饰先行词 knowledge。

[3] Only through a simultaneous development of the basic IT skills and personal qualifications can it be ensured that the individual, companies and society will reap the full benefit of information technology.

**译文**：只有同时发展基本的信息技术技能和个人技能，个人、企业以及社会才能真正享受到信息技术带来的全部好处。

• that the individual, companies and society will reap the full benefit of information technology 是宾语从句。

• can it be ensured that the individual, companies and society will reap the full benefit of information technology 是倒装语序，only 位于句首，主句需倒装。

## Selected Translation

### Text C

### 信息技术与教育

利用信息技术和电子通信能够在几秒钟的时间内将建立在最新的研究和对现有知识的替代性解释基础上的新知识传送到世界各地。知识正在不断改变，或者说知识如此迅速地就过时，以至于知识的传播者——教师——并非总是切合时宜。

知识不是静态的而是动态的，且在信息社会中以极快的速度发展着。信息技术为更个性化的教学形式提供了机会，学习者可以自己控制学习过程，并且老师不一定要在教学现场。教学要采取这样一种组织方式，即学习者学会学习并且自己承担教育责任。以信息技术为基础的教育课程可以用更有效的新方法来支持每一个学习者，包括支持那些在学习基本技能，如阅读、写作和算术方面特别薄弱的学习者群体。因此，有必要修订关于教师角色的传统观点。当信息技术与教育融合的同时，教师也要发展教学的策划者和调解人这两种角色。对信息进行分类的需求以及将积累的信息转化为实用知识的需求也日益增长。在将来，老师还必须能够作为学习者的引导者和辩论伙伴。

另外，在工作时间之外，在周末，在公司和教育机构合作的工作时间里，并且在另一个完全不熟悉的地方开课的情况下，学习者也可以通过信息技术受到教育。因此，我们可以说教育是"无限制的"。同时，我们也可以说，信息技术为更大程度的教育国际化创造了机会。

## Exercises

**Short Answers**：

1. In what terms do most people think of the information age nowadays?

2. Why do we think that the use and production of ICT plays an important part in the ability of nations to participate in global economic activities?

3. What effects does IT have in the field of education?

4. According to the text, what are basic IT skills and personal qualifications?

# 英汉语序的对比与翻译

英译汉、汉译英的翻译方法和技巧是建立在英汉两种语言语句结构和语序的对比之上的。翻译的本质是不同思维方式的转换,思维的方式决定着语言的表达形式。西方民族的思维形式是重在分析,这种思维形式使西方人惯于"由一列多"的思维,句子结构以主语和谓语为核心,统摄各种短语和从句,结构复杂,形成了"树杈形"的句式结构;而东方民族思维形式是重在综合,这种思维形式使中国人注重整体和和谐,强调"从多而一"的思维形式,句子结构以动词为中心,以时间顺序为语序链,形成"流水型"的句式结构。

例如:He had flown yesterday from Beijing where he spent his vocation after finishing the meeting he had taken part in in Tianjin.

他本来在天津开会,会议一结束,他就去北京度假了,昨天才坐飞机回来。

从以上句子来看,汉语句子以动词为关键词,以时间顺序为语序链;而英语句子则以主要动词为谓语,以分词、介词、不定式、动名词或介词等短语(或从句)表示汉语中相应动词的语义和动作的先后顺序。汉语的几个短句往往可以译成一个由英语关联词及各种短语连接在一起的一个英语长句。因此翻译时,必须按照东西方民族思维方式的特点,调整语句结构,以符合汉语的表达习惯。

从语言上看,英语句子结构复杂,多长句;汉语多短句。英语多用被动,汉语多用主动。英语多变化,汉语多重复。英语较抽象,汉语较具体。如:

There is no race of men anywhere on earth so backward that it has no language, no set of speech sounds by which the people communicate with one another.

世界上的任何种族,不论其多么落后,都有自己的语言,都有人们用以交流的语言体系。

从语序上看,英汉两种语句中的主要成分主语、谓语、宾语或表语的词序基本上是一致的,但各种定语的位置,各种状语的次序和从句的次序在英、汉语句中则有同有异。下面分别加以说明。

## 一、定语语序的对比

1. 形容词、分词作定语。英语中,形容词和分词作定语通常放在所修饰的名词之前,但在有些情况下,如修饰 some, any, every, no 和 body, thing, one 组成的合成词时,形容词必须后置。而在汉语中,形容词作定语一般都前置。例如:

We were pleased at the inspiring news.(前置)
听到这个鼓舞人心的消息我们很高兴。(前置)
The excited people rushed into the building.(前置)
激动的人们冲进了这幢大楼。(前置)
I've got something important to tell you.(后置)
我有重要的事要告诉你。(前置)

He was the only person awake at the moment.(后置)

他是那时唯一醒着的人。(前置)

2. 短语作定语。英语中,修饰名词的短语一般放在名词之后,而汉语则往往反之,例如:

The next train to arrive was from New York.(不定式作定语,后置)

下一列到站的火车是从纽约开来的。(前置)

There was no time to think.(不定式作定语,后置)

已经没有时间考虑了。(后置)

The man standing by the window is our teacher.(分词短语作定语,后置)

站在窗户旁的那位男士是我们的老师。(前置)

### 二、状语语序的对比

英语中状语短语可放在被修饰的动词之前或之后,译成汉语时则大多数放在被修饰的动词之前。例如:

He is sleeping in the bedroom.(位于动词之后)

他正在卧室里睡觉。(位于动词之前)

英语中时间状语、地点状语的排列一般是从小到大,而汉语中则是从大到小。例如:

Fourier was born on March 21, 1768, in Auxerre, France.

傅立叶1768年3月21日生于法国奥克斯雷市。

### 三、从句语序的对比

英语复合句中,从句的位置比较灵活,可以放在主句之前,也可以放在主句之后。而汉语中,通常是偏句在前,正句在后。如对于时间状语从句,一般是按时间的先后来描述,对于原因状语从句,一般是原因在前,结果在后。例如:

I went out for a walk after I had my dinner.(后置)

After I had my dinner, I went out for a walk.(前置)

我吃了晚饭后出去散步。(前置)

I will go on with the work when I come back tomorrow.(后置)

我明天回来时会继续干这份工作的。(前置)

I haven't seen him since I came here.(后置)

我来这儿后还没见过他呢。(前置)

He had to stay in bed because he was ill.(后置)

因为他病了,他只好待在床上。(前置)

根据汉英两种语言的句子语序特点和表达习惯,采取一些必要的手段来调整语句的顺序,在翻译当中是必要的,因此,只有了解汉英两种语言在语序上的不同,才能在汉英互译时,以符合汉英语言的表达形式进行翻译。

Part 3  Media, Technology and Learning

# Unit 10  The Development Trends of Media and Technologies

## Knowledge Objectives

When you have completed this unit, you will be able to:
- State the reasons why we continue to use traditional media
- State the current situations of telecommunications and interactive technologies and their effects
- List the development trends of technology
- Explain the meanings of E-learning

## Professional Terms

| | |
|---|---|
| projector | 投影仪 |
| slide | 幻灯片 |
| Global Position System (GPS) | 全球定位系统 |
| electronic learning (e-learning) | 电子学习 |
| blended learning | 混合学习 |
| Virtual Learning Environment (VLE) | 虚拟学习环境 |
| Management Information System (MIS) | 管理信息系统 |

## Text A

### Continuing Use of Traditional Media[①]

Many teachers want to forget traditional media and focus on "new technologies". However, traditional media will be with us for many years because they accomplished many tasks as well as or even better than the new technology. Like a carpenter, we need to know how to use all tools, both old and new, and more importantly, we must be able to select the best tool for our particular task. Teachers and students need to know how to select from all available media those materials that will best promote learning.[1] For example, most classrooms will continue to have chalkboards (Figure 10-1), so teachers must learn to use them to their maximum effectiveness. The overhead projector continues to be an effective tool for gaining and maintaining students' attention (Figure 10-2). Instructors can not just brush off traditional media in favor of computers and digital technology.

---

① Sharon E. Smaldino, James D. Russell, Robert Henich and Michael Molenda, *Instructional Technology and Media for Learning*, Eighth Edition.

Figure 10-1　Chalkboard is still very popular in most schools.

Figure 10-2　Projector is an effective traditional media in assisting instruction.

Although they do not attract the attention that newer computer-based media do, traditional media are still used far more often than computer-based media, in both the school and the corporate realm. In the United States, for example, print material is the dominant media format, according to teacher self-report. Textbooks and other printed materials are the most common instructional tools throughout the world.

Organizations implement technology with the hope that it will increase their benefits or decrease their costs. In the case of higher education, technology has not proven to be a cost reducer on the educational side of their operations. Colleges and universities continue to struggle to support the traditional analog media-audio—and videocassettes, slides, and overhead transparencies-still preferred by many instructors and the digital media, which are seen as potential cost reducers.

Both traditional and digital technologies will continue to be used. You need to know the advantages, limitations, and appropriate applications of a range of media and technology options in order to know when to use each type. All media and technology have their place in education and training.

## Text B

### Advancing Telecommunications and Interactive Technologies[1]

Technology is becoming more useful, more prevalent, more "intelligent", and more powerful, while at the same time becoming less intimidating, less noticeable, less demanding and less expensive. User interfaces are becoming simpler and devices are becoming increasingly user friendly.

Advanced interactive technologies include multimedia, hypermedia and virtual reality. Multimedia CD-ROM products are commonly found in school media centers, primarily in the form of encyclopedias or other reference databases. There is still relatively little application of

---

[1] Sharon E. Smaldino, James D. Russell, Robert Henich and Michael Molenda, *Instructional Technology and Media for Learning*, Eighth Edition.

multimedia and hypermedia to core instruction in schools. In higher education there is widespread experimentation with locally produced multimedia and hypermedia, but standard formats or universal acceptance of such technologies for core instruction across institutions remain to be established.

Telecommunications offers the potential for both students and teachers to break down the walls of classrooms in elementary schools and middle schools and share ideas and information with colleagues collaboratively. In the business word, telecommunications has had the same effect—leading to a more national and international business community.

Business and industry have experienced steady growth in the use of telecommunication networks. These networks—satellite based for video conferencing or wired networks for digital communication—are typically established for purposes such as sales meeting. Video conferencing (Figure 10-3) allows real-time, synchronous interaction among participants at widely dispersed locations, saving companies money formerly spent on travel. Once in place, businesses can then use these communication systems to deliver distance education.

Figure 10-3  Businesses benefit a lot from video conferencing.

Interactive media formats have gained a foothold in corporate training, primarily to deliver basic courses across multiple sites. Lack of hardware and software compatibility has restricted the availability of off-the-shelf courseware. Organizations are beginning to incorporate more multimedia courseware into their training programs as compatibility improves; thus, the supply of less expensive off-the-shelf materials is increasing as the demand rises. We believe this trend will continue well.

## Text C

### Predictions of Technology Trends[①]

What's going to happen about technology? What will happen to the identity of people in the web? Will traditional TV survive the impacts of the Internet? Will GPS (Global Position System) be popular in the near future? All of these issues are discussed in Predictions—the critical trends that will influence the development of technology.

Trend one: from anonymity to authenticity—It is often argued that one of the great benefits of the web is anonymity. There may be an increasing clamor from regulators, users and online traders, for internet to provide authenticated identity every time people undertake any

---

① http://www.deloitte.com/dtt/research/0,1015,sid%3D1012&cid%3D108298,00.html
   http://www.merinews.com/catFull.jsp? articleID = 132262

transaction via the web. A move to process online authentication could ultimately be good for both business and users.

Trend two: the rising value of digital protection—Some owners will spend more on virus protection, online backup and insurance to enhance the lifetime of their computer. This trend could extend beyond the PC (personal computer) to other devices such as MP3 players, mobile phones, external hard drives and others, as all these forms hold valuable data.

Trend three: innovation blowback—Technology industries are demonstrating increased interest and investment in developing products to reach large, low-income populations in emerging economies such as India, China, and Latin America. In a phenomenon called innovation blowback, we can also expect to see innovative products, services, or management practices be introduced back into western economies.

Figure 10-4  Television brings a lot of fun to our life, and broadens our horizons.

Trend four: long live traditional television (Figure 10-4), thanks to Internet television—The global traditional television sector, despite the occasional shock, should remain in good health throughout the year, and there is a good chance that Internet television will have contributed to traditional television's fortunes.

Trend five: capitalize on mobile phones—Lower priced mobile handsets are popular gifts in China, but the major opportunity for mobile phones may be the market for machines, rather than for people. Lower priced handsets are likely to increase overall mobile penetration rates but as global mobile ownership approaches 50 percent. Embedding mobile phone functionality in machines from ATMs (Automatic Teller Machines) to vending machines could be a potential market for the mobile industry.

Trend six: overcoming online privacy may not mean the end of counterfeit content—Steady growth in the number of broadband connections around the world has allowed online piracy to grow and the increasing speed of broadband connections has made movie, television and software piracy feasible. The Chinese authorities attach great importance in cracking down online piracy by closing down illegal websites, imposing fines on violators and controlling "virtue communities" of the Internet. But the rapid growth of the Internet and wider access will continue to pose challenges to anti-piracy efforts.

Trend seven: giving mobile GPS (Global Position System) (Figure 10-5) direction—Prices for GPS functionality have fallen to such an extent that a growing number of mobile phones now incorporate GPS navigation. The number of devices that incorporate the technology is expected to grow rapidly. The mobile industry may overlook several critical differences between how satellite navigation is used in vehicles and how people on foot may use it. Thus, while a growing number of GPS-enabled mobile phones may be shipped and sold, aside from the novelty, their use may be infrequent in the near future.

Trend eight: exploiting new media's growing need to communicate—Digital communications will become more varied, vibrant and vital to the way we live than ever before. New media companies, such as social networks, synthetic worlds and blogs, are likely to offer the services through which, newer forms of communication are initiated. However, the telecommunications sector should consider how to earn a greater share of revenues from communications in new media websites.

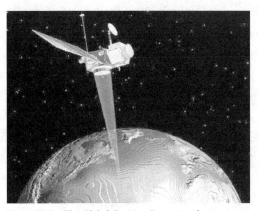

Figure 10-5  The Global Position System is playing a more and more important role nowadays.

## Text D

### Electronic Learning[①]

Electronic learning (or e-learning) is a type of education where the medium of instruction is computer technology. No in-person interaction may take place in some instances. E-learning is used interchangeably in a wide variety of contexts. In companies, it refers to the strategies that use the company network to deliver training courses to employees. In the USA, it is defined as a planned teaching/learning experience that uses a wide spectrum of technologies, mainly Internet or computer-based, to reach learners at a distance. Lately in most Universities, e-learning is used to define a specific mode to attend a course or programs of study where the students rarely attend face-to-face for on-campus access to educational facilities, because they study on-line.[2]

Figure 10-6  E-learning is a type of education, and learners can enjoy the convenience it brings.

E-learning is naturally suited to distance learning and flexible learning (Figure 10-6), but can also be used in conjunction with face-to-face teaching, in which case the term Blended learning is commonly used. E-Learning pioneer Bernard Luskin argues that the "E" must be understood to have broad meaning if e-learning is to be effective. Luskin says that the "e" should be interpreted to mean exciting, energetic, enthusiastic, emotional, extended, excellent, and educational in addition to "electronic" that is a traditional national interpreta-

---

① http://en.wikipedia.org/wiki/E-learning

tion. This broader interpretation allows for 21st century applications and brings learning and media psychology into the equation.

Figure 10-7  With computer and internet, we can create a virtual learning environment.

In higher education especially, the increasing tendency is to create a Virtual Learning Environment (VLE) (Figure 10-7) (which is sometimes combined with a Management Information System to create a Managed Learning Environment) in which all aspects of a course are handled through a consistent user interface standard throughout the institution.[3] A growing number of physical universities, as well as newer online-only colleges, have begun to offer a select set of academic degree and certificate programs via the Internet at a wide range of levels and in a wide range of disciplines. While some programs require students to attend some campus classes or orientations, many are delivered completely online. In addition, several universities offer online student support services, such as online advising and registration, e-counseling, online textbook purchase, student governments and student newspapers.

E-Learning can also refer to educational web sites such as those offering learning scenarios, worksheets and interactive exercises for children. The term is also used extensively in the business sector where it generally refers to cost-effective online training.

## New Words

carpenter   *n.* 木匠
realm   *n.* 领域
analog   *n.* 类似物，相似体
encyclopedia   *n.* 百科全书
telecommunications   *n.* （与单数动词连用）电讯，长途通讯，无线电通讯，电信学
synchronous   *adj.* 同时的，［物］同步的
foothold   *n.* 立足处
portable   *adj.* 轻便的，手提（式）的，便携式的
transistor   *n.* ［电子］晶体管
battery   *n.* 电池，殴打
anonymity   *n.* 匿名，作者不明（或不详）
clamor   *n.* 喧闹，叫嚷，大声的要求 *v.* 喧嚷，大声地要求
backup   *n.* 后援，支持，阻塞 *vt.* 做备份 *adj.* 候补的，支持性的 ［计］文件备份
blowback   *n.* 后座，后坐力
counterfeit   *n.* 赝品，伪造品 *adj.* 伪造的，假冒的 *vt.* 伪造，假冒
broadband   *n.* 宽带

vibrant　　*adj.* 振动的
synthetic　　*adj.* 合成的，人造的，综合的
vending machine　　自动售货机

## Notes

[1] Teachers and students need to know how to select from all available media those materials that will best promote learning.

译文：老师和学生都必须知道怎样从可利用的媒体中选择最能促进学习的那些素材。

* how to select from all available media those materials 是宾语从句的省略形式。
* that will best promote learning 是定语从句，修饰先行词 materials。

[2] Lately in most Universities, e-learning is used to define a specific mode to attend a course or programs of study where the students rarely attend face-to-face for on-campus access to educational facilities, because they study on-line.

译文：最近在大多数大学中，电子化学习被用来定义一种上课或参加学习课程的具体模式，在这样的学习中学生很少参加面授，也没有机会接触学校的教学设施，因为他们是在网上学习。

* where the students rarely attend face-to-face for on-campus access to educational facilities 是定语从句，修饰限定先行词 study。
* because they study on-line 是原因状语从句。
* face-to-face　　*adv.* 面对面地

[3] In higher education especially, the increasing tendency is to create a Virtual Learning Environment (VLE) (which is sometimes combined with a Management Information System to create a Managed Learning Environment) in which all aspects of a course are handled through a consistent user interface standard throughout the institution.

译文：尤其是在高等教育中，渐增的趋势是创造一个虚拟学习环境（虚拟学习环境有时与管理信息系统组合在一起，以创造一种管理学习环境），在这种环境中，一门课程的各个方面都通过学校内部一致的用户界面标准来处理。

* which is sometimes combined with a Management Information System (MIS) to create a Managed Learning Environment 是定语从句，修饰先行词 Virtual Learning Environment。
* in which all aspects of a course are handled through a consistent user interface standard throughout the institution 是定语从句，修饰先行词 Virtual Learning Environment。

## Selected Translation

## Text B

### 先进的远程通信和交互技术

技术现在变得越来越有用，越来越普及，越来越智能化，功能越来越强大；同时，技术

也变得不那么陌生,不引人注意,不需要高级的操作技巧,价格也越来越便宜。用户界面变得更加友好,设备越来越便于使用。

先进的交互技术包括多媒体、超媒体和虚拟现实。多媒体 CD-ROM 在学校媒体中心很容易找到,它们主要是百科全书或其他参考资料数据库。中小学核心课程中,使用多媒体和超媒体还相对较少。在高等教育领域,各大学纷纷尝试开发多媒体和超媒体,但是对于各大学都开设的核心课程来说,如何制订标准化格式,如何使开发的课程得到普遍接受,都还有待解决。

远程通信为中小学教师和学生提供了一种可能,即打破中小学教室围墙的限制,与大学合作,共享理念和信息。在商业领域,远程通信也有同样的影响——它能实现真正全国性、国际化的商业联盟。

在使用远程通信网络方面,商业界和企业界都经历了稳步的增长。建设这些网络(卫星支持的视频会议系统和有线网络支持的数字交流网络)的目的是为了跨国或跨洲召开销售会议。视频会议可以让广泛分布在各个地区的参与者进行实时的、同步的交互,这样就节省了公司花费在旅程上的费用。一旦网络装备完毕,公司就可以使用这些系统来开展远程教育。

在企业培训中,交互媒体已经取得了一席之地,其主要作用是在多个站点传播基础课程。不同公司出品的软件系统和硬件设备之间缺少兼容性,制约了不同公司制作的课件的应用范围。随着兼容性的提高,一些机构已经开始把更多的多媒体课件整合到公司的培训项目中。而且由于需求的增加,一些价格低廉的成品课件正在增多。我们相信这种趋势会持续发展。

## Exercises

**Short Answers:**

1. How can we choose an appropriate medium for instruction from the available media?
2. What do advanced interactive technologies include? And what are their current situations in application?
3. What are the effects of telecommunications in education, business and industry?
4. What does e-learning mean in both education and business?

# 文献检索简介

文献信息检索是指从任何文献信息集合中查出所需信息的活动、过程和方法。广义的文献信息检索还包括文献信息存储,两者又往往合并称为"文献信息存储与检索"。当然,对于信息用户来说,信息检索仅指信息的查找过程。

一、文献检索的意义

1. 充分利用已有的文献信息资源,避免重复劳动。

科学研究具有继承和创造两重性,科学研究的两重性要求科研人员在探索未知或从事研究工作之前,应该尽可能地占有与之相关的资料、情报。研究人员在开始研究某一课题前,必须利用科学的文献信息检索方法来了解课题的进展情况,在前人的研究基础上进行研究。可以说一项科研成果中95%是别人的,5%是个人创造的。科研人员只有通过查找文献信息,才能做到心中有数,防止重复研究,将有限的时间和精力用于创造性的研究中。

2. 缩短查找文献信息的时间,提高科研效率。

目前文献信息的数量和类型增加十分迅速,科研人员不可能将世界上所有的文献都阅读完。据美国科学基金会统计,一个科研人员花费在查找和消化科技资料上的时间占全部科研时间的51%,计划思考占8%,实验研究占32%,书面总结占9%。由上述统计数字可以看出,科研人员花费在科技出版物上的时间为全部科研时间的60%左右。如果科研人员掌握好科学的文献信息检索方法,就可以缩短查阅文献的时间,获取更多的文献信息,提高科研效率。

3. 促进专业学习,实现终身学习

掌握了科学的文献信息检索方法,可以把学生引导到超越教学大纲的更广的知识领域中去,促进学生的专业学习。在当代社会,人们只有终身学习,不断更新知识,才能适应社会发展的需求。而掌握了科学的文献信息检索方法,在研究实践和生产实践中根据需要查找文献信息,就可以无师自通,很快找到一条吸取和利用大量新知识的捷径。

**二、国内检索系统**

目前我国高校和科研机构一般都是根据自己的专业设置和科研需要来购置不同的数据库。下面是常见和常用的一些数据库:

《中国期刊网全文数据库》(http://www.cnki.edu.cn);
《万方数据资源系统》(http://www.wfdata.com.cn);
《重庆维普中文科技期刊数据库》(http://www.cqvip.com.cn);
《中国专利数据库》(http://www.sipo.gov.cn);
《中国生物医学文献数据库》(http://cbm.imicams.ac.cn);
《中国科技论文在线》(Figure 10-8)(http://www.paper.edu.cn);
《国家科技成果网》(http://www.nast.org.cn);
《国家科技图书文献中心》(Figure 10-9)(http://www.nstl.gov.cn)。

**三、国际著名的六大检索系统**

1. 美国《科学引文索引》(Science Citation Index,简称SCI)。
2. 美国《工程索引》(Engineering Index,简称EI)。
3. 美国《化学文摘》(Chemical Abstracts,简称CA)。CA报道的化学化工文献量占全世界化学化工文献总量的98%左右,是当今世界上最负盛名、收录最全、应用最为广泛的查找化学化工文献的大型检索工具。
4. 英国《科学文摘》(Science Abstracts,SA;或INSPEC)。包括:

《物理文摘》(Section A-Physics Abstracts, PA);

《电子与电气文摘》(Section B-Electrical Engineering & Electronics Abstracts, EEA);

《计算机与控制文摘》(Section C-Computers and Control Abstracts, CCA);

《信息技术》(Information Technology, IT)。

5. 俄罗斯《文摘杂志》(Abstract Journals, 简称 AJ)。

6. 日本《科学技术文献速报》,现扩充为大型数据库"日本科学技术情报中心"(Japan Information Center Science and Technology, 简称 JICST)。

Figure 10-8　中国科技论文在线

Figure 10-9　国家科技图书文献中心

# Part 4  Instructional Systems Design

## Unit 11  Instructional Systems and Instructional Systems Design

▲ Knowledge Objectives
  • State the five subsystems included in the instructional system and their outputs
  • Understand the cybernetic system and the differences between the cybernetic system and "one-shot" system
  • Know the inputs of instructional design, the procedures and the outputs

▲ Professional Terms
  instructional system    教学系统
  instructional design    教学设计

## Text A

### Instructional Systems[①]

An instructional system represents an organized, planned, and arranged means for teaching effectively. As a system it meets R. Buckminster Fuller's basic definition of "system". Moreover, any set of methods that works will qualify as an instructional system.

An instructional system has organization, and involves planning, deployment, operation, and evaluation. We can view an instructional system, therefore, as one organized into various subsystems. These subsystems include (1) design of the system, (2) development of the system, (3) deployment of the system, (4) evaluation of the system, and (5) re-design of the system (see Table 1 below). Note that not all instructional systems include the last subsystem, redesign. Redesign makes an instructional system "cybernetic." That is, such a system becomes self-corrective and evolves over time.

---

① http://members.aol.com/johneshleman/insys.html

Table 1  Component Steps of a Cybernetic Instructional System

| System Step: | Result: |
| --- | --- |
| 1. Design of the System | a "blueprint" for development |
| 2. Development of the System | a working system for deployment |
| 3. Deployment of the System | learning data for evaluation |
| 4. Evaluation of the System | recommendations for redesign |
| 5. Redesign of the System | a revised system for further development |

Each component step of an instructional system has a set of inputs. Each step also results in a set of outputs. The table above lists the principal output produced at each phase.

**Types of Instructional Systems**

The type of system described has been named, by E. A. Vargas, as "cybernetic". The word "cybernetic" has Greek origins, and means "to steer". Steering, in this case, further means that the system "changes course". Think of a helmsman steering a vessel. The destination appears in the form of a better system, one that increases in efficiency, effectiveness, and productivity. Any instructional system can be made cybernetic. A few examples of cybernetic systems exist.

A cybernetic system contains multiple feedback loops. The principal feedback loop concerns the efficiency, effectiveness, and productivity of the system back into the system. Accordingly, a cybernetic system contains two important steps beyond implementation, delivery, and deployment of the system. These two steps include (1) evaluation of the data generated by the system, and (2) redesign of the system based on the evaluation. This results in a somewhat revised system. The steps then proceed around again, through the same steps in the same loop. Once a system has been redesigned, it then gets redeveloped, redeployed, and reevaluated. The cycle can continue indefinitely. (Figure 11-1)

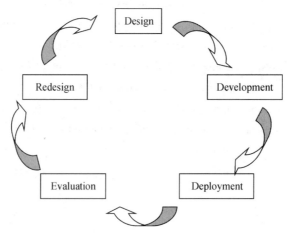

Figure 11-1  the indefinite loop of a cybernetic system

Another way of looking at feedback in a cybernetic system of instruction goes like this:

The system gets designed so that the verbal behavior of the designer comes under effective stimulus control of the changes to learner behavior affected by the system.[1] In such a system, the behavior of the teacher becomes just as important as the behavior of the learner. Change to the behavior of both becomes an overall objective of the system.

Because a cybernetic system is both iterative and cyclical, one can illustrate it with a circular loop.

A cybernetic system of instruction differs from what I refer to as "one-shot", or linear systems. A "one-shot" system typically has only the first three phases—design, development, and deployment. Such a system lacks an explicit feedback loop. Any improvement to such a system will thus run haphazardly, and may not happen at all. A "one-shot" system can remain unchanged. And even if change does get made to a "one-shot" system, the basis for change may include factors other than the system's efficiency, effectiveness, and productivity. In fact, those data may not serve as a basis for change at all. Changes, if it occurs, probably do so if the content of the instruction changes, the target population changes, or for other purposes such as new agreements with an end client or profits that allow an expansion of a curriculum.[2]

"One-shot" systems also differ with respect to the three steps shared with a cybernetic system. A "one-shot" system may display less concern with precision in pinpointing behavior, and in writing objectives. The resulting "blueprint" may thus appear sparse and less exact. Additionally, in a "one-shot" system there may be less attention on changing behavior, because any data on behavior change would have no feedback and revision purpose. Thus, the resulting instructional activities may be fewer in number, involve far less active student responding, involve little or no measurement of student responding, and center mainly on presenting content to learners. In a "one-shot" system, therefore, deployment becomes largely a matter of delivery. If you think of delivery in the same terms as the Post Office delivering a letter, or a radio station delivering a broadcast, you will have a fairly good picture of what delivery means in a "one-shot" system.

In a "one-shot" instructional system, "teaching" usually gets accomplished with the delivery. In such instances, teaching does not explicitly mean changing behavior. Nor does it mean explicitly arranging conditions so that student behavior will change. If student behavior does change, it typically does so in large part outside of the instructional system.

A "one-shot" instructional system can become fairly good, however, if effective instructional principles are followed during the design, development, and deployment phases. To the extent that this happens, a "one-shot" system works and achieves some measure of real education. So, the difference between a "one-shot" system and a cybernetic system does not reduce to a false dichotomy based on one being ineffective and the other effective. Rather, a cybernetic system can make an already effective system even more effective (and more efficient and productive as well).

## Text B

# Instructional Design[①]

### Overview of the Design of Instruction Phase

A field of "Instructional Design" exists, has practitioners, issues publications, and holds meetings. To some people "instructional design" represents all that one needs to know about in order to create materials and arrange conditions for learning to occur. [3] Most often and for many people, "instructional design" refers mainly to how information will be presented to learners.

In the view taken here, however, Instructional Design forms only part of the development of a larger Instructional System. Design typically forms the first step when developing a complete instructional system. It also represents the first step in any subsequent redesign of a system. Instructional Design results in a "blueprint" for a course of instruction, ready for development into a completed package. The "blueprint" consists of the named course, lists of content resources, assumptions that limit the range and scope of the course, knowledge and skills to be taught, the set of pinpointed behaviors necessary and relevant to the knowledge and skills to be taught, and the set of named units and modules, with each module containing a set of one or more behavioral objectives, each objective tagged and classified by learning category.

### Inputs to the Instructional Design Phase

Instructional design represents the first step in building a system of instruction.

There has to be some reason to begin working on an instructional system, however. There must be some rationale for choosing to instruct people versus implementing other solutions to problems. Instead of opting for instruction, a problem may be solved by developing a performance management program or changing ergonomic variables. Not all problems require teaching as a solution. However, the development of an instructional system assumes that some need for instruction has been determined.

The principal inputs to the design phase include either (1) a contract agreed upon with a client for whom the system will be produced, (2) an assignment or work order, or (3) a decision to create a course "on spec." Without any of these decisions being made, little reason would exist to begin designing and developing courses. Note that a course developed "on spec" typically means one developed for potential general use. In that case the end product becomes available "off the shelf."

Courses developed on a contract basis for clients should have some up-front agreement, and probably some up-front consideration, before work proceeds. [4] Note that the design phase can be used to determine cost estimates for development. In point of fact, the end product of the design phase—the so-called "blueprint"—can itself represent a deliverable product.

---

① http://members.aol.com/johneshleman/design.html

**Instructional Design Procedure**

Instructional Design typically follows a sequence of steps. While one does not have to adhere to a hard and fast ordering, the following list presents a useful, complete, and efficient sequence:

1. Naming the course.
2. Specifying available financial resources.
3. Determining content resources, references, and available human expertise.
4. Identifying knowledge and skills to be taught.
5. Specifying assumptions about the target audience and the prerequisite knowledge and skill levels.
6. Pinpointing the behaviors representative of fluent knowledge and skilled performance.
7. Stating behavioral pinpoints in terms of behavior channels or learning channels.
8. Defining the behavioral objectives.
9. Tagging and classifying the behavioral objectives.
10. Organizing the behavioral objectives into designated modules of instruction.
11. Assembling the final "blueprint" for instructional development.

**Outputs**

The principal output of the instructional design process, as defined here, is a "blueprint" for subsequent development of the course. The "blueprint" consists of all of the outputs and materials produced and assembled in this phase, as listed above.

With an effective and useful "blueprint" at hand, one can proceed to the next major phase of creating an instructional system, development of the system.

## New Words

deployment　　*n.* 展开,部署,调度
cybernetic　　*adj.* 控制论的
steer　　*vt. & vi.* 架势,掌舵
helmsman　　*n.* 舵手
feedback loop　　反馈回路,反馈环
verbal　　*adj.* 1. 词语的,言语的,字句的 2. 口头的 3. 动词的
cyclical　　*adj.* 轮转的,循环的
one-shot　　*adj.* 只有一次的
haphazard　　*adj.* 偶然的,随意的,无计划的
sparse　　*adj.* 稀疏的;稀少的
practitioner　　*n.* 1. 习艺者,实习者 2. 从业者(尤指医师)
rationale　　*n.* 理由;逻辑依据
ergonomic　　*adj.* 人类环境改造学的
spec　　*n.* 投机,说明,规格

off the shelf   现货供应
adhere to   遵循,依附;坚持
prerequisite   *n.* 先决条件,前提
designated   指定的,派定的

## Notes

[1] The system gets designed so that the verbal behavior of the designer comes under effective stimulus control of the changes to learner behavior affected by the system.

**译文**:由于学习者行为受系统的影响,因此,设计系统的目的是想让学习者行为的变化有效地刺激设计者的语言行为。

- so that 引导的是目的状语从句,用来修饰主句 The system gets designed。
- affected by the system 是过去分词作后置定语,用来修饰先行词 learner behavior。
- comes under 归入,受到

[2] Changes, if it occurs, probably do so if the content of the instruction changes, the target population changes, or for other purposes such as new agreements with an end client or profits that allow an expansion of a curriculum.

**译文**:如果发生变化,并且如果教学内容发生变化、目标人群发生变化,或者出现其他的一些情况,例如与客户端的新协议或允许课程拓展所带来的好处,那么,上述数据很可能成了变化的基础。

- if it occurs 是 if 引导的条件状语从句,用来修饰主语 changes。
- so 指代的是前一句中的内容,即 those data may serve as a basis for change。
- agreements with 与……达成的协议
- 后一个 if 引导的也是条件状语从句,用来修饰主句中的谓语 do。

[3] To some people "instructional design" represents all that one needs to know about in order to create materials and arrange conditions for learning to occur.

**译文**:对某些人来说,"教学系统设计"代表了所有需要知道的内容,以此来制作学习材料,并为学习的发生创造条件。

- that one needs to know about 是由 that 引导的定语从句,用来修饰先行词 all。
- know about 知道,了解
- arrange for 为……做准备(安排)

[4] Courses developed on a contract basis for clients should have some up-front agreement, and probably some up-front consideration, before work proceeds.

**译文**:为客户开发的基于合同的课程必须在工作进行之前有一些预先的协议,并大概有一些预先的考虑。

- developed on a contract basis for clients 是过去分词作后置定语,用来修饰限定先行词 courses。
- before work proceeds 是由连词 before 引导的时间状语从句,用来修饰主句。

# Selected Translation

## Text A

### 教 学 系 统

教学系统提供了一种有组织、有计划并且是已经安排好的方法来有效地教学。作为一个系统,它符合 R. Buckminster Fuller 关于"系统"的基本定义。并且,任何一套起作用的方法都可以被认为是教学系统。

教学系统有着系统性的组织,包括计划、部署、操作和评价这几个步骤。因此,我们可以将教学系统看成是由许多不同的子系统组织而成的。这些子系统包括:(1) 系统设计,(2) 系统开发,(3) 系统部署,(4) 系统评价和(5) 系统重设计(如下表1)。需要注意的是,并不是所有的教学系统都包括最后一个子系统,即重设计。重设计使教学系统能自我控制。也就是说,这种系统会变成自我矫正的系统,并且能够一直演变下去。

表1 控制教学系统的组成步骤

| 系统步骤 | 输出结果 |
| --- | --- |
| 系统设计 | 用于开发的"蓝图" |
| 系统开发 | 用于部署的工作系统 |
| 系统部署 | 用于评价的学习数据 |
| 系统评价 | 用于重设计的建议 |
| 系统重设计 | 有待进一步开发的修订系统 |

教学系统的每一个组成步骤有一系列的输入,同样导致一系列的输出。上表列出了每一阶段的最重要的输出。

**教学系统的类型**

以前所描述的教学系统类型被 E. A. Vargas 命名为"控制性的"。"控制性的"这个单词起源于希腊,意思是"操控,驾驶"。既然这样,操控的更深一层意思就是,这个系统能够"改变航向"。想一想舵手操控船舰的情形。操控的目的是想产生一种更优越的系统形式,这种系统增加了效率、效用和生产率。任何一个教学系统能够做成"控制性"的。其中存在一些控制系统的例子。

控制系统包括多重反馈回路。主反馈关注的是返回系统的系统效率、效用和生产率。于是,控制系统除了执行、传递和部署系统外,还包括两个重要的步骤。这两个步骤就是:(1) 评价系统所产生的数据;(2) 基于这种评价来重设计系统。这将产生一个略微有所修改的系统。然后这两个步骤又继续在同样的循环回路并通过同样的步骤循环进行。一旦系统被重设计,那么它将被重开发、重部署和重评价。这个循环无限继续下去。

另一种看待教学控制系统的反馈是这样的:由于学习者行为受系统的影响,因此,设计系统的目的是想让学习者行为的变化有效地刺激设计者的语言行为。在这种系统中,老师的行为变得和学习者的行为同样重要了。两者行为的变化成了系统的总目标。

控制系统既反复迭代,又循环,因此可以用一个圆形回路来说明它。

教学控制系统与我提到的"一次"系统或线性系统不同。"一次"系统典型地只有前三个阶段——设计、开发和部署。这种系统缺少一个明确的反馈回路。于是这种系统的任何改进只偶然发生,并且可能从不发生。"一次"系统能始终保持不变,而且即使发生了变化,这种变化的基础也可能不包含系统效率、效用和生产率。事实上,这些数据根本不可能成为变化的基础。如果发生变化,并且如果教学内容发生变化、目标人群发生变化,或者出现其他一些情况,例如与客户端的新协议或允许课程拓展所带来的好处,那么上述数据很可能成了变化的基础。

"一次"系统同样不同于控制系统的三个步骤。"一次"系统更少关注定位行为和写作目标的精确性。由此产生的"蓝图"因此可能出现松散且精确度不高的状况。并且由于在行为改变上的任何数据都没有反馈和修改目标,因此在"一次"系统中将可能更少关注行为上的改变。因此,由此产生的教学活动可能在数量上会减少,包括学生的反应越来越不积极、对学生的反应没有或只有很少的衡量和主要集中在向学习者介绍内容。因此,在"一次"系统里,部署这个环节很大程度上变成了传递。如果你将传递想象为邮局投递信件,或广播站发送广播,那么就相当正确地理解了传递在"一次"系统里的意思。

在"一次"教学系统中,"教学"通常是通过传递的方式来完成。在这个例子里,教学并不明确地意味着改变行为,也不明确地意味着安排能使学生的行为发生改变的条件。如果学生行为的确发生了改变,那么它大多数情况下是超出了教学系统的范围了。

然而,如果在设计、开发和部署的阶段中按照有效的教学原则进行设计的话,"一次"教学系统能变得相对好一点。当这种情况发生时,"一次"系统能够起作用,并完成某种程度的真正教育。那么,"一次"系统和控制系统之间的区别没有降低至"假二歧分枝"现象,即一种无效而另一种有效的极端情况。在一定程度上,控制系统能使一个已经有效的系统变得更加有效(并且更加高效和多产)。

### Exercises

**1. Short Answers:**

(1) What are the subsystems included in the instructional system and what are their respective result?

(2) What are the differences between the cybernetic system and "one-shot" system?

(3) What are the inputs and outputs of instructional design?

# 文献检索方法简介

文献检索是科学研究工作中的一个重要步骤,它贯穿研究的全过程。文献为选题提供了依据,研究者确定选题以后必须围绕选题广泛地查阅文献资料。能否正确地掌握文献检索方法,关系到研究的过程、质量以及能否出成果,因此必须掌握文献检索的技能。了解和掌握文献的分类及其特点,是迅速有效地查找所需信息的必要前提。

### 一、文献的类型

一级文献,即原始文献,是由亲自经历事件的人所提供的各种形式的材料和各种原著。这种文献是我们从事研究的第一手资料,对研究工作有很大的价值。

二级文献,指对一级文献加工整理而成的系统化、条理化的文献资料,如索引、书目、文摘以及类似内容的各种数据库等。

三级文献,指在二级文献的基础上对一级文献进行分类后,经过加工、整理而成的带有个人观点的文献资料。如数据手册、年鉴、动态综述述评等。

### 二、检索文献的步骤

1. 分析研究课题。在检索之前首先要分析检索的课题,一要分析主题内容,弄清课题的关键问题所在,确定检索的学科范围;二要分析文献类型,不同类型的文献各具特色,研究者应根据自己的检索需要来确定检索文献的类型范围;三要确定检索的时间范围;四要分析已知的检索线索,逐步扩大。

2. 确定检索工具。正确地确定检索工具,能使我们在浩瀚的文献海洋中畅游无阻,从而以最简捷的方法,迅速、准确地获得研究所需的文献信息。下面是几种检索工具:

索引:把文献的一些特征,如书目、篇名、作者以及文献中出现的人名、地名、概念、词语等组织起来,按一定的顺序(字母或笔画)排列,供人检索。

文摘:它是一种概括地介绍原文献内容的简短摘要,使人们不必看全文就可以大致了解文章的内容,是一种使用广泛的检索工具,如《新华文摘》、《教育文摘》等。

书目:是将各种图书按内容或不同学科分类进行编制的目录,如《全国总书目》。

参考性与资料性工具书:它的范围很广,如辞典、百科全书、年鉴等。

计算机和互联网:可以通过搜索引擎等对文献进行查询。

3. 确定检索方法。常用的检索方法主要有:

顺序查找法:从课题研究的起始年代开始往后顺时查找,直到近期为止,这种方法查全率高,但费时。

回溯查找法:这是以某一篇论文(或专著)后面所附的参考资料为线索,跟踪追查的方法。这种查找方法针对性更强、直接、效率高。

计算机检索:计算机以其强大的数据处理和存储能力成为当今最为理想的信息检索工具。计算机检索有以下优点:检索速度快,检索范围大。它可以同时对跨越几年甚至几十年的数据做检索,检索途径多。计算机的数据库能提供十几种甚至几十种的检索工具,还可以使用逻辑的方法把它们组合起来使用,非常灵活;可以同时检索多个数据库。计算机可以同时打开几个数据库以备检索,并且可以去掉其中重复的数据;可以立刻得到原文。由于早期的检索系统大多提供索引、文摘等二级文献,有时我们不得不再去寻找原文即一级文献。现在使用计算机全文检索系统,当场就能看到全文,并且还可以根据需要打印出来。

### 三、计算机的检索方式

当前广泛使用的计算机检索包括:联机检索、光盘检索和国际互联网检索。

联机检索(online retrieval)是指用户利用计算机终端设备,通过通讯线路,从信息中心的计算机(主机)数据库中检索出所需要的信息的过程。它允许用户以人机对话、联机会话这样交互的方式(interactive)直接访问系统及数据库,检索是实时(real time)、在线(online)进行的。用户的提问一旦传到主机被接收后,机器便立刻执行检索运算,很快将检索结果传送到用户终端,用户可反复修改检索式,最后获得较满意的检索结果。联机检索能远程登录到国内外检索系统。大型检索系统不仅数据库多,而且数据库的文献报道量大,高达数百万条记录,数据更新及时,系统检索点多,组合方式多样,输出形式、输出方式多样。用户容易得到最新、最准确和最完全的检索效果。

基于 Web 方式的联机检索使用 WWW 浏览器在 windows 界面下交互作业,给用户揭示了一篇篇文章的信息,有很强的直观性,此外,用户也可以借以检索多媒体信息。Web 版数据库检索大量采用超文本。超文本(hypertext)的内容排列是非线性的,它按知识(信息)单元及其关系建立起知识结构网络,如具有图形、画面的信息又称作超媒体(hypermedia),超文本(媒体)的检索是通过超文本链接(hyperlink)来实现的。其形式是:有的在网页的文字处有下划线,或以图标方式标志,用户点击(point-and-click)这些标志便能进入与此信息相关的下一页,在该页面上通过超文本链接进入另一个页面,超文本在其中起信息导向作用。这样,用户在从一个页面转向另一个页面的控制过程中获取自己所需要的信息。

Web 版文献数据库检索在采用超文本的基础上又将命令检索、菜单检索方式融合其中,交互使用,集各种检索机制为一体。许多大型国际联机检索系统在互联网上开设了自己的站点,提供用户检索服务。

## Unit 12　Instructional Systems Design Models

▲ Knowledge Objectives

◆ Understand the ADDIE model and the five phases during the Instructional Design

◆ Understand the ASSURE model and know the situation it is used in

◆ Understand the Dick and Carey model and the nine stages in the model

◆ Understand the Rapid Prototyping model, the situations it can be used in and the rapid design techniques for instructional development in each phase of the ADDIE model

▲ Professional Terms

Instructional System Design (ISD)　　教学系统设计
Entry Behaviors　　入门技能
performance objectives　　绩效目标
subject-matter expert (SME)　　主题问题专家
Rapid prototyping　　快速原型法

# Text A

## Instructional System Design (ISD): Using the ADDIE Model[①]

Instructional design is the systematic approach to the Analysis, Design, Development, Implementation, and Evaluation of learning materials and activities.

Instructional design aims for a learner-centered rather than the traditional teacher-centered approach to instruction, so that effective learning can take place. This means that every component of the instruction is governed by the learning outcomes, which have been determined after a thorough analysis of the learners' needs. [1]

These phases sometimes overlap and can be interrelated; however, they provide a dynamic, flexible guideline for developing effective and efficient instruction.

**Table 1　The ADDIE Model**

| | Sample Tasks | Sample Outputs |
|---|---|---|
| **Analysis** the process of defining what is to be learned | • Needs assessment<br>• Problem identification<br>• Task analysis | • Learner profile<br>• Description of constraints<br>• Needs, Problem Statement<br>• Task analysis |
| **Design** the process of specifying how it is to be learned | • Write objectives<br>• Develop test items<br>• Plan instruction<br>• Identify resources | • Measurable objectives<br>• Instructional strategy<br>• Prototype specification |
| **Development** the process of authoring and producing the materials | • Work with procedures<br>• Develop workbook, flowchart, program | • Storyboard<br>• Script<br>• Exercises<br>• Computer assisted instruction |
| **Implementation** the process of installing the project in the real world context | • Teacher training<br>• Tryout | • Student comments, data |
| **Evaluation** the process of determining the adequacy of the instruction | • Record time data<br>• Interpret test results<br>• Survey graduates<br>• Revise activities | • Recommendations<br>• Project report<br>• Revised prototype |

The ADDIE Model is an iterative instructional design process, where the results of the formative evaluation of each phase may lead the instructional designer back to any previous phase. [2] The end product of one phase is the starting product of the next phase. (Figure 12-1)

### Analysis

The Analysis phase is the foundation for all other phases of instructional design. During this phase, you must define the problem, identify the source of the problem and determine possible solutions.

---

① http://www.seas.gwu.edu/~sbraxton/ISD/general_phases.html

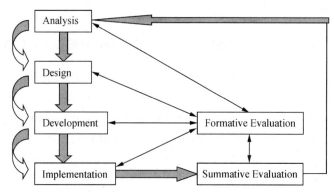

Figure 12-1    the flow chart of the ADDIE Model

The phase may include specific research techniques such as needs analysis, job analysis and task analysis. The outputs of this phase often include the instructional goals, and a list of tasks to be instructed. These outputs will be the inputs for the Design phase.

**Design**

The Design phase involves using the outputs from the Analysis phase to plan a strategy for developing the instruction. During this phase, you must outline how to reach the instructional goals determined during the Analysis phase and expand the instructional foundation.

Some of the elements of the Design Phase may include writing a target population description, conducting a learning analysis, writing objectives and test items, selecting a delivery system, and sequencing the instruction. The outputs of the Design phase will be the inputs for the Develop phase.

**Development**

The Develop phase builds on both the Analysis and Design phases. The purpose of this phase is to generate the lesson plans and lesson materials. During this phase you will develop the instruction, all media that will be used in the instruction, and any supporting documentation. This may include hardware (e.g., simulation equipment) and software (e.g., computer-based instruction).

**Implementation**

The Implementation phase refers to the actual delivery of the instruction, whether it's classroom-based, lab-based, or computer-based. The purpose of this phase is the effective and efficient delivery of instruction. This phase must promote the students' understanding of material, support the students' mastery of objectives, and ensure the students' transfer of knowledge from the instructional setting to the job.

**Evaluation**

This phase measures the effectiveness and efficiency of the instruction. Evaluation should actually occur throughout the entire instructional design process—within phases, between phases, and after implementation. Evaluation may be Formative or Summative.

**Formative Evaluation** is ongoing during and between phases. The purpose of this type of evaluation is to improve the instruction before the final version is implemented.

**Summative Evaluation** usually occurs after the final version of instruction is implemented. This type of evaluation assesses the overall effectiveness of the instruction. Data from the Summative Evaluation is often used to make a decision about the instruction (such as whether to purchase an instructional package or continue/discontinue instruction).

## Text B

## The ASSURE Model[①]

The ASSURE model is an ISD (Instructional Systems Design) process that was modified to be used by teachers in the regular classroom. The ISD process is one in which teachers and trainers can use to design and develop the most appropriate learning environment for their students. You can use this process in writing your lesson plans and in improving teaching and learning.

The ASSURE model incorporates Robert Gagne's events of instruction to assure effective use of media in instruction.

### Analyze learners

Before you can begin, you must know your target audience (your students). You need to write down the following information about your students:

General characteristics—grade, age, ethnic group, sex, mental, emotional, physical, or social problems, socioeconomic level, and so on.

Specific entry competencies—prior knowledge, skills, and attitudes.

Learning styles—verbal, logical, visual, musical, structured, and so on.

### State objectives

Once you know your students, you can begin writing the objectives of your lesson. Objectives are the learning outcomes, that is, what will the student get out of the lesson?

The ABCD's of writing objectives are:

- Audience (who are your students?)
- Behavior to be demonstrated
- Conditions under which the behavior will be observed
- Degree to which the learned skills are to be mastered

Example: Fifth grade social studies students (Audience) will be able to name at least 90% (Degree) of the state capitols (Behavior) when given a list of states (Condition).

### Select instructional methods, media, and materials

Once you know your students and have a clear idea of what they should get out of the lesson, then you are ready to select the following:

---

[①] http://www.unca.edu/education/edtech/techcourse/assure.htm

• Instructional method that you feel is most appropriate to meet the objectives for these particular students.

• Media that would be best suited to work with your instructional method, the objectives, and your students. Media could be text, still images, video, audio, and computer multimedia.

• Materials that provide your students with the help they need in mastering the objectives. Materials might be purchased and used as they are or they might need some modifications. You can also design and create your own materials for the students to use. Materials would be specific software programs, music, videotapes, images, but would also be equipment, i.e., overhead projector (Figure 12-2), computer, printer, scanner, TV, laserdisc player (Figure 12-3), VCR, and so on.

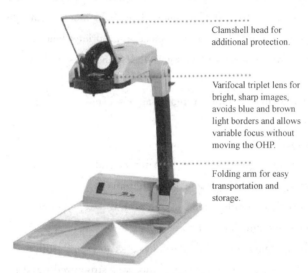

Figure 12-2　Overhead projector

Figure 12-3　Laserdisc player

Part 4    Instructional Systems Design

### Utilize media and materials

Now it's time to do your lesson and use the media and materials that you have selected. You should always preview the materials before using them in a class and you should also use the equipment in advance to be sure it works and you know how to use it. [3] If you use electronic equipment, don't assume that everything will work. Be sure to have a plan B. Hardware and software are created by humans. Humans make mistakes and so software has mistakes in it. Hardware can malfunction. Don't get discouraged if technology lets you down. Make sure that your instructional materials are suitable and work the best you can and then use it in the classroom.

### Require learner participation

Remember, students learn best when they are actively involved in the learning. The passive learner has more trouble learning whatever we try to pour into his/her brain. Whatever your teaching strategy, you can incorporate questions and answers (Figure 12-4), discussions, group work, hands-on activities (Figure 12-5), and other ways of getting students actively involved in the learning of the content. It is up to you, the teacher, to make sure that all your students have opportunities to participate in the learning activities in the unit plan. Avoid lecturing for an entire hour. Listen to your students and allow them to become aware of the content. Allow them to learn as opposed to trying to "teach" them.

Figure 12-4   The students are actively answering their teacher's questions.

Figure 12-5   In their lab coats, sixth graders participate in a variety of hands-on activities, including figuring out how to clean up a mini-oil spill in a pie plate using only the supplies provided to them.

**Evaluate and revise**

This last stage is often neglected but it is the most important one. Anyone can develop a lesson and deliver it, but really good teachers must reflect upon the lesson, the stated objectives, the instructional strategy, the instructional materials, and the assessment and determine if these elements of the lesson were effective or if one or more of them need to be changed the next time the lesson is done.[4] Sometimes a lesson may seem like it would be great, at least on paper. But then when you actually teach the lesson with a specific set of students, you might discover there were several things that did not seem to work. Your expectations might be too high or too low. The materials used might not have been appropriate for the grade level or the material might not be very motivating. The instructional strategy might not have got students interesting in participation or the strategy might have been difficult for you to manage. The assessment you used might have shown that students didn't learn what you tested for. This might mean that you did not accurately test for the stated objectives, the method of assessment needs to be revised, or the lesson did not permit enough time for the students to master the objectives.

You are not a bad teacher if a lesson does not work. You are a bad teacher if you don't reflect upon your lessons and work on revising elements of the lesson until your students become successful learners.[5]

# Text C

## Dick and Carey Model①

This model describes all the phases of an iterative process that starts by identifying instructional goals and ends with summative evaluation. This model is applicable as shown below.

**Table 2  the Application of Dick and Carey Model**

| Expertise Level | Novice | Expert |
| --- | --- | --- |
| Orientation | Descriptive | Prescriptive |
| Knowledge Structure | Procedural | Declarative |
| Purpose & Uses | Small Scale (Unit, Module, Lesson) | Large Scale (Course, Instruction) |
| Theoretical Basis | Learning Theory | Analysis Functions |
| Context | K-12/Higher Education | Business/Government |

**Stage 1: Instructional Goals**

• Instructional Goal: Desirable state of affairs by instruction

• Needs Analysis: Analysis of a discrepancy between an instructional goal and the present state of affairs or a personal perception of needs

---

① http://www.umich.edu/~ed626/Dick_Carey/dc.html

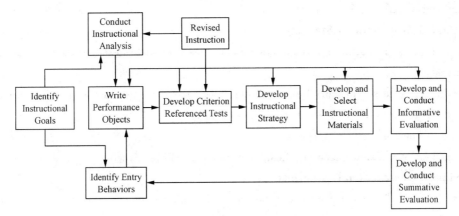

Figure 12-6　Dick and Carey Model

## Stage 2：Instructional Analysis
- Purpose：To determine the skills involved in reaching a goal
- Task Analysis（procedural analysis）：about the product of which would be a list of steps and the skills used at each step in the procedure
- Information-Processing Analysis：about the mental operations used by a person who has learned a complex skills
- Learning-Task Analysis：about the objectives of instruction that involve intellectual skills

## Stage 3：Entry Behaviors and Learner Characteristics
- Purpose：To determine which of the required enabling skills the learners bring to the learning task
- Intellectual skills
- Abilities such as verbal comprehension and spatial orientation
- Traits of personality

## Stage 4：Performance Objectives
- Purpose：To translate the needs and goals into specific and detailed objectives
- Functions：Determining whether the instruction related to its goals.

Focusing the lesson planning upon appropriate conditions of learning

Guiding the development of measures of learner performance

Assisting learners in their study efforts.

## Stage 5：Criterion-Referenced Test Items
- To diagnose an individual possessions of the necessary prerequisites for learning new skills
- To check the results of student learning during the process of a lesson
- To provide document of students progress for parents or administrators
- Useful in evaluating the instructional system itself（Formative/Summative evaluation）
- Early determination of performance measures before development of lesson plan and

instructional materials

### Stage 6: Instructional Strategy

- Purpose: To outline how instructional activities will relate to the accomplishment of the objectives
- The best lesson design: Demonstrating knowledge about the learners, tasks reflected in the objectives, and effectiveness of teaching strategies

e. g. Choice of delivering system.

Teacher-led, Group-paced vs. Learner-centered, Learner-paced

### Stage 7: Instructional Materials

- Purpose: To select printed or other media intended to convey events of instruction.
- Use of existing materials when it is possible
- Need for development of new materials, otherwise
- Role of teacher: It depends on the choice of delivery system

### Stage 8: Formative Evaluation

- Purpose: To provide data for revising and improving instructional materials
- To revise the instruction so as to make it as effective as possible for larger number of students
- One on One: One evaluator sitting with one learner to interview
- Small Group
- Field Trial

### Stage 9: Summative Evaluation

- Purpose: To study the effectiveness of system as a whole
- Conducted after the system has passed through its formative stage
- Small scale/Large Scale
- Short period/Long period

## Text D

## Rapid Prototyping[①]

Rapid prototyping can be used in situations to: test out a user interface, test the database structure and flow of information in a training system, test the effectiveness and appeal of a particular instructional strategy, develop a model case or practice exercise that can serve as a template, give clients and sponsors a more concrete model of the intended instructional product, and to get user feedback and reactions to two competing approaches. [6]

### Techniques for Rapid Instructional Design

George M. Piskurich lists the following rapid design techniques for instructional

---

① http://en.wikibooks.org/wiki/Instructional_Technology/Instructional_Design/Rapid_Prototyping

development in each phase of the ADDIE model:
### A-ANALYZE
1. Use retro assessment—ask the "right questions" to fill in the background on the program you are creating
2. Interview the top 10 people most and first for an organizational assessment
3. Perform a quick approach to a performance gap by
- Identify the problem
- Analyze the tasks and conditions of the job
- Analyze the current performance level
- Identify the causes of the problem
- Identify the desired performance outcome
- Identify the expectations of your training related to the outcome

4. Forego time-intensive interviews and focus groups of a training needs assessment
5. Use electronic bulletins instead of live meetings to collect data
6. Interview two at a time or use net-based surveys to gather information
7. Choose individuals who are not over-experienced to do a job analysis so that the information is not too complicated or use job descriptors that are well-detailed for job analysis
8. Spend a day observing a SME at work and ask questions for task analysis
9. Videotape experts do their jobs and analyze it for the component points

### D-DESIGN
1. Use job analysis and distribute completed objectives and distribute
2. Keep formal reporting to a minimum-jot down what you need to know
3. Create a series of tests at various levels and distribute them to the trainees along with the objectives they are based on
4. Use logical sequencing of steps

### D-Development
1. Use existing polices, procedures, annual reports, magazine articles, pamphlets, etc. for training material
2. Use games that let you alternate the content for instructional use or use templates
3. Strip training of "nice to know" to "must know"
4. Short cut video production by taping short video clips of SMEs doing their work and describing the process or tape an SME as he/she does the training process

### I-Implementation
1. Have reviewers or validators of the design meet as a group
2. Allow the trainers train the trainers

### E-Evaluation
1. Evaluate only what you need to evaluate
2. Use performance checklists as a transfer evaluation to re-check performance

With Rapid Prototyping the ADDIE model is not used as designed. It typically has several steps merged together to streamline the process. Rapid Prototyping should not be used by a novice, because even though it cuts out steps of ADDIE, the designer still must have knowledge of the whole process.

**Representation of the Rapid Prototyping Model:**

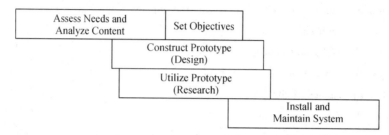

Figure 12-7 the Rapid Prototyping Model

### Advantages of Rapid Prototyping

There are many advantages to using RP in instructional design. It allows for better communication between the designer and users because the needs are clearly expressed from the beginning. The user is able to offer immediate feedback which results in a better product. Its non-linear approach allows for more flexibility in the instruction and can catch problems early in the development stages. Moreover, RP reduces development time and costs.

### Disadvantages of Rapid Prototyping

Some people believe that rapid prototyping is not an effective model of instructional design because it does not replicate the real thing. They believe that many important steps of instructional design are forfeited for a faster, cheaper model. Many problems may be overlooked and results in endless revision.

## New Words

overlap   *vt.* & *vi.* 部分重叠
interrelated   *adj.* 相互关联的
prototype   *n.* 原型,雏形,蓝本
ongoing   *adj.* 继续进行的;不断前进(发展)中的
ethnic group   同种同文化的民族
socioeconomic   *adj.* 社会经济学的
capitol   *n.* 国会大厦,州议会大厦,(古罗马的)主神殿
overhead projector   高射投影仪
laserdisc player   激光视盘机
prescriptive   *adj.* 1. 规定的,指定的,制定(规则)的 2. 约定俗成的,惯例的
procedural   *adj.* 程序上的
declarative   *adj.* 宣言的,公布的

discrepancy　　*n.* 差异,不符合(之处);不一致(之处)
spatial　　*adj.* 空间的,立体空间的,三维空间的
criterion-referenced　　*adj.* 效标参照的
prerequisite　　*n.* 先决条件,前提
retro　　*n.* 制动火箭,减速火箭
forego　　*vt.* (在位置时间或程度方面)走在……之前,居先
bulletin　　*n.* 1. 公告,新闻快报 2. 小报,期刊
jot　　*n.* 一点,少量
pamphlet　　*n.* 小册子
validator　　*n.* 总监制
streamline　　*vt.* 1. 把……做成流线型 2. 简化……使效率更高
forfeit　　*vt.* (因违反协议、犯规、受罚等)丧失,失去

## Notes

[1]　This means that every component of the instruction is governed by the learning outcomes, which have been determined after a thorough analysis of the learners' needs.

**译文:** 这意味着,教学的每一部分都被学习结果所控制,而学习结果则取决于对学习者需求的彻底分析。

◆ which have been determined after a thorough analysis of the learners' needs 是由 which 引导的非限制定语从句。

[2]　The ADDIE Model is an iterative instructional design process, where the results of the formative evaluation of each phase may lead the instructional designer back to any previous phase.

**译文:** ADDIE 模型是一种交互式教学系统设计过程,在这个过程中,每个阶段的形成性评价结果可以导致教学设计者回到以前的任何一个阶段。

◆ where the results of the formative evaluation of each phase may lead the instructional designer back to any previous phase 是由 where 引导的地点状语从句。

◆ lead...to 把……带到,领到

[3]　You should always preview the materials before using them in a class and you should also use the equipment in advance to be sure it works and you know how to use it.

**译文:** 你必须在课堂上使用它们之前预览一下这些资料,而且你同样必须事先使用仪器来确保它能正常工作以及知道怎样操作它。

◆ in advance 1. 在前头 2. 预先,事先

◆ it works 是由 that 引导的宾语从句,其中 that 省略掉了。

◆ how to use it 是由 how 引导的宾语从句。

[4]　Anyone can develop a lesson and deliver it, but really good teachers must reflect upon the lesson, the stated objectives, the instructional strategy, the instructional materials, and the assessment and determine if these elements of the lesson were effective or if one or

more of them need to be changed the next time the lesson is done.

译文：任何人都可以对课程内容进行探究并给学生授课，但真正的好老师必须对课程、规定的目标、教学策略、教材和评估持怀疑态度，并且弄清楚这些课程因素是否有效，或者它们其中一个或几个需要下次上课时进行修改。

- reflect upon 怀疑
- if these elements of the lesson were effective 是由 if 引导的宾语从句。
- if one or more of them need to be changed the next time the lesson is done 是由 if 引导的宾语从句。
- the lesson is done 是同位语从句，用来修饰 the next time。

[5] You are a bad teacher if you don't reflect upon your lessons and work on revising elements of the lesson until your students become successful learners.

译文：如果你不对你的课程持怀疑态度并在学生成为成功的学习者之前致力于修改课程要素，那么你就是一个很差的老师。

- if you don't reflect upon your lessons and work on revising elements of the lesson until your students become successful learners 是由 if 引导的同位语从句，用来修饰 teacher。
- work on 致力于……
- not... until 直到……才

[6] Rapid prototyping can be used in situations to: test out a user interface, test the database structure and flow of information in a training system, test the effectiveness and appeal of a particular instructional strategy, develop a model case or practice exercise that can serve as a template, give clients and sponsors a more concrete model of the intended instructional product, and to get user feedback and reactions to two competing approaches.

译文：快速原型法可以用在以下情况：对用户接口进行彻底检验，测试数据库培训系统中的数据库结构和信息流动，测试某一特定教学策略的有效性和感染力，开发示范个案或能充当模板的实践练习，向客户和赞助商提供预期教学产品的更具体的模型，以及获得用户对两种竞争方法的反馈和反应。

- test out 对……进行彻底检验
- that can serve as a template 是由 that 引导的定语从句，用来修饰限定先行词 practice exercise。
- serve as 充当，担任

## Selected Translation

### Text A

#### 教学系统设计(ISD)：运用 ADDIE 模型

教学系统设计是对学习教材和学习活动进行分析、设计、开发、执行和评价的系统化方法。

教学系统设计意在寻求以学生为中心的，而不是传统的以老师为中心的教学方法，只有这样,学习才能变得有效。这意味着,教学的每一部分都被学习结果所控制,而学习结果则取决于对学习者需求的彻底分析。

这些阶段有时候重叠在一起,相互关联,但是它们为开发有效用的和有效率的教学提供了一种动态的、灵活的指导方针。

表 1　ADDIE 模型

| | 任务举例 | 输出举例 |
| --- | --- | --- |
| 分析<br>明确需要学什么的过程 | • 评估需求<br>• 找出问题<br>• 分析任务 | • 学习者概况<br>• 限制描述<br>• 陈述需求与问题<br>• 任务分析 |
| 设计<br>详述怎样去学习的过程 | • 撰写目标<br>• 开发测试项目<br>• 教学计划<br>• 找出问题来源 | • 可衡量的目标<br>• 教学策略<br>• 原型说明 |
| 开发<br>著述和创作教材的过程 | • 依程序运行<br>• 开发教材,流程图和程序 | • 情节串联图板<br>• 讲稿<br>• 练习<br>• 计算机辅助教学 |
| 执行<br>将此工程在现实世界背景下加以运行的过程 | • 教师培训<br>• 试验 | • 学生意见,数据 |
| 评价<br>决定教学系统适合性的过程 | • 录制时间数据<br>• 说明测试结果<br>• 调查毕业生<br>• 修改活动 | • 建议<br>• 项目报告<br>• 修改后的原型 |

ADDIE 模型是一种交互式教学系统设计过程,在这个过程中,每个阶段的形成性评价结果可以导致教学设计者回到以前的任何一个阶段。一个阶段的输出产品是另一个阶段的输入产品。(图 12-1)

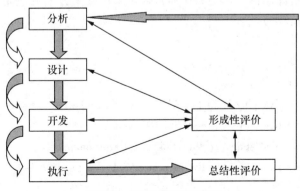

图 12-1　ADDIE 模型的流程图

**分析**

分析阶段是教学系统设计的其他阶段的基础。在这个阶段中,你必须界定问题,找出问题的根源,并确定可能的解决办法。

这个阶段可能包括一些具体的研究技术,例如需求分析、工作分析和任务分析。这个阶段的输出通常包括教学目标和一列需要教的任务。这些输出将作为设计阶段的输入。

**设计**

设计阶段需要使用分析阶段的输出来计划用来开发教学的策略。在这个阶段中,你必须概述怎样达到在分析阶段所决定的教学目标,并扩大教学基础。

设计阶段的一些元素可能包括撰写有关目标人群的描述、进行学习分析、撰写目标和测试项目、选择传输系统和教学排序。设计阶段的输出将作为开发阶段的输入。

**开发**

开发阶段是建立在分析和设计阶段之上的。这个阶段的目的是产生出课程计划和课程教材。在这个阶段,你将开发出教学、将在教学中使用的所有媒体,以及任何一种支持文件。这可能包括硬件(例如模拟设备)和软件(例如基于计算机的教学)。

**执行**

执行阶段指的是教学的实际传输,而不管这种教学是基于教室、基于实验室或基于计算机。这个阶段的目标是教学的有效用和高效率的传输。这个阶段必须提高学生对教材的理解,支持学生对目标的掌握,并且保证学生能将所学的知识从教学环境运用到工作中去。

**评价**

这个阶段测试的是教学的效用和效率。评价必须在整个教学系统设计过程中真实存在:在各阶段内,在各阶段间,以及在执行后。评价可以是形成性的或总结性的。

**形成性评价**在各阶段内以及在各阶段间存在。这种类型的评价的目的是,在最后一个环节被执行之前改善教学。

**总结性评价**通常在教学最后一个环节执行之后发生。这种类型的评价评定的是教学的总体效能。总结性评价产生的数据通常被用来做教学方面的决定(例如是否购买教学套件或连续/离散教学)。

## Exercises

**1. Short Answers:**

(1) What are the five phases in the ADDIE model and what are their main functions?

(2) What are the five steps in the ASSURE model?

(3) What are the nice stages in the Dick and Carey model?

(4) What are the situations the Rapid prototyping can be used in?

# Internet 上常用的教育技术文献资源

Internet 上常用的教育技术文献资源主要以教育网站的形式存在。教育网站是 Internet 上教育资源的主要体现形式,它是指通过收集、加工、存储教育资源等方式建立教学资源库或者建立网上教育平台与开发信息获取及信息搜索的工具等,通过互联网服务提供单位(ISP)接入互联网,向上网用户提供教学和其他有关教育信息服务的机构。在 Internet 上常用的教育技术文献资源主要有下面几种。

1. 国内综合教育网站

(1) 中华人民共和国教育部网址:http://www.moe.edu.cn。

中华人民共和国教育部网站包括教育动态、教育法规、教育部文件、重要文献等栏目,提供了关于国家教育工作的方针政策以及教育部机构设置、主要职能介绍与部属机关、直属机构、所属高校和各教育工程、教育基金会的主页链接等方面的信息。

(2) 中国教育与科研计算机网,网址:http://www.edu.cn。

该网站由中国教育和科研计算机网络中心制作,是了解中国教育、科研现状的窗口,能及时介绍各地教育进展、各学校的基本情况及科研成果、研究机构的最新科研成果。

(3) 人教网,网址:http://www.pep.com.cn。

该网站由人民教育出版社课程教材研究所主办,下设栏目主要包括教育信息、课程研究、人教图书、人教期刊、学科教育、科学知识、中华文化等,还提供交互式论坛、网上购书等服务。

(4) 中国教育信息网,网址:http://www.chinaedu.edu.cn。

该网站旨在通过设置教育动态、招考中心、科普长廊、教育图书、教研天地、学生社区、家长时段、海外视窗、信息化成就展等栏目为学生、教师、家庭、学校提供全方位的服务。

(5) 中国基础教育网,网址:http://www.cbe21.com.cn。

该网站是教育部基础教育课程教材发展中心与北京师范大学共同主办的综合性专业服务网站。该网站强调在基础教育的改革与发展、教育观念、素质教育等方面的导向性,开辟了教育新闻、课程改革、行政管理、教育社区、招生咨询、教育用品、附校中心等栏目。

(6) K12 中国中小学教育教学网,网址:http://www.K12.com.cn。

教育网的目标是建设网上教育资源中心、教育信息中心、教育研究中心、学习交流中心、教育电子商务平台,目前围绕这个目标提供了教育新闻教师频道、学生频道、家长频道、K12 教育论坛、学校与教师免费主页空间、免费电子邮件等大量服务,是中小学教师教学过程中的良师益友。

(7) 其他综合教育网站。

中国教育报,网址:http://www.jyb.com.cn;

中国高校网,网址:http://www.china-school.net;

中国学生网,网址:http://www.6to23.com;

中国教育在线,网址:http://www.cer.net;

中国高等教育网,网址:http://www.h-edu.com/indexl.htm;

香港教育研究所,网址:http://www.fed.cuhk.edu.hk/%7Ehkier/indexc.htm;

香港教育研究协会,网址:http://www.fed.cuhk.edu.hk/%7Ehkera;

美国教育部,网址:http://www.ed.gov。

2. 教育技术学网站

(1) 国内教育技术学网站。

教育技术在线,网址:http://www.iteonline.net;

中国中小学信息技术教育网,网址:http://www.nrcce.com/index.php3;

现代教育装备信息,网址:http://www.eduienet.com/yumai.htm;

全国信息技术及应用远程培训教育工程网,网址:http://www.itat.com.cn/index-1.php;

教育技术通讯,网址:http://www.etc.edu.cn;

现代教育技术网,网址:http://202.112.88.33:91/index.asp;

中国教育技术网,网址:http://www.etr.com.cn;

中国电化教育,网址:http://www.net-edu.com;

中国教育技术,网址:http://www.jyjs.net;

(2) 国外教育技术学网站。

美国教育通讯与技术协会(AECT),网址:http://www.aect.rog;

美国国际教育技术协会,网址:http://www.iste.org;

美国教育技术办公室,网址:http://www.etr.com.cn;

美国教育技术首席执行总裁论坛,网址:http://www.ceoforum.org;

美国教育技术联合会,网址:http://www.rtec.org;

# Unit 13　Automating Instructional Design

▲ **Knowledge Objectives**

• Know about the Automating Instructional Design and understand the advantages about it

• State the four types of Automated Instructional Design tools and know their functions

• Know about the electronic performance support systems (EPSS) as the current trends in automated tools

▲ **Professional Terms**

Automating Instructional Design(AID)　　教学设计自动化

expert systems　　　　　　　　　　　　专家系统

| | |
|---|---|
| advisory systems | 咨询系统 |
| information management systems | 管理信息系统 |
| Electronic Performance Support Systems (EPSS) | 电子绩效支持系统 |
| Instructional Transaction Theory | 教学事务理论 |
| Guided Approach to Instructional Design Advising (GAIDA) | 教学设计建议指导方法 |
| Experimental Advanced Instructional Design Advisor (EAIDA) | 先进的实验教学设计顾问 |
| Advanced Instructional Design Advisor (AIDA) | 先进的教学设计顾问 |
| Instructional Design Advanced Workbench | 教学设计先进工作台 |
| Instructional Design Environment (IDE) | 教学设计环境 |
| Computer-based Instruction (CBI) | 基于计算机的教学 |
| Computer-based Training (CBT) | 基于计算机的训练 |

# Text A

## Automating Instructional Design[①]

Instructional designers are constantly faced with many demands working in various settings, but one common challenge across job settings is to reduce the time required to plan and produce quality instruction. Although instructional content differs among projects, there are common design stages necessary to produce quality instruction. Regardless of the content, designers consider the learner characteristics, instructional context, goals, objectives, instructional strategies, sequencing approaches, evaluation techniques, and production of instructional materials. These common stages are identified in automated tools and align with the ADDIE acronym that describes the major stages.

There have been numerous efforts to automate the instructional design process. Early attempts to automate instructional design followed the proliferation of computers in other industries and educational settings. The attempts concentrated on the development of technological tools that would aid in the user's decision making and in the production of instructional materials.[1] These efforts resulted in the development of job aids to support novice instructional designers in the military. There are four common types of automated instructional design tools: (a) expert systems, (b) advisory systems, (c) information management systems, and (d) electronic performance support systems.

The primary goal of these tools and systems is to aid instructional designers and others in producing instructional materials to enhance learning. They assist and provide support to the

---

① http://www.sciencedirect.com/science?_ob=ArticleURL&_udi=B6VDC-4DW34R5-4&_user=1529636&_rdoc=1&_fmt=&_orig=search&_sort=d&view=c&_version=1&_urlVersion=0&_userid=1529636&md5=b1eb9babae44adbd7f349de178f539c4#secx2

users in the creation of courseware, in the development of computer-based instruction, in the general designer decision making, and may contribute to the elimination of certain instructional design tasks such as story boarding. The research suggests that automated instructional design tools are especially useful in their ability to aid and support the novice designer or subject-matter expert (SME) working as a designer, and others through the instructional design process to produce quality instruction. [2]

## Text B

## Four Types of Automated Instructional Design Tools[①]

### Expert Systems

An expert system contains a domain-specific knowledge-base and performs decision-making and analysis functions for the designer using natural language queries. Expert systems for instructional design have been developed to provide advice to novice instructional designers and to facilitate the development process for experienced designers.

ID Expert from the ID2 Research Group was created to develop and deliver computer-based instruction more efficiently. ID Expert is based on Instructional Transaction Theory, a "second generation" theory of instructional design. According to Instructional Transaction Theory, instruction is based on transactions (sets of interactions) between the system and the learner in order to accomplish a given task. ID Expert assists designers in creating transactions by presenting a set of decision-making steps involving instructional components, formatting, resources, etc. ID Expert is considered a prototype system and has not yet been released commercially.

The United States Air Force Armstrong Laboratory proposed two AID approaches that use expert system technology to provide expertise to novice instructional designers and subject matter experts in the design, production, and implementation of courseware used in Air Force training. Guided Approach to Instructional Design Advising (GAIDA) uses tutorials and context-specific advice and examples. Experimental Advanced Instructional Design Advisor (XAIDA) uses the Instructional Transaction Theory framework to encapsulate context-specific knowledge. Both of these environments are results of the Advanced Instructional Design Advisor (AIDA) research project.

Reactions to Expert Systems: While expert systems for instructional design can teach theory validation and function as authoring tools, they are limited by their inability to support analysis and design tasks. ID expert systems attempt to control the instructional design process, a process involving a large number of interrelated elements, and so must rely heavily on the knowledge and experience of the individual practitioner. [3] Several instructional technologists

---

① http://www.ericdigests.org/1999-1/tools.html

have proposed systems that more subtly advise the instructional designer, rather than prescribe a set of solutions.

**Advisory Systems**

Duchastel challenges the expert system model by providing an advisory system model. Instead of controlling the problem-solving process with expert knowledge, advisory systems assist or coach users in accomplishing a given task. A prototype for the advisory system approach is the Instructional Design Advanced Workbench, architecture for a computer-based workbench that supports the cognitive tasks of instructional design without constraining the designer. [4]

**Information Management Systems**

Instructional Design Environment (IDE) from the Institute for Research on Learning is a computer-aided design environment that supports an ID methodology for teaching the use of software in real-life problem-solving contexts. IDE helps document design and development options. It is intended for experienced instructional designers.

**Electronic Performance Support Systems**

Electronic performance support systems (EPSS) are self-instructional electronic environments that provide access to "software, guidance, advice, data, tools, and assessment with minimum support and intervention by others". EPSS have become popular in the 1990s for business and educational contexts that require "just-in-time" learning and a high level of a particular skill. Some examples of EPSS are listed below.

Building on Duschastel's "workbench," Paquette et al introduced a performance support system called AGD (a French acronym meaning Didactic Engineering Workbench). AGD provides procedural instructional design information to guide users in defining the learning system (e.g., analyzing training needs, designing pedagogical structures). AGD includes a rules-based advisory component that offers advice regarding specific design decisions made by users (e.g., amount and nature of objectives).

Other performance support systems tools include Designer's Edge (Figure 13-1) from Allen Communication and Instructional DesignWare from Langevin Learning Services (Langevin Learning Services). Like AGD, these tools support the planning phases of instructional design, but contain a much more general advisory component (e.g., context-specific online help, wizards, and tutorials).

In contrast to AGD, Designer's Edge and Instructional DesignWare lead designers through all tasks involved in instructional design, but place more emphasis on the ultimate production phase. Both tools provide a graphical representation of the instructional systems design model, thus leading to additional support for completing each step of the model. Data entered by users are cross-referenced with all steps to enhance continuity between phases. Usable reports and documents such as evaluation instruments, content outlines, lesson plans, and checklists can be generated by the users.

The primary difference between the two products lies in their intended audiences and

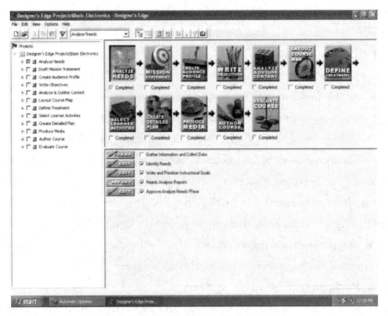

Figure 13-1　Main window of Designer's Edge

purposes. Designer's Edge is for both novice and experienced instructional designers planning computer-based instruction. The product includes support for scripts, storyboards and other CBI production needs. Integration with external software applications is also supported. Instructional Design Ware is intended for course designers and trainers interested in producing either computer-based or classroom training. For this reason, more support is provided for decisions regarding media selection and course and presentation materials (Langevin Learning Services).

## Text C

## Current Trends in Automated Tools[①]

The most recent automated instructional design tools are in the form of electronic performance support systems (EPSS, See Figure 13-2). The nature of electronic performance support systems varies based in focus. Gery defines EPSS as a program that is able to automate many job-related mental skills and to provide instant instructions to help users make whatever human judgments and decisions necessary.[5] For this study, EPSS is defined as a system of online job aids, support tools, and information systems designed to assist users with workplace performance. This technology is expected to simplify performance by reducing the complexities or

---

① http://www.sciencedirect.com/science?_ob=ArticleURL&_udi=B6VDC-4DW34R5-4&_user=1529636&_rdoc=1&_fmt=&_orig=search&_sort=d&view=c&_version=1&_urlVersion=0&_userid=1529636&md5=b1eb9babae44adbd7f349de178f539c4#secx2

series of functions needed to perform, and by providing guidance to the performer throughout the task.

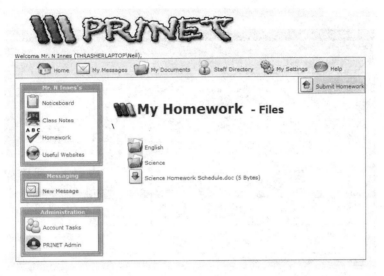

Figure 13-2 An example of electronic performance support systems (EPSS)—PRINET, which is an integrated electronic performance support system designed for Primary schools. It allows Teachers to increase communication with their students via notice boards, easily publish files and receive electronic homework and create lists of useful websites. PRINET uses context sensitive help to aid the user in their tasks.

Some of the clearly identified components of an EPSS include tools, interactive software, information database, training modules or learning experiences, advisors, glossaries, and references. Typical tools incorporated in an EPSS are word processing programs, spreadsheets, templates, and forms used to support performance and training. Information databases include on-line documentation, reference materials, case database, and history data. Advisors are designed as interactive expert advice, coaching algorithms, and context-sensitive on-line help systems. The learning experience components of an EPSS are presented in various formats such as computer-based training (CBT), tutorials, simulations, and scenarios.

Designer's Edge is an instructional design electronic performance support system for both novice and experienced designers. Designer's Edge is described as a task driven automated instructional design application with a visual interface that allows navigation to any step to guide both novice and expert designers through the entire development process. The tool supports all the phases in instructional design from analysis, design, development, implementation, to evaluation as described by the ADDIE acronym. The primary interface is based on typical Instructional Design model, and the steps of the process are embedded and enhanced to facilitate navigation and ease of use.

Designer's Edge interface allows the user to navigate to any step in the design process. The steps included are analyzing needs, drafting mission statement, creating audience profile, writing objectives, analyzing and outlining content, laying out course map, selecting learner activities, creating detailed plan, producing media, authoring the course and evaluating and implementing the course. Designer's Edge has a visual interface (Figure 13-3) that is meant to provide guidance for those who have not been formally trained in the field of instructional design.

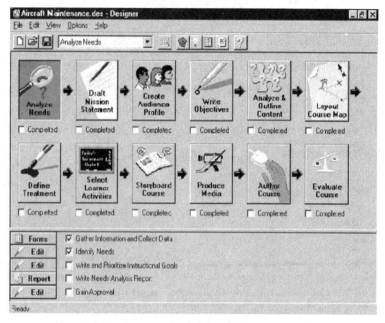

Figure 13-3  Phase designer's edge interface

Chapman suggests this system provides a central performance support that accelerates the instructional development process and provides guidance for non-designers to design partial or full courses for delivery on any medium. Allen Communication posits that Designer's Edge ensures instructional integrity by guiding the user through the entire traditional ISD process. They report that the use of Designer's Edge resulted in a 36% increase in trainers' productivity. Additional benefits include:

• Provides a starting point and step-by-step guidance through critical decision-making stages and design processes.

• Standardizes the design process for entire development team.

• Integrates data and displays it in a visual course map for easy access.

• Provides a fully integrated script-storyboard with visual screen layout capabilities, showing thumbnails of graphics used.

• Puts a virtual encyclopedia of learning strategies and instructional design expertise at your fingertips through a powerful online help.

• Customize the interface and wizards to support their own design methodology.

Prior research suggests that expert designers and novice designers use different approaches in designing instruction. This study examined how the experienced, novice, and naive designers used Designer's Edge while designing instruction for a novel task. This study was guided by the three research questions. First, how does each of the designer groups use the automated tool? Second, are there any relationships between the designer's perceptions of the tool and the quality of the final product? Third, how does the automated tool affect the quality of the design?

## New Words

sequencing　*n.* 先后顺序
acronym　*n.* 只取首字母的缩写词
proliferation　*n.* 增殖,分芽繁殖
domain-specific　*adj.* 领域特定的
transaction　*n.* 1. 处理,办理,执行 2. (一笔)交易;(一项)事务
context-specific　*adj.* 针对具体情况的,具体情况具体对待的,因情况而异的
encapsulate　*vt.* 1. 装入胶囊 2. 总结;扼要概括;囊括
workbench　*n.* 工作台,手工台
just-in-time　*adj.*,*n.* 1. 及时(的) 2. 及时盘存调节法(的)
graphical representation　图示
cross-referenced　对比参照
spreadsheet　*n.* 电子制表软件,电子数据表
algorithm　*n.* 运算法则
context-sensitive　*adj.* 上下文相关的
posit　*vt.* 假定,设想,假设
thumbnail　*adj.* 极小的,极短的 *n.* 拇指甲,极小的东西
encyclopedia　*n.* 百科全书;(某一学科的)专科全书
wizard　*n.* 1. 尤指故事中的男巫,术士 2. 〈褒〉有特殊才干的人;奇才

## Notes

[1] The attempts concentrated on the development of technological tools that would aid in the user's decision making and in the production of instructional materials.

译文:这些努力主要集中在开发出能够帮助使用者做决策和制作教材的技术工具上。

• concentrate on 专心于,把思想集中于
• that would aid in the user's decision making and in the production of instructional materials 是由 that 引导的定语从句,用来修饰限定先行词 technological tools。
• decision making 决策,判定

[2] The research suggests that automated instructional design tools are especially useful in their ability to aid and support the novice designer or subject-matter expert (SME) working as a designer, and others through the instructional design process to produce quality instruction.

**译文:** 这个研究表明,教学设计自动化工具在协助和支持设计新手或作为设计师的学科内容专家(SME)方面,以及在协助和支持其他一些在教学设计过程中做出高质量的教学系统的设计师方面尤其有帮助。

* that 引导的从句是宾语从句,用来说明主句中的谓语。
* work as 任……职,当……

[3] ID expert systems attempt to control the instructional design process, a process involving a large number of interrelated elements, and so must rely heavily on the knowledge and experience of the individual practitioner.

**译文:** 教学设计专家系统试图控制教学设计进程,即一个包括许多相互关联元素的进程,因此它在很大程度上必须取决于个别实习者的知识和经验。

* a process involving a large number of interrelated elements 是 the instructional design process 的同位语。
* rely on 信赖,依赖

[4] A prototype for the advisory system approach is the Instructional Design Advanced Workbench, architecture for a computer-based workbench that supports the cognitive tasks of instructional design without constraining the designer.

**译文:** 咨询系统方法的一个原型是教学设计先进工作台——基于计算机的工作台结构,这种工作台支持教学系统设计的认知任务但并不限制设计者。

* architecture for a computer-based workbench that supports the cognitive tasks of instructional design without constraining the designer 是同位语从句。
* that supports the cognitive tasks of instructional design without constraining the designer 是由 that 引导的定语从句,用来修饰限定先行词 computer-based workbench。

[5] Gery defines EPSS as a program that is able to automate many job-related mental skills and to provide instant instructions to help users make whatever human judgments and decisions necessary.

**译文:** Gery 将 EPSS(电子绩效支持系统)定义为一种项目,它能够使许多与工作相关的心理技巧自动化和提供即时说明以帮助用户做出任何必要的判断和决定。

* define as 定义为,解释为
* that 引导的从句是定语从句,用来修饰现场先行词 program。

# Selected Translation

## Text A

### 教学设计自动化

教学系统设计者经常面对许多在不同背景下工作的要求,但是在不同的工作环境中,共同的挑战就是减少计划的时间和创造有质量的教学。虽然教学内容因项目而有不同,但是为了创造出有质量的教学系统,它们有共同的设计阶段。不管内容怎样,设计者们考虑的是学习者的性格、教学内容、目标、目的、教学策略、排序方法、评价技术和制作教材。这些共同的阶段是以自动化工具为特征的,并且与描述主要阶段的 ADDIE 模型相结合。

我们在教学系统设计的过程自动化中曾付出过许多努力。早期的自动化教学系统设计的产生是由于其他的工业与教学环境下电脑的增多。这些努力主要集中在开发出能够帮助使用者做决策和制作教材的技术工具上。这些努力使得用来支持军事领域里的教学系统设计新手的工作辅助程序发展起来了。教学设计自动化工具有四个共同类型:(a) 专家系统,(b) 咨询系统,(c) 管理信息系统,和(d) 电子绩效支持系统。

这些工具和系统的主要目的是要帮助教学系统设计者以及帮助其他制作教材以提高学习的人。它们帮助用户创作课件、开发基于计算机的教学和给一般设计师做决策,并且可能有助于消除类似于故事板这样的教学设计任务。这个研究表明教学设计自动化工具在协助和支持设计新手或作为设计师的学科内容专家(SME)方面,以及在协助和支持其他一些在教学设计过程中做出高质量的教学系统的设计师方面尤其有帮助。

## Exercises

### 1. Short Answers:

(1) What are the four common types of automated instructional design tools and what are the advantages of automated instructional design tools?

(2) What are the main functions of Automated Instructional Design tools?

(3) What are the benefits of the Designer's Edge?

# 教育技术期刊——Your Guide to Educational Technology Journals on the Web(Ⅰ)

• Australian Journal of Educational Technology (AJET) (Figure 13-4)—a refereed academic journal publishing research and review articles in educational technology, instructional design, educational applications of computer technologies, educational telecommunications and related areas.

• British Journal of Educational Technology (BJET) (Figure 13-5)—provides readers with the widest possible coverage of developments in international educational and training technology.

• Canadian Journal of Learning and Technology (CJLT)—a peer-reviewed, scholarly journal published 3 times annually by AMTEC.

• Computer Assisted Language Learning (CALL)—international, peer-reviewed journal which leads the field in its total dedication to all matters associated with the use of computers in language learning. It provides a forum to discuss the discoveries in the field and to exchange experience and information about existing techniques.

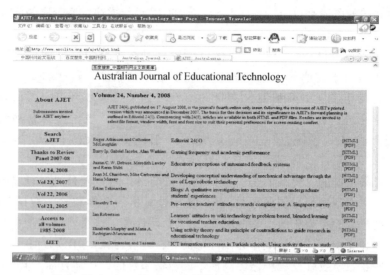

Figure 13-4　Australian Journal of Educational Technology (AJET)

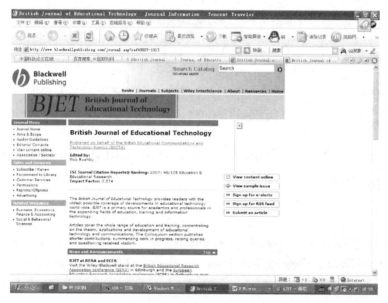

Figure 13-5　British Journal of Educational Technology (BJET)

◆ Computers & Education—journal discussing the educational aspects of computers.

◆ Computers in the Schools—articles emphasize the practical aspect of any application, but also tie theory to practice, relate present accomplishments to past efforts and future trends, identify conclusions and their implications, and discuss the theoretical and philosophical basis for the application.

◆ Educational Technology and Society (Figure 13-6)—a quarterly journal which seeks academic articles on the issues affecting the developers of educational systems and educators who implement and manage such systems.

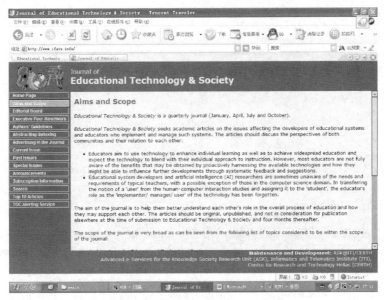

Figure 13-6　Educational Technology and Society

◆ Educational Technology Review—publication which is designed to provide a multi-disciplinary forum to present and discuss all aspects of educational technology in all learning environments.

◆ From Now On (FNO)—journal on educational technology for engaged learning and literacy.

◆ Interactions—termly electronic journal of the Educational Technology Service at the University of Warwick. This web-based publication aims to keep staff informed about teaching and learning technology methods, media, support and innovation going on.

◆ Interactive Educational Multimedia—journal intended as a space for dialogue and reflection about the application of the multimedia technologies in education.

◆ International Journal of Instructional Media—focuses on quality research and presents articles about ongoing programs in instructional media and education.

◆ International Journal of Technology and Design Education—encouraging research and development in any aspect of technology and design education.

◆ Interpersonal Computing and Technology Journal (IPCT-J)—focus is on computer-mediated communication, and the pedagogical issues surrounding the use of computers and technology in educational settings.

# Part 5　Developing Learning Resources

## Unit 14　Audio

▲ **Knowledge Objectives**

When you have completed this unit, you will be able to:

• Know the two kinds of audio formats most often used for instructional purposes and understand how they work

• Understand the instructional applications used to describe the advantages of producing materials on cassette tapes

• Understand the ASSURE model that preparing lessons incorporating the use of audio

▲ **Professional Terms**

| | |
|---|---|
| compact cassette | 小型带盒(双磁带盘) |
| compact disc | 激光唱片,压缩磁盘,光盘 |
| Non-return-to-zero, inverted (NRZI) | 倒转不归零 |
| Eight-to-Fourteen Modulation | 8到14比特调制编码 |
| the Cross-Interleaved Reed-Solomon Coding | 颠倒交叉交织 RS 编码 |
| index of refraction | 折射率 |
| HD DVD | 高清晰度 DVD |
| CD-I | 交互式 CD |
| LP (long playing) record | 黑胶唱片 |

## Text A

### Audio Formats

Audio formats that are most often used for instructional purposes are Compact Cassette and compact discs. Let's talk about them as follows:

**Compact Cassette**[①]

The Compact Cassette (Figure 14-1), often referred to as audio cassette, cassette tape,

---

① http://en.wikipedia.org/wiki/Compact_Cassette

cassette, or simply tape, is a magnetic tape sound recording format. Although intended for dictation, improvements in fidelity led the Compact Cassette to supplant reel-to-reel tape (Figure 14-2) recording in most non-professional applications.[1] Its uses ranged from portable audio to home recording to data storage for early microcomputers. Between the early 1970s and late 1990s, the cassette was one of the two most common formats for prerecorded music, first alongside the LP (Figure 14-3) and later the Compact Disc. The word cassette is a French word meaning "little box."

Figure 14-1  Typical 60-minute Compact Cassette

Figure 14-2  An example of reel to reel tape recorder

Figure 14-3  An example of LP Record

Compact Cassettes consist of two miniature spools, between which a magnetically coated plastic tape is passed and wound. These spools and their attendant parts are held inside a protective plastic shell. Two stereo pairs of tracks (four total) or two monaural audio tracks are available on the tape; one stereo pair or one monophonic track is played or recorded when the tape is moving in one direction and the second pair when moving in the other direction.[2] This reversal is achieved either by manually flipping the cassette or by having the machine itself change the direction of tape movement ("auto-reverse").

The cassette was a great step forward in convenience from reel-to-reel audio tape recording, though because of the limitations of the cassette's size and speed, it initially compared poorly in quality. [3] Unlike the 4-track stereo open reel format, the two stereo tracks of each side lie adjacent to each other rather than being interleaved with the tracks of the other side. This permitted monaural cassette players to play stereo recordings "summed" as mono tracks and permitted stereo players to play mono recordings through both speakers. The tape is 3.81 mm (0.150 in) wide, with each stereo track 0.6 mm wide and an unrecorded guard band between each track. The tape moves at 4.76 cm/s (1 7/8 in/s) from left to right. For comparison, the typical open reel format in consumer use was 1/4 inch (6.35 mm) wide, each stereo track nominally 1/16 inch (1.59 mm) wide, and running at either 9.5 or 19 cm/s (3.75 or 7.5 in/s).

The first cassette machines were simple mono record and playback units. Early machines required attaching an external dynamic microphone. Most units after the 1970s also incorporated built-in condenser microphones, which have extended high frequency response, but may also pick up noises from the recorder motor. [4] A common portable recorder format still common today is a long box, with a speaker at the top, a cassette bay in the middle, and "piano key" controls at the bottom edge. (Figure 14-4) The markings of "piano key" controls near the handle were soon standardized and are a legacy still emulated on many software control panels, though many DVD panels have eliminated the fast forward and rewind buttons in favor of next and previous tracks, which are only implemented on machines which have logic to search for blank spots in the tape. [5] These symbols are commonly the square for stop, right pointing triangle for play, double triangles for fast forward and rewind, red dot for record, and a vertically-divided square (two rectangles side-by-side) for the pause button. Another format is only slightly larger than the cassette, also adapted for stereo "Walkman" player applications.

Figure 14-4   Cassette Portable Recorder and Player

**Compact Discs**①

A Compact Disc (also known as a CD) (Figure 14-5) is an optical disc used to store digital data, originally developed for storing digital audio. The CD, available on the market since late 1982, remains the standard playback medium for commercial audio recordings to the present day.

A Compact Disc is made from a 1.2 mm thick disc of almost pure polycarbonate plastic and weighs approximately 16 grams. A thin layer of aluminum or, more rarely, gold is applied to the surface to make it reflective, and is protected by a film of lacquer. The lacquer is normally spin coated directly on top of the reflective layer. On top of that surface, the label print

---

① http://en.wikipedia.org/wiki/Compact_discs

Part 5  Developing Learning Resources 149

Figure 14-5  The closely spaced tracks on the readable surface of a Compact Disc cause light to diffract into a full visible color spectrum.

is applied. Common printing methods for CDs are screen-printing and offset printing.

Table 14-1  Novelty shaped CDs are available in a number of shapes and sizes, and are mostly used for marketing.

| Physical size | Audio Capacity | CD-ROM Data Capacity | Note |
| --- | --- | --- | --- |
| 12 cm | 74—80 min | 650—703 MB | Standard size |
| 8 cm | 21—24 min | 185—210 MB | Mini-CD size (Figure 14-6) |
|  | ~ 6 min | ~ 55 MB | "Business card" size |

CD data is stored as a series of tiny indentations (pits), encoded in a tightly packed spiral track molded into the top of the polycarbonate layer. The areas between pits are known as "lands". Each pit is approximately 100 nm deep by 500 nm wide, and varies from 850 nm to 3.5 μm in length.

The spacing between the tracks, the pitch, is 1.6 μm. A CD is read by focusing a 780 nm wavelength (near infrared) semiconductor laser through the bottom of the polycarbonate layer. The change in height between pits and lands results in a difference in intensity in the light reflected. By measuring the intensity change with a photodiode, the data can be read from the disc.

The pits and lands themselves do not directly represent the zeros and ones of binary data. Instead, Non-return-to-zero, inverted (NRZI) encoding is used: a change from pit to land or land to pit indicates a one, while no change indicates a zero. This in turn is decoded by reversing the Eight-to-Fourteen Modulation used in mastering the disc, and then reversing the Cross-Interleaved Reed-Solomon Coding, finally revealing the raw data stored on the disc.

While CDs are significantly more durable than earlier audio formats, they are susceptible

Figure 14-6  A Mini-CD is 8 centimeters in diameter.

to damage from daily usage and environmental factors. Pits are much closer to the label side of a disc, so that defects and dirt on the clear side can be out of focus during playback. Discs consequently suffer more damage because of defects such as scratches on the label side, whereas clear-side scratches can be repaired by refilling them with plastic of similar index of refraction, or by careful polishing. [6] Early music CDs were known to suffer from "CD rot" or "laser rot" where the internal reflective layer itself degrades. When this occurs the CD may become unplayable.

The digital data on a CD begins at the center of the disc and proceeds outwards to the edge, which allows adaptation to the different size formats available. Standard CDs are available in two sizes. By far the most common is 120 mm in diameter, with a 74 or 80-minute audio capacity and a 650 or 700 MB data capacity. This diameter has also been adopted by later formats, including Super Audio CD, DVD, HD DVD, and Blu-ray Disc. 80 mm discs ("Mini CDs") were originally designed for CD singles and can hold up to 21 minutes of music or 184 MB of data but never really became popular. Today nearly all singles are released on 120 mm CDs, which is called a Maxi single.

The technology was later adapted and expanded to include data storage (CD-ROM), write-once audio and data storage (CD-R), rewritable media (CD-RW), Super Audio CD (SACD), Video Compact Discs (VCD), Super Video Compact Discs (SVCD), PhotoCD, PictureCD, CD-i, and Enhanced CD. CD-ROMs and CD-Rs remain widely used technologies in the computer industry. The CD and its extensions have been extremely successful: in 2004, worldwide sales of CD audio, CD-ROM, and CD-R reached about 30 billion discs. By 2007, 200 billion CDs had been sold worldwide.

# Text B

## Produce Materials on Cassette Tapes[①]

Students and teachers can easily prepare their own cassette tapes. Students can use cassette tapes for gathering oral histories and preparing oral book reports. Teachers can prepare tapes for use in direct instruction; for example, a vocational technical school instructor can create audiotapes with directions for students to follow. Skills practice, such as pronunciation of a foreign language, can also be provided by audiocassette.

A popular project in 12th-grade social studies classes is the recording of oral histories. The students interview local senior citizens regarding the history of their community. (Figure 14-7) Only one student interviews each senior citizen, but the interviewing task is rotated among the students, and the entire class assists in determining which questions to ask. In preparation for this project, students study both national and local history. All the tapes prepared during the interviews are kept in the school media center. Excerpts are duplicated and edited into programs for use with other social studies classes and for broadcast by the local radio station. This audiotape project serves the dual purpose of informing students and local residents about local history and collecting and preserving information that might otherwise be lost.

Figure 14-7  The student is interviewing an angler about the history of their community.

The cassette recorder can be used for presenting book reports. Students may record their book reports during study time in the media center or at home. You can evaluate the reports and keep the best ones on file in the media center. Encourage other students to listen to them before selecting books to read. Limit reports to ideas from the book and to read. Limit reports to three minutes, and require students to extract the main ideas from the book and to organize their thoughts carefully. During the taping, they practice their speaking skills. Encourage them to make the report as exciting as possible to interest other students in reading the book.

Tape recorders can be used to record information gleaned from a field trip. On returning to the classroom, students can play back the tape for discussion and review. Many museums, observatories, and other public exhibit areas now supply visitors with prerecorded messages about various items on display, which may (with permission) be recorded for playback in the classroom.

Students can also record themselves reciting, presenting a speech, performing music, and so on. (Figure 14-8) They can then listen to the pate privately or have the performance

---

[①] Sharon E. Smaldino, James D. Russell, Robert Heinich and Michael Molenda, *Instruction Technology and Media for Learning*, Eigth Edition, Chapter 11 Audio.

Figures 14-8  Students are asked to review their journals, think reflectively, and make a personal connection to the novel. They should go through the writing process to create a digital story reflective of what they have learned.

critiqued by the teacher or other students. Initial efforts can be kept for comparison with later performances and for reinforcement of learning. Many small-group projects can include recorded reports students present to the rest of the class. These recordings can become part of each student's portfolio.

In a vocational-technical school, dental laboratory technology students are instructed on the procedures for constructing prosthetic devices (Figure 14-9) such as partial plates and bridges by listening to an audiotape prepared by their instructor. To be efficient and effective in their work, these students must have both hands free and their eyes much be on their work, not on a textbook or manual. Audiotapes allow the students to move at their own pace, and the instructor is free to circulate around the laboratory and discuss each student's work individually.

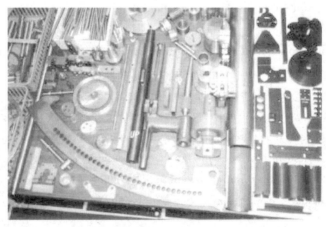

Figure 14-9  A part of prosthetic devices

A teacher of ninth-grade students with learning difficulties (but average intelligence) provides instruction on how to listen to lectures, speeches, and other oral presentations. The students practice their listening skills with tapes of recorded stories, poetry, and instructions. The teacher also uses commercially available tapes of speeches and narration. After the students have practiced their listening skills under teacher direction, they are evaluated using a tape they have not heard before. The students listen to the five-minute tape without taking notes; the teacher then gives them a series of questions dealing with important content from the passage.

An often overlooked use of audio materials is for evaluating student attainment of lesson objectives. For example, you may prerecord test questions for members of the class to use individually. You may ask students to identify sounds in a recording (e.g., to name the solo instrument being played in a particular musical movement) or to identify the composer of a particular piece of music. Students in social studies classes could be asked to identify the historical person most likely to have made excerpted passages from famous speeches, or to identify the time period of excerpted passages based on their content. Testing and evaluating in the audio mode is especially appropriate when teaching and learning have also been in that particular mode.

## Text C

### Using Audio Files in Multimedia[①]

One way to enhance multimedia files such as *PowerPoint* or *HyperStudio* is to add audio files. Using audio within a multimedia presentation can enhance the interest or focus of the topic being presented. In addition, audio files can compensate for possible reading or learning problems that students might have. For example, when doing a presentation of great composers, a teacher can add short samples of the composers' work by inserting a link to an audio file stored on the hard drive. This can provide the students with a better understanding of that particular piece of music. Or, a *HyperStudio* (Figure 14-10) stack designed for readers can be used by nonreaders with the addition of teacher-prepared scripts that actually read the text to the student using software such as *Blabbermouth*.

To accomplish this is relatively easy if you have the right equipment and enough memory on the computer as audio files can be quite large unless compacted. Both *PowerPoint* and *HyperStudio* have audio files included in their software packages. Or, using a CD or audiotape, audio files can be created using a program such as *SoundEdit*. The digital audio file can then be added to the presentation. Or, using a microphone and *SoundEdit*, the teacher or student can create original audio to enhance the information presented. The process for creating a digital audio file is similar to that of creating an audiotape.

Then we use the ASSURE model to prepare lessons incorporating the use of audio.

**Analyze Learners**

Lesson development begins by identifying your students' unique attributes and learning

---

① Sharon E. Smaldino, James D. Russell, Robert Heinich and Michael Molenda, *Instruction Technology and Media for Learning*, Eigth Edition, Chapter 11 Audio.

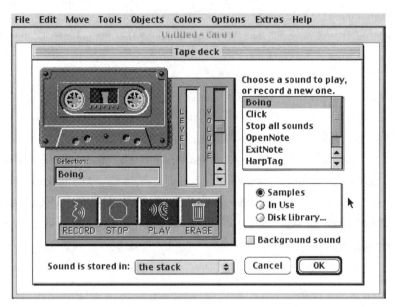

Figure 14-10  A demonstration of how to access sounds in HyperStudio

characteristics. You also will wish to determine their various levels of experience with using audio.

**State Objectives**

Before stating specific objectives, you may wish to explore how to use audio in support of student learning. Sometimes it is more appropriate to state specific objectives after you have identified the direction you will take with the content and what materials you will use.

**Select Methods, Media, and Materials**

Use the information on audio as the basis for selecting, modifying, or designing your materials. Adjust the specific applications to suit the specific nature of your topic and objectives.

In selecting audio materials to use in your instruction, first consult with your school media specialist to determine what is available at your media center. (Figure 14-11) For materials that are unavailable, consult the appropriate directory: For general audio sources see the *Schwann Record and Tape Guide*; for music CDs see *Best Rated CDs: Classical* and *Best Rated CDs: Jazz and Pop*.

You should preview and appraise both commercially and locally produced materials before using them with your students. You may wish to use the "Selection Rubric: Audio Materials" to guide your selection decisions.

**Utilize Media and Materials**

Follow the suggestions to facilitate your students' learning, modifying each of the materials you use to fit your needs. The audio equipment and source materials you have access to, as well as its location, will determine how you schedule your students' learning experiences. If you have access to an audio playback system for the classroom, you may want all students to

Figure 14-11 This School Media Center serves a variety of purposes within Information Literacy. The media center provides students with the knowledge and skills that are necessary for success in our multi-cultural, multi-media world.

listen simultaneously. If you have limited access to equipment and audio source materials, you may consider creating a learning center.

**Require Learner Participation**

Introduce and explain the audio involved in your specific objective. Have the students do specific activities that rely on their ability to use audio. Students will find more value in the materials if they are able to connect what they are doing to what they are learning. Have them create slide shows with synchronized sound using PowerPoint and audio files either downloaded from the Internet or from sources you prepare, that they can then share with other students. [7] Or, have them record a soundtrack to accompany an oral presentation.

**Evaluate and Revise**

It is important to consider how materials that rely on audio help students to interpret information. You can assess students on the quality of their created audio materials, and on how well they integrated them into their other learning. As with all media—and technology-based lessons, you may choose to revise your selection of materials after you have determined how well they have worked. In addition, you want to be certain that all materials used have been cleared of any potential copyright issues.

## New Words

fidelity　　*n.*　1. 忠诚,忠实 2. 忠贞 3. 翔实,精确,(声音、色彩等)逼真
supplant　　*vt.*　把……排挤掉,取代
spool　　*n.*　(绕线、铁线、照相软片等的)管、筒、线轴
wind　　*vt.*　1. 缠绕,卷绕 2. 给……上发条
monaural　　*adj.*　单耳(听觉)的,非立体声的
nominally　　*adv.*　有名无实,名义上

incorporate   *vt.* 1. 包含,加上,吸收 2. 把……合并,使并入 3. 组成公司
condenser   *n.* 1. 冷凝器 2.（尤指汽车发动机内的）电容器
emulate   *vt.* 仿真
polycarbonate   *n.* 聚碳酸酯
lacquer   *n.* 1. 漆 2.（固定发行的）发蜡,定性剂
screen-printing   *n.* 丝网印刷术
offset printing   *n.* 橡皮版印刷,胶印
indentation   *n.* 1. 凹进,缩格 2. 凹口,缺口
pit   *n.* 1. 坑 2. 煤矿,矿坑
spiral   *adj.* 螺旋形的
pitch   *n.* 1. 程度；强度；高度 2. 斜度,坡度
infrared   *adj.* 〈物〉红外线的
photodiode   *n.* 光敏二极管,光电二极管
senior citizens   *n.* 老人
excerpt   *n.* 摘录,摘要
glean   *vt.* 一点点地收集(资料、事实)*vt.* & *vi.* （收割后）拾穗
pate   *n.* 〈口〉脑袋,头顶
critique   *n.* 评论文章；评论
narration   *n.* 叙述事情的经过；故事

## Notes

[1] Although intended for dictation, improvements in fidelity led the Compact Cassette to supplant reel-to-reel tape recording in most non-professional applications.

**译文**：虽然刚开始是为听写而制作的,但是在精度方面的改进使得盒式磁带取代了卷到卷录音带而应用到大多数非专业领域。

• Although intended for dictation 是过去分词做后置定语,用来修饰限定 improvements。

• intend for 1. 希望……加入…… 2. 为……而准备

• lead to 导致,引起

[2] Two stereo pairs of tracks (four total) or two monaural audio tracks are available on the tape; one stereo pair or one monophonic track is played or recorded when the tape is moving in one direction and the second pair when moving in the other direction.

**译文**：磁带上有两对立体声轨道（即四个）或两个非立体声音频轨道；当磁带向一个方向运动的时候,其中一对立体声或单声道的轨道在播放或录制,而当磁带向另一个方向运动时,另一对立体声或单声道轨道在播放或录制。

• when the tape is moving in one direction 是由 when 引导的时间状语从句,第二个由 when 引导的从句也是时间状语从句。

[3] The cassette was a great step forward in convenience from reel-to-reel audio tape

recording, though because of the limitations of the cassette's size and speed, it initially compared poorly in quality.

**译文:** 虽然由于盒式磁带的尺寸和速度的限制使得它刚开始在质量上处于劣势,但是从便利性而言,盒式磁带相对于卷到卷录音磁带录制是一大进步。

- a step forward 前进一步
- though because of the limitations of the cassette's size and speed, it initially compared poorly in quality 是由连词 though 引导的让步状语从句。
- because of 因为,由于

[4] Most units after the 1970s also incorporated built-in condenser microphones, which have extended high frequency response, but may also pick up noises from the recorder motor.

**译文:** 在 20 世纪 70 年代后,大部分的单元同样内置了电容器麦克风,这种电容器麦克风提高了高幅频响应,但同样可能从记录装置电动机上录制了噪声。

- built-in *adj.* 是……的组成部分的;嵌入式的;内置的
- which have extended high frequency response 是非限制性定语从句,用来修饰限定先行词 condenser microphones。
- frequency response 录放幅频响应
- pick up 拾起,捡起;抬起

[5] The markings of "piano key" controls near the handle were soon standardized and are a legacy still emulated on many software control panels, though many DVD panels have eliminated the fast forward and rewind buttons in favor of next and previous tracks, which are only implemented on machines which have logic to search for blank spots in the tape.

**译文:** 在把手附近的"钢琴键"控制器的标识立刻就被标准化了,并且是一个现今仍然被许多软件控制面板模仿的先例。但是,许多 DVD 面板已经淘汰了快速前进和重绕按钮以支持下一个和前一个轨道,其中这些轨道仅仅在那些通过逻辑电路在磁带上寻找空白点的播放器上执行。

- emulated on many software control panels 是过去分词做后置定语,用来修饰限定 The markings of "piano key" controls。
- though many DVD panels have eliminated the fast forward and rewind buttons in favor of next and previous tracks 是由 though 引导的让步状语从句,表转折关系。
- in favor of 1. 赞成(支持) 2. 以……取代
- which are only implemented on machines which have logic to search for blank spots in the tape 是非限制定语从句,用来修饰先行词 next and previous tracks。
- which have logic to search for blank spots in the tape 是由 which 引导的状语从句,用来修饰限定先行词 machines。

[6] Discs consequently suffer more damage because of defects such as scratches on the label side, whereas clear-side scratches can be repaired by refilling them with plastic of similar index of refraction, or by careful polishing.

**译文:** 因为像刮伤这样的瑕疵在有标签的一面上,所以光盘会遭受更多的损坏,而清楚一面的刮伤可以通过用具有相似折射率的塑料填充或通过仔细的打磨来修复(从而对光盘的伤害较小)。

- refill with 填充
- index of refraction 折射率

[7] Have them create slide shows with synchronized sound using PowerPoint and audio files either downloaded from the Internet or from sources you prepare, that they can then share with other students.

译文:让他们用 PowerPoint 和一些从网上下载的或你所准备的音频资源来制作具有同步声音的幻灯片,这样他们就能与其他同学一起分享了。

- either or ……或……
- that they can then share with other students 是由 that 引导的定语从句,用来修饰先行词 slide shows。
- share with 1. 与……分享(合用) 2. 把(自己的感受)告诉(某人)

## Selected Translation

### Text A

### 音 频 格 式

教学中最经常用到的音频格式是盒式磁带和光盘。下面,我们开始讨论它们。

**盒式磁带**

盒式磁带通常指的是盒式录音磁带、盒式录音带,或者仅仅是录音带而已,它是一种磁带录音格式。虽然刚开始是为听写而制作的,但是在精度方面的改进使得盒式磁带取代了卷到卷录音带而应用到大多数非专业领域。它的用途从便携式音频到家庭录制再到早期微型计算机的数据存储。从 20 世纪 70 年代早期到 90 年代晚期,盒式磁带是两种事先录制音乐的最常用的格式之一,另外一种首先是黑胶唱片,然后是光盘。Cassette 这个单词是法语词,意思是"小盒子"。

盒式磁带由 2 个小型的线轴组成,在它们中间绕行通过的是磁性涂粉塑料磁带。这些线轴和其他的部件被包裹在具有保护性的塑料外壳中。磁带上有两对立体声轨道(即四个)或两个非立体声音频轨道;当磁带向一个方向运动的时候,其中一对立体声或单声道的轨道在播放或录制,而当磁带向另一个方向运动时,另一对立体声或单声道轨道在播放或录制。这种反向既可以通过手动转动盒式磁带,也可以通过机器自己来改变磁带的运动方向("自动反向")。

虽然由于盒式磁带的尺寸和速度的限制使得它刚开始在质量上处于劣势,但是从便利性而言,盒式磁带相对于卷到卷录音磁带录制是一大进步。不像四轨道立体声开放卷筒格式,每一边的两立体声轨道彼此相连,而不是被轨道另一边交叉干扰。这样的话,非立体声盒式磁带播放器就既可以播放由单声道"加"在一起的立体声录音,也可以通过两个喇叭来播放单音频录音了。盒式磁带宽 3.81 毫米(0.150 英尺),其中每一个立体声轨道宽 0.6 毫米,并且在每一个轨道中间都有未录制的保护带。盒式磁带以每秒 4.76 厘米(每秒1 7/8 英尺)的速度从左向右转动。相比之下,典型的开放卷筒格式总体上来说宽 1/4 英尺 (6.35 毫米),每一边的立体声轨道通常都是宽 1/16 英尺(1.59 毫米),并且以每秒9.5 或 19 毫米(每秒3.75 或 7.5 英尺)的速度转动。

  第一个盒式磁带播放器仅仅是单声道的录制和重放单元。早期的播放器需要附上一个外部电动式传声器麦克风。在 20 世纪 70 年代后,大部分的单元同样内置了电容器麦克风,这种电容器麦克风提高了高幅频响应,但同样可能从记录装置电动机上录制了噪声。现在仍然普遍使用的便携式录音机格式是一个长盒子,顶部有一个麦克风,中间有个镭射湾,底部边缘有"钢琴键"控制器。在把手附近的"钢琴键"控制器的标识立刻就被标准化了,并且是一个现今仍然被许多软件控制面板模仿的先例。但是,许多 DVD 面板已经淘汰了快速前进和重绕按钮以支持下一个和前一个轨道,其中这些轨道仅仅在那些通过逻辑电路在磁带上寻找空白点的播放器上执行。这些符号通常是用方形表示停止,用向右指的三角形表示播放,用两个三角形表示快进和快绕,用红点表示录制,以及用垂直分开的方形(即两个并排的三角形)表示暂停。另一种格式只是比盒式磁带稍许大些,同样是为了适应立体声"随身听"的应用。

### 光盘

  光盘(也被称为 CD)是一个频闪观测盘,用来存储数字数据,起初是用来存储数字音频。自从 1982 年末 CD 才出现在市场上,现今仍然是商业录音播放媒体的标准。

  光盘是由几乎非常纯的聚碳酸酯塑料制作而成的,厚 1—2 毫米,重大约 16 克。一层薄铝或更少被用到的黄金被覆盖到光盘表面以使它能够反光,并且被一层薄漆保护着。这种漆通常直接旋转覆盖在反光层上。在那个表面上制有光盘标签。CD 通常采用网版印刷和平版印刷。

| 实际尺寸 | 音频容量 | 只读光盘数据容量 | 标注 |
| --- | --- | --- | --- |
| 12 厘米 | 74—80 分钟 | 650—703 兆比特 | 标准大小 |
| 8 厘米 | 21—24 分钟 | 185—210 兆比特 | 迷你 CD 大小 |
|  | ~6 分钟 | ~55 兆比特 | "名片"大小 |

  光盘数据是以一系列小凹凸(槽)的形式来存储的,并且这些凹凸槽被编码在紧紧相连的、并被浇铸在聚碳酸酯层之表面的螺旋轨道上。凹凸槽中间的区域被认为是"陆地"。每一个凹凸槽大约100 纳米深,500 纳米宽,长度从 850 纳米到 3.5 微米不等。

  轨道间的间距,即高度,是 1.6 微米。CD 数据通过从聚碳酸酯层底部聚焦 780 纳米波长(接近红外线)半导体激光器来读取。每一个凹凸槽间的高度和陆地的变化导致了反射光有强有弱。通过使用光电二极管来测量改变的强度,就能从光盘中读取数据。

  高度和陆地本身并不直接代表数据比特的 0 和 1。取而代之的是采用倒转不归零编码方法:从槽到陆地的改变或从陆地到槽的改变表示 1,而没有改变表示 0。通过首先颠倒控制光盘使用的 8 到 14 比特调制编码来依次解码,然后颠倒交叉交织 RS 编码来最终展现光盘上存储的原始数据。

  光盘比以往的音频格式都更耐用,但是它们容易因为日常使用和环境因素而遭到损害。凹凸槽更靠近光盘的标签边,这样的话在光盘清楚一面上的瑕疵和污垢在播放的时候就不用被考虑。因为像刮伤这样的瑕疵在有标签的一面上,所以光盘会遭受更多的损坏,而清楚一面的刮伤可以通过用具有相似折射率的塑料填充或通过仔细的打磨来修复(从而对光盘的伤害较小)。早期的音乐光盘被认为会遭受"CD 腐烂"或"激光腐烂",即内部的反射层自己分解。当这发生的时候,CD 可能就不能播放了。

　　CD 上的数字数据从光盘的中心开始,然后一直向外到光盘边沿,这样可以根据可得到的不同的格式大小来进行调整。标准的 CD 有两种大小。目前最常用的是直径为 120 毫米的光盘,它有 74 或 80 分钟的音频容量,并且有 650 或 700 兆比特的存储数据容量。这个直径同样被以后的格式(包括超级音频光盘、数字化视频光盘、高清数字化视频光盘和蓝光盘)所采用。起初单曲 CD 被设计为直径 80 毫米的光盘("迷你 CD"),可以存储多达 21 分钟的音乐或 184 兆的数据,但是从来没有真正流行过。现在发行的几乎所有的单张 CD 都是直径为 120 毫米的 CD,被称为主打单碟。

　　这个技术后来被修改了并扩展到包括数据存储(CD-ROM)、一次性写入音频和数据存储(CD-R)、可擦写光盘(CD-RW)、超级音频 CD(SACD)、视像光碟(VCD)、超级视像光碟(SVCD)、相片光盘、图片光盘、交互式 CD 和加强型 CD。CD-ROM 和 CD-Rs 仍然是电脑行业广泛使用的技术。CD 及其扩展形式已经极度成功了:在 2004 年世界范围内的音频 CD、CD-ROM 和 CD-R 的销售达到三百亿张。到 2007 年,全世界已卖了两千亿张 CD。

## Exercises

**1. Short Answers:**

(1) What is the general structure of Compact Cassettes?

(2) How is data stored on Compact Disk and how is it read from disc?

(3) Can you give some examples on producing materials on cassette tapes?

(4) What are the advantages in using audio within a multimedia presentation? And can you give a brief description on how to use the ASSURE model to prepare lessons incorporating the use of audio?

# 教育技术期刊——Your Guide to Educational Technology Journals on the Web(Ⅱ)

• **Journal of Computing in Higher Education**—publishes peer-reviewed essays, reviews, reports, and research articles that contribute to our understanding of the issues, problems, and research associated with instructional technology and educational environments.

• **Journal of Computing in Teacher Education**—a refereed journal published quarterly by the Special Interest Group for Teacher Educators (SIGTE) of the International Society for Technology in Education (ISTE). The journal provides a forum for sharing information among departments, schools, and colleges of education that are confronting the issues associated with providing computer and technology education for preservice and inservice teachers.

• **Journal of Educational Computing Research**—a refereed journal discussing the use of computer-based technologies at all levels of the formal education system, business and industry, home-schooling, lifelong learning and unintentional learning environments.

• **Journal of Educational Media ( Figure 14-12 )**—aim is to stimulate and represent international and interdisciplinary discussion in the field with a particular focus on research contributing to practice and practical experiences with media in education.

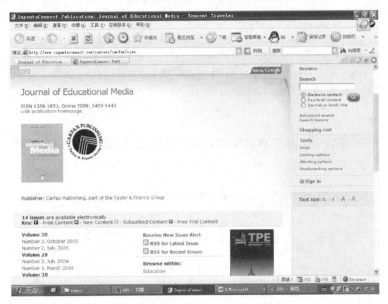

Figure 14-12  Journal of Educational Media

• **Journal of Instructional Science and Technology ( JIST ) ( Figure 14-13 )**—international peer reviewed journal on instructional technology.

• **Journal of Interactive Learning Research ( JILR )**—publishes papers related to the underlying theory, design, implementation, effectiveness, and impact on education and training of interactive learning environments.

• **Journal of Interactive Media in Education ( JIME )**—publication discussing interactive media in education.

• **Journal of Research on Technology in Education ( Figure 14-14 )**—publishes articles that report on original research, system or project descriptions and evaluations, syntheses of the literature, assessments of the state of the art, and theoretical or conceptual positions that relate to educational computing.

• **Journal of Technology Education**—provides a forum for scholarly discussion on topics relating to technology education. In addition, the Journal publishes book reviews, editorials, guest articles, comprehensive literature reviews, and reactions to previously published articles.

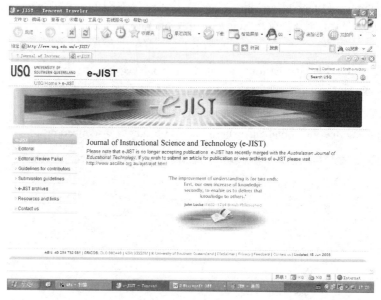

Figure 14-13  Journal of Instructional Science and Technology (e-JIST)

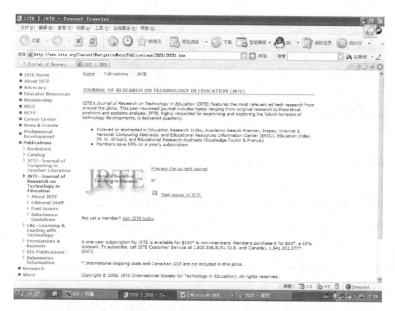

Figure 14-14  Journal of Research on Technology in Education

- **Journal of Technology & Teacher Education (JTATE)**—serves as a forum for the exchange of knowledge about the use of information technology in teacher education.
- **Language Learning & Technology (LLT)**—a refereed journal for second and foreign language educators.
- **Meridian**—electronic journal dedicated to research and practice of computer technology in middle school classrooms.
- **The New Curriculum (TNC)**—designed to provide essential resources to help

teachers integrate technology into their classes, including annotated links and a biweekly column or two on practical tech-integration ideas. You will also find columns on issues, such as leadership and school policies, that are important to the successful integration of technology at schools.

- **Teaching English with Technology**—journal for teachers of English.
- **Teaching Horizons in Education (THE) Journal**—longest running, most widely read education technology publication.
- **TECHNOS**—online version of the Agency for Instructional Technology Journal.

## Unit 15  Video

### Knowledge Objectives

When you have completed this unit, you will be able to:
- Know the three kinds of video formats and be familiar with how they work
- State the three aspects in selecting videos
- Know the In-house Video and understand the production of analog video and edition of digital video

### Professional Terms

| | |
|---|---|
| video tape recorder(VTR) | （磁带）录像机 |
| video cassette recorder(VCR) | （磁带）录像机 |
| Video Home System(VHS) | 家用录像系统 |
| HDV | 高清数码摄像机 |
| HDTV | 高清晰度电视 |
| HDDs | 高密度数据系统 |
| non-linear editing(NLE) | 非线性编辑 |
| MPEG | 运动图像专家组（一种压缩比率较大的视频压缩标准） |
| Liquid Crystal Display(LCD) | 液晶显示屏 |

## Text A

### Video Formats

Video is the technology of electronically capturing, recording, processing, storing, transmitting, and reconstructing a sequence of still images representing scenes in motion. The most common video formats are Videotapes, Digital Video and DVD.

## Videotapes[①]

Videotape (Figure 15-1) is a means of recording images and sound onto magnetic tape as opposed to movie film.

Figure 15-1  An assortment of video tapes, used in both video tape recorders (VTRs or, more common, video cassette recorders [VCRs] and video cameras)

In most cases, a helical scan video head rotates against the moving tape to record the data in two dimensions, because video signals have a very high bandwidth, and static heads would require extremely high tape speeds. Video tape is used in both video tape recorders (VTRs or, more common, video cassette recorders [VCRs]) and video cameras. Tape is a linear method of storing information, and since nearly all video recordings made nowadays are digital, it is expected to gradually lose importance as non-linear/random access methods of storing digital video data are becoming more common.[1]

Figure 15-2  Bottom view of VHS videotape cassette with magnetic tape exposed

The size of a standard VHS tape cassette (Figure 15-2) is 1″ x 4″ ″x 7 1/2″. Following in the footsteps of standard VHS came other consumer videotape formats such as 8mm video, Hi8, and digital 8, VHS-C (compact) and S-VHS-C.

Presently, MiniDV (Figure 15-3) is the most popular format for tape-based consumer camcorders, providing near-broadcast quality video and sophisticated nonlinear editing capability on consumer equipment; however, though intended as a digital successor to VHS, MiniDV VCRs are not widely available outside professional circles.[2]

For high definition, the most promising system seems to be HDV (Figure 15-4), which uses MiniDV media to store a roughly broadcast-quality HDTV data stream.

The latest trend in consumer camcorders is to switch from tape-based to tapeless solutions,

---

① http://en.wikipedia.org/wiki/Videotape

like built-in HDDs, optical disks and solid-state media.

**Digital Video**[①]

Digital video is a type of video recording system that works by using a digital rather than an analog video signal. The terms camera, video camera, and camcorder are used interchangeably in this article.

Digital video cameras come in two different image capture formats: interlaced and progressive scan. (Figure 15-4) Interlaced cameras record the image in alternating sets of lines: the odd-numbered lines are scanned, and then the even-numbered lines are scanned, then the odd-numbered lines are scanned again, and so on. One set of odd or even lines is referred to as a "field", and a consecutive pairing of two fields of opposite parity is called a frame.

Figure 15-3  A reel of 2 inch quad videotape compared with a modern-day miniDV videocassette

A progressive scanning digital video camera records each frame as distinct, with both fields being identical. Thus, interlaced video captures twice as many fields per second as progressive video does when both operate at the same number of frames per second. This is one of the reasons video has a "hyper-real" look, because it draws a different image 60 times per second, as opposed to film, which records 24 or 25 progressive frames per second.

Figure 15-4  An example of camcorder

Digital video can be copied with no degradation in quality. No matter how many generations a digital source is copied, it will be as clear as the original first generation of digital footage.

Digital video can be processed and edited on an NLE, or non-linear editing station, a device built exclusively to edit video and audio. These frequently can import from analog as well as digital sources, but are not intended to do anything other than edit videos.

Many types of video compression exist for serving digital video over the internet, and onto DVDs. While DV video is not compressed beyond its own codec while editing, the file sizes that result are not practical for delivery onto optical discs or over the internet, with codecs such as the Windows Media format, MPEG2, MPEG4, Real Media, the more recent H.264, and the Sorenson media codec. Probably the most widely used formats for delivering video over the internet are MPEG4 and Windows Media, while MPEG2 is used almost exclusively for DVDs, providing an exceptional image in minimal size but resulting in a high level of CPU

---

① http://en.wikipedia.org/wiki/Digital_video

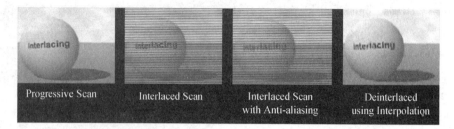

Figure 15-5　this animation demonstrates the interline twitter effect. The two interlaced images use half the bandwidth of the progressive one. The interlaced scan (second from left) precisely duplicates the pixels of the progressive image (far left), but interlace causes details to twitter. Real interlaced video blurs such details to prevent twitter, as seen in the third image from the left, but such softening (or anti-aliasing) comes at the cost of resolution. A line doubler could never restore the third image to the full resolution of the progressive image. *Note—Because the frame rate has been slowed down, you will notice additional flicker in simulated interlaced portions of this image.*

consumption to decompress. [3]

**DVD**①

Figure 15-6　DVD

| | |
|---|---|
| Media type | Optical disc |
| Capacity | ~4.7 GB (single-sided single-layer), ~8.54 GB (single-sided double-layer) |
| Read mechanism | 650 nm laser, 10.5 Mbit/s (1×) |
| Write mechanism | 10.5 Mbit/s (1×) |
| Usage | Data storage, video, audio, games |

DVD (also known as "Digital Versatile Disc" or "Digital Video Disc"—see Etymology) (Figure 15-6) is a popular optical disc storage media format. Its main uses are video and data storage. Most DVDs are of the same dimensions as compact discs (CDs) but store more than six times as much data.

Variations of the term DVD often describe the way data is stored on the discs: DVD-ROM has data which can only be read and not written, DVD-R and DVD+R can only record data once and then function as a DVD-ROM. DVD-RW and DVD+RW can both record and erase data multiple times. The wavelength used by standard DVD lasers is 650 nm, and thus has a red color.

DVD-Video and DVD-Audio discs respectively refer to properly formatted and structured audio and video content. Other types of DVDs, including those with video content, may be referred to as DVD-Data discs.

The basic types of DVD are referred to by a rough approximation of their capacity in gigabytes. The 12 cm type is a standard DVD, and the 8 cm variety is known as a mini-DVD. These are the same sizes as a standard CD and a mini-CD, respectively. The capacity by surface (MiB/cm2) differs from 6.92MiB/cm2 in the DVD-1 to 18.0 MiB/cm2 in the DVD-18.

---

① http://en.wikipedia.org/wiki/DVD#cite_note-1

Each DVD sector contains 2418 bytes of data, 2048 bytes of which are user data.

## Text B

## Selecting Video[①]

### Locating Materials

Program guides and directories can help keep you abreast of available materials in your areas of interest and guide you toward selection of materials best suited to your particular teaching needs. Librarians, media specialists, and teachers working as partners should communicate constantly concerning the resources needed for instruction. A basic resource for you, then, is a collection of catalogs of rental agencies you are most likely to use. To be more thorough in your search you will want *The Educational Film/Video Locator*, a comprehensive list of the videotapes available in various college and university rental collection. (Figure 15-7) The most comprehensive list of current educational video is "A-V Online," which is in CD-ROM format. Other broad listings are *Bowker's Complete Video Directory* and *Video Source Book*.

Figure 15-7   The video rental collection contains over 7000 DVD and VHS titles available for rental by special Library card holders. This is a diverse collection with an emphasis on international films as well as current releases and cinema classics. VHS tapes may be rented for one week for $1. DVD's are available for $2 per week.

### Appraising Video

After you have located some potentially useful videos, you will want to preview and appraise them. Some schools and organizations have standard appraisal forms ready to use. Some of these are meticulously detailed, covering every possible factor; others are much more perfunctory. A good appraisal form will be brief enough not to be intimidating but complete enough to help individuals choose materials that may be useful for current and future applications. It should also stand as a public record that you can use to justify the purchase or rental of specific

---

[①]   Sharon E. Smaldino, James D. Russell, Robert Heinich and Michael Molenda, *Instruction Technology and Media for Learning*, Eigth Edition, Chapter 12 Video.

titles. The "Selection Rubric: Video" includes the most commonly used criteria, particularly those that research indicates really do make a difference.

Appraising and previewing also give you the opportunity to make notes for class discussion of the video, and to note key points in the program to explain or emphasize to student.

**Sponsored Videos**

Private companies, associations, and government agencies sponsor videos for a variety of reasons. Private companies may make them to promote their products or to enhance their public image. Associations and government agencies sponsor videos to promote causes, such as better health habits, conservation of natural resources, and proper use of park and recreation areas. Many of these sponsored videos make worthwhile instructional materials. They also have the considerable advantage of being free.

A certain amount of caution, however, is called for in using sponsored programs for instructional purposes. Some privately produced materials may be too flagrantly self-serving. Or they may deal with products not very suitable for certain instructional settings, for example, the manufacturing of alcoholic beverages or cigarettes. Some association and government materials may contain a sizable number of propaganda or special pleading for pet causes along with their content. You must *always* preview sponsored materials.

When properly selected, many sponsored materials can be valuable additions to classroom instruction. Modern Talking Picture Services is one of the major distributors of sponsored videos. The best single source of information on sponsored films is *Free Videotapes*.

# Text C

## Producing Video[①]

**In-house video** refers to videos produced within one's own classroom or company. With in-house video production, students and instructors are not limited to off-the-shelf materials but can with reasonable ease prepare custom materials. This feature sets video apart from some of the other media. Do-it-yourself has become commonplace since the popularization of the battery-operated portable video recording systems.

The development of the camcorder (camera and recorder built into a single book-size unit) has increased the ease and portability of video recording. It allows video production to be taken into the field, wherever that might be: the science laboratory (Figure 15-8), the classroom, the counseling office, the athletic field (Figure 15-9), the factory assembly home, the hospital, the neighborhood, and even the home. Equally important, the simplicity of the system has made it feasible for nonprofessionals, instructors, and students alike to create their

---

① Sharon E. Smaldino, James D. Russell, Robert Heinich and Michael Molenda, *Instruction Technology and Media for Learning*, Eigth Edition, Chapter 12 Video.

own video materials.

Figure 15-8  General Science Laboratory—Introductory science students use this room to investigate and construct models; classify and explore properties, changes, and conservation of matter and energy; and conduct investigations of consumer products and water samples.

Figure 15-9  Soccer Field/Track

Locally produced video can be used for virtually any of the purposes described earlier. Its unique capability is to capture sight and sound for immediate playback. This medium thus works well with activities that are enhanced by immediate feedback: group dynamics sessions, athletic practice, skills training, and interpersonal techniques.

Other applications that emphasize the local aspect of video production include the following:

- Dramatization of student stories, songs, and poems
- Student documentaries of school or neighborhood issues
- Preservation of local folklore
- Demonstrations of science experiments and safety drills
- Replays of field trips for in-class followup
- Career information on local businesses

Growing numbers of school library media centers are now adding to their environments a small video studio for student productions. Many students come to school with home experience in using portable cameras. Student production will increase as equipment continues to become less expensive, more light sensitive, and easier to use. Elementary and secondary students can be involved in scripting, recording, editing, and revising their own video productions.

As with all media production, preproduction planning is necessary. Storyboarding (Figure 15-10) can be used by students of all ages to facilitate planning and production of video. Storyboarding is particularly helpful when a group of students is cooperatively involved in designing a video.

**Analog Video Production**

Video production requires a camera, a recorder, a microphone, and perhaps editing

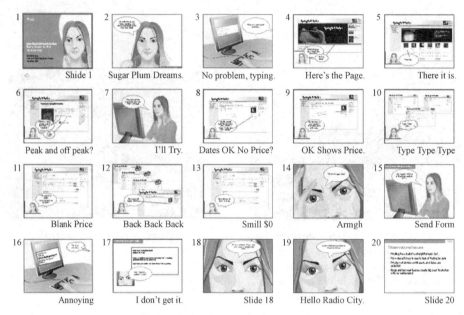

Figure 15-10　An example of storyboarding

equipment. Most cameras are of the viewfinder type. The viewfinder camera (Figure 15-11) is so named because it has built into it a small TV set that allows the operator to monitor the image received by the pickup tube.[4] Even small hand-held cameras typically contain build-in viewfinders with one-inch screens.

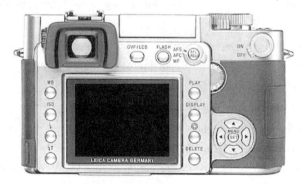

Figure 15-11　An example of optical viewfinder camera—Monitor preview

Hand-held cameras (Figure 15-12) usually come with a microphone built into the front of the camera. This microphone has an automatic lever control, a feature that automatically adjusts the volume to keep the sound at an audible level. The camera "hears" as well as "sees." The problem is that these microphones amplify all sounds within their range, including shuffling feet, coughing, street noises, and equipment noise, along with the sounds you want. You may therefore want to bypass the built-in microphone by plugging in a separate microphone better suited to your particular purpose.

Part 5 Developing Learning Resources 171

1600MA 2~3 Hours battery life
900Mw output

Figure 15-12 High Power Hand Held Video Camera/Bluetooth Jammer

Figure 15-13 An example of microphone head

The *lavaliere*, or neck mike, is a good choice when recording a single speaker. It can be clipped to a tie or dress, hung around the neck, or even hidden under lightweight clothing. A desk stand may be used to hold a microphone for a speaker or several discussions seated at a table. For situations in which there is unwanted background noise or the speaker is moving, a highly directional microphone (Figure 15-13) is best.

Standard video editing equipment is very expensive. However, you and your students can do your own video editing with two VCRs, connecting them by a patch cord or cable to record from one tape to another. It is also possible to record from a videodisc to videotape using a similar setup.

### Digital Video Editing

Digital video editing refers to the means by which video can be taken apart and put back together using a compute and appropriate software. [5] It is also called *nonlinear editing*. Digital video camcorders are smaller than analog video cameras and are simple to operate. With some digital camcorders there is no videotape, while others use specialized videotape to record in a digital mode.

After shooting video, you can watch it on the camera's built-in LCD monitor. You can also connect the camcorder to the television monitor, or you can transfer the images to the computer. Many camcorders allow you to edit right in the camera.

Using a special video transfer cable or FireWire connection, you can connect the camcorder, either analog or digital, to the computer hard drive. You and your students can then edit the video within the computer, without using the videotape equipment. You can also use the computer as a display device; using a digitizing camera for motion media, moving images from any of the analog sources can be displayed on the screen without being stored.

There are several methods for storing video on a computer. One format is *QuickTime*, for use with *Mac OS*, and *Windows* operating systems. Many applications, such as *Compton's Multimedia Encyclopedia*, incorporate *QuickTime* "movies." Students can produce their own to add visuals, graphics, and text to their portfolios or projects.

By doing your own video productions, you can target your video to a specific audience with specific content. The productions can be readily and easily updated. Once the equipment (cameras, computers, and software) has been purchased, the production of in-house video is very inexpensive. Software for in-house production includes Apple's *iMovie* 4 and Avid Technology's *Cinema* and *VideoShop*. These types of software are readily available, inexpensive (iMovie 4 comes preloaded on new Apple computers), and easy to use. Very young children can learn to use software and video cameras quickly.

## New Words

camcorder    *n.* （VCR）摄像机
solid-state    *adj.* 使用电晶体的,不用真空管的
interlaced    *adj.* 交织的,交错的
progressive    *adj.* 1. 不断前进的,逐渐上升的 2. 进步的,先进的
consecutive    *adj.* 连续的,连贯的
abreast    *adv.* 并排,并列
meticulous    *adj.* 极仔细的;一丝不苟的
perfunctory    *adj.* 1. 敷衍的,马虎的,例行公事的 2. 肤浅的,浅薄的
intimidate    *vt.* 恐吓,威胁
sponsor    *vt.* 赞助,发起,主办
flagrantly    *adv.* 千真万确地,极恶地
propaganda    *n.* 宣传,宣传运动
special pleading    *n.* 间接答辩法,诡辩术
in-house    *adj.* 内部的
dramatization    *n.* 编剧,改编成戏剧
folklore    *n.* 民间传统;民间故事;民俗
storyboarding    *n.* （电影、电视节目或商业广告等的）情节串联图板
viewfinder    *n.* （照相机）取景器
shuffle    *vt. & vi.* 1. 拖着脚步走 2. 洗（纸牌）;弄混;乱堆 3. 粗心地做
patch cord    调度塞绳

## Notes

[1] Tape is a linear method of storing information, and since nearly all video recordings made nowadays are digital, it is expected to gradually lose importance as non-linear/random access methods of storing digital video data are becoming more common.

译文：磁带采用的是一种线性存储信息的方法,并且既然现在几乎所有的音频录制都是数字的,所以当存储数字视频数据所采用的非线性的/随机存取方法变得更普遍时,磁带将会逐渐失去其现有的重要性。

• since nearly all video recordings made nowadays are digital 是由连词 since 引导的原

因状语从句。

- it 指代的是 tape。
- as non-linear/random access methods of storing digital video data are becoming more common 是由连词 as 引导的原因状语从句。

[2] Presently, MiniDV is the most popular format for tape-based consumer camcorders, providing near-broadcast quality video and sophisticated nonlinear editing capability on consumer equipment; however, though intended as a digital successor to VHS, MiniDV VCRs are not widely available outside professional circles.

译文：现在，迷你 DV 是基于录像带的消费者摄像机最欢迎的格式，它提供了近乎广播质量的录像和在消费者设备上精密的非线性编辑能力。然而，虽然迷你 DV 想要成为 VHS 的数字形式的接替者，但是它在专业领域以外并没有广泛使用。

- providing near-broadcast quality video and sophisticated nonlinear editing capability 是现在分词引导的定语从句，用来修饰限定先行词 MiniDV。
- though intended as a digital successor to VHS 是过去分词引导的定语从句，用来修饰限定先行词 MiniDV VCRs。
- intend sth. (as sth.) 打算，意欲，想要

[3] Probably the most widely used formats for delivering video over the internet are MPEG4 and Windows Media, while MPEG2 is used almost exclusively for DVDs, providing an exceptional image in minimal size but resulting in a high level of CPU consumption to decompress.

译文：在将视频发送到因特网上的格式中，最广泛使用的是 MPEG4 和视窗媒体格式，而 MPEG2 专门用于 DVD，能够产生最小存储空间的独特图像，不过压缩时将导致高的 CPU 消耗。

- providing an exceptional image in minimal size but resulting in a high level of CPU consumption to decompress 是现在分词引导的定语从句，修饰限定先行词 MPEG2。
- result in 引起，导致；以……为结局

[4] The viewfinder camera is so named because it has built into it a small TV set that allows the operator to monitor the image received by the pickup tube.

译文：取景器照相机之所以如此取名，是因为它内部装有的一个小电视机能够让操作员监视通过摄像管所采集到的图像。

- because it has built into it a small TV set 是由 because 引导的原因状语从句。
- that allows the operator to monitor the image 是由 that 引导的定语从句，用来修饰限定先行词 TV set。
- received by the pickup tube 是过去分词引导的定语从句，用来修饰限定先行词 image。

[5] Digital video editing refers to the means by which video can be taken apart and put back together using a compute and appropriate software.

译文：数字视频编辑指的是通过使用计算和合适的视频编辑软件将视频拆分和重组

在一起的方法。
- by which video can be taken apart and put back together 是由 which 引导的定语从句,用来修饰限定先行词 means。
- refer to 1. 提及 2. 暗指 3. 有关,针对
- take apart 拆开;拆卸

## Selected Translation

### Text A

视 频 格 式

录像带是一种以电子的方式获取、录制、处理、存储、传播和重现一系列静像以描绘运动中的景象的技术。最常用的视频格式是录像带、数字视频和 DVD(数字化视频光盘)。

**录像带**

录像带是一种将图像和声音录制到磁带上的方法,这与电影相反。

在大多数情况下,因为视频信号带宽非常大,而且静止的视频头将需要极度大的录制速度,所以螺线扫描视频头对着转动的带子旋转转动,以此能从两个方向来录数据。录像磁带在磁带录像机[VTRs,更普遍的叫法是磁带录像机(VCRs)]和摄影机中都得到了使用。磁带采用的是一种线性存储信息的方法,并且既然现在几乎所有的音频录制都是数字的,所以当存储数字视频数据所采用的非线性的/随机存取方法变得更普遍时,磁带将会逐渐失去其现有的重要性。

标准家用录像系统的大小是 1×4×7 1/2。在这种标准下又产生了另外一些消费者录像带格式,例如 8 毫米录像带、Hi8、数字 8、VHS-C(压缩)和 S-VHS-C。

现在,迷你 DV 是基于录像带的消费者摄像机最欢迎的格式,它提供了近乎广播质量的录像和在消费者设备上精密的非线性编辑能力。然而,迷你 DV 虽然想要成为 VHS 的数字形式的接替者,但是它在专业领域以外并没有广泛使用。

就高清晰度而言,最有前途的系统似乎是 HDV(高清数码摄像机),它运用迷你 DV 来存储大致上达到广播质量的 HDTV(高清晰度电视)数据流。

消费者摄像机最近的趋势就是从基于磁带的方法转变到无磁带的方法,例如内置 HDDs(高密度数据系统)、光盘和液晶媒体。

**数码摄像机**

数码摄像机是一种录制视频系统,它通过使用数字而非模拟视频信号来工作。录像机、视频录像机和摄像机这些术语都在本文中交替使用。

数码照相机有两种不同的获取图像的格式:交错扫描和循序扫描。交错式照相机用交互的线条来录制图像——奇数线条被扫描后,偶数线条再被扫描,然后奇数线条又被扫描,等等。这一套奇数或偶数线条被认为是一"场",连续配对的反奇偶的两场就成为一帧。

循序扫描数字视频摄像机非常清晰地录制每一帧,两场都是完全相同的。因此,当

它们都以同样的速率运作时,交错扫描录像机每秒扫描的场数是循环扫描数字视频摄像机的两倍。这就是摄像机有"超真实"录像的原因之一,因为它每秒提取60幅不同的图像,与电影不同的是,电影只能每秒交错扫描24或者25帧。

数码摄像机被复制时在质量上不会有所降低。不管数字源被复制了多少次,它都将与原始第一代的数字影片一样清晰。

数字视频信号能在NLE,或非线性编辑工作站上进行处理和编辑,这种设备是专门用来编辑视频和音频的。它们能够频繁地将模拟或数字源输入进来,但是除了编辑视频外,并不会做任何其他处理。

有许多视频压缩类型能将数字视频传送到因特网及DVD上。DV视频在压缩编辑时并没有超出自身的编解码器,其输出文件并不适用于借助视窗媒体格式、MPEG2、MPEG4、实时媒体、最近的H.264和索伦森媒体编解码器等传送到光盘或网上去。在将视频发送到因特网上的格式中,最广泛使用的是MPEG4和视窗媒体格式,而MPEG2专门用于DVD,能够产生最小格式的独特文件,不过压缩时将导致高的CPU消耗。

**DVD**

DVD(同样被称为"数字式激光视盘"或"数码视像光碟"——参考词源学)是一种广受欢迎的存储媒体光盘格式。它主要的用途是视频和数据存储。大多数的DVD与光盘的尺寸一样大,但是存储的数据却是光盘的六倍多。

不同的DVD术语通常描述了数据存储在光盘上的方式:DVD-ROM是以只读的方式存储数据,DVD-R和DVD+R只能录制一次数据,DVD-ROM DVD-RW和DVD+RW的作用是能多次录制和擦除数据。标准DVD激光器的波长是650纳米,因此发出的光是红色的。

视频DVD和音频DVD光盘分别指的是被适当格式化和组织的音频和视频内容。DVD的其他类型,包括那些有视频内容的,可以被称为DVD光盘。

DVD的基本类型指的是大约用十亿字节来衡量其容量。

直径为12厘米的DVD为标准DVD,直径为8厘米的种类被认为是迷你DVD。它们分别与标准CD和迷你CD一样大。表面的容量(兆字节/每平方厘米)从DVD-1的每平方厘米6.92兆字节到DVD-18的每平方厘米18.0兆字节不等。

DVD的每个扇形包含2418个字节的数据,其中2048个字节是用户数据。

## Exercises

**1. Short Answers:**

(1) What are the two different image capture formats used in digital video cameras and how they work?

(2) What are the three aspects of selecting videos?

(3) Can you state some applications of the local aspect of video productions?

(4) What is the disadvantage of the microphones built in the front of the hand-held cameras and how people overcome it according to different situations?

(5) What does digital video editing refer to?

# 科技论文的结构与写作初步（Ⅰ）

科技资料主要包括科技图书与科技论文。一般而言，图书的篇幅比论文要长得多，通常可分为两大类：专著和普及性读物。专著通常是对某一问题或某一类问题进行深入的探论，所包含的内容往往比较难。普及性读物则是对某一问题较为全面、实用的论述，通常注重实践性。两类图书具有相同的结构：前言、目录、正文、附录、索引和参考文献。这里我们主要讨论科技论文的结构与写作问题。

科技论文一般包括：报刊科普论文、学术论文、毕业论文、学位论文。科技论文是在科学研究、科学实验的基础上，对自然科学和专业技术领域里的某些现象或问题进行专题研究、分析和阐述，揭示出这些现象和问题的本质及其规律性而撰写成的文章。也就是说，凡是运用概念、判断、推理、论证和反驳等逻辑思维手段，来分析和阐明自然科学原理、定律和各种问题的文章均属科技论文。科技论文主要用于科学技术研究及其成果的描述，是研究成果的体现。运用它们能进行成果推广、信息交流，并能促进科学技术的发展。它们的发表标志着研究工作的水平，为社会所公认，载入人类知识宝库，成为人们共享的精神财富。科技论文还是考核科技人员业绩的重要标准。

科技论文一般具备以下五个特点：

1. 学术性。科技论文是科学研究的成果，是客观存在的自然现象及其规律的反映。它要求运用科学的原理和方法，对自然科学领域的新问题进行科学分析，严密论证，抽象概括。学术论文的科学性，要求作者在立论上不得带有个人好恶，不得主观臆造，必须切实地从客观实际出发，从中引出符合实际的结论。在论据上，应尽可能多地占有资料，以最充分的、确凿有力的论据作为立论的依据。在论证时，必须经过周密的思考，进行严谨的论证。可见，学术性是科技论文最基本的特征。

2. 创造性。科技论文不同于教科书和综述性的科学报告，后者的主要任务在于传授知识，能否提出新的内容并不起决定作用，而科技论文则必须有新的内容，因为科学研究是对新知识的探求。创造性是科学研究的生命。学术论文的创造性在于作者要有自己独到的见解，能提出新的观点、新的理论。这是因为科学的本性就是"革命的和非正统的"，"科学方法主要是发现新现象、制定新理论的一种手段，旧的科学理论就必然会不断地被新理论推翻"。因此，没有创造性，学术论文就没有科学价值。

3. 理论性。学术论文在形式上是属于议论文的，但它与一般议论文不同，它必须有自己的理论系统，不能只是材料的罗列，应对大量的事实、材料进行分析、研究，使感性认识上升到理性认识。一般来说，学术论文具有论证色彩，或具有论辩色彩。论文的内容必须符合历史唯物主义和唯物辩证法，符合"实事求是"、"有的放矢"、"既分析又综合"的科学研究方法。

4. 专业性。不同专业的科技论文的内容和表现形式不尽相同。科技论文可分为理论型、实验型和描述型三种。理论型论文的主要研究方法是理论分析；实验型论文的主要研究方法是设计实验、实验过程研究和实验结果分析；描述型论文的主要研究方法是描述说明,目的是介绍新发现的事物或现象及其所具有的科学价值,重点说明这一新事物是什么现象或不是什么现象。

5. 平易性。指的是要用通俗易懂的语言表述科学道理,不仅要做到文从字顺,而且要准确、鲜明、和谐、力求生动。也就是说,要为人所用,不要让别人看不懂。

随着科学技术飞速发展,科技论文大量发表,这越来越要求论文作者以规范化、标准化的固定结构模式(即通用型格式)来表达他们的研究过程和成果。这种通用型结构形式,是人们经过长期实践之后总结出来的论文写作的表达形式和规律。它是最明确、最易令人理解的表达科研成果的好形式,并逐步形成了科学技术报告、学位论文和学术论文的编写格式国家标准(GB 7713-87),其通用型基本结构如下:

```
1. 标题
2. 作者及其工作单位
3. 摘要
4. 引言
5. 正文
6. 结论
7. 致谢
8. 参考文献
9. 附录
```

英文科技论文的阅读是迅速了解科技与工程动态的必要手段,而英文科技论文的写作是进行国际学术交流必须掌握的技能,也是科技成果得到世界同行认可的最佳方式。在撰写英文科技论文时,除了需要遵循科技论文的基本要求,还需要注意英文科技论文的写作风格。其原因主要在于中国人和西方人思维方式、文化习惯等方面上的差异,这种差异突出地表现在文章的结构与表达上。比如说,中国人行文比较含蓄,因此文章各段之间可能存在不明显的内在关联;而西方人则比较直截了当,他们的文章结构往往一目了然。因此,即使已有一篇现成的中文论文,在其基础上写英文论文时,也不能采用"拿来主义"逐字逐句翻译。

理解与撰写英文科技论文的第一步就是要了解英文科技论文的分类。英文科技论文一般分为:

1. 综述文章(Review paper)
2. 研究论文(Research paper)
3. 简报(Brief/Note/Short article)
4. 评论/回复(Comments/Reply)
5. 书评(Book Review)。

综述文章一般是对某项研究的总结,它不是情况的罗列,除了需要占有文献,还需要对这个问题进行分析和发表看法。原因在于,已经发表的研究报告,有些是重要的,但大多数是无关紧要的,综述必须能够根据自己的研究经验去粗取精,以便供其他研究者参考。如何去粗取精,这就需要比较,需要考虑理论的进展、技术的有效,以及应用的条件等方面。此外,问题的演变与发展也是综述必须包括的内容。因此,只有本行当内有较大影响的学者才可能写出较好的综述。

研究论文通常是指对科学领域中的某些现象和问题进行比较系统的研究,以探讨其本质特征及其发展规律等的理论性文章。英文研究论文通常又分为长论文与短论文。本章主要讨论研究论文的结构与写作问题。

简报是传递某方面信息的小论文,具有简洁、精悍、快速、新颖和连续性等特点,一般针对的是某项科学研究的初步进展与新的发现。

评论通常是针对该杂志先前发表的某篇研究论文或简报所做出的评论性文章,且一般是评判性地指出该论文所存在的问题与错误;而回复则是原论文作者就评论文章指出的问题给出的回复。

理解与撰写英文科技论文的第二步就是要了解并推敲科技论文的结构,使之能被西方人理解。尽管目前中文科技论文与英文科技论文在论文整体结构上已经趋于一致,但东西方文化的表达与逻辑思维上存在不小的差异,特别是由于科技论文本身的严肃性,因此即使是西方本土的大学生也需要接受科技论文的正规训练。

## Unit 16　Developing Online Courses

▲ Knowledge Objectives

When you have completed this unit, you will be able to:

◆ State the three approaches to build a web page or website and know their respective advantages and disadvantages

◆ Be familiar with the six steps in creating a web page

▲ Professional Terms

| | |
|---|---|
| Internet Service Providers (ISPs) | Internet 服务提供者 |
| Hypertext Markup Language (HTML) | 超文本链接标示语言 |
| Uniform Resource Locator (URL) | Internet 的 WWW 服务程序上用于指定信息位置的表示方法 |
| File Transfer Protocol (FTP) | 文件传送[输]协议 |

## Text A

### Creating a Web Page[①]

There are three approaches to building a Web page or a website (multiply Web pages connected together). The first is to hire someone to build your site for you. The second is to buy a software package that will assist you in building your website. The third is to build the website yourself.

---

① Robent Heinich, Michael Molenda, James D. Russell and Sharon E. Smaldino, *Instructional Media and Technologies for Learning* (Seventh Edition).

The first option is often expensive. Custom Web page design can cost 150 dollars per hour or more. Additionally, contracting a Web page designer means you lose a measure of control over the content and design of the site. For these reasons, this option should be a last resort. As you will see, basic website design can be easy and inexpensive.

The second option is to buy a software package to assist you in designing your website. Popular packages include Macromedia Dreamweaver™ and Adobe PageMill™. However, as with most other computer technologies, this software is evolving rapidly. Consult a knowledgeable friend or computer store associate to find the latest software available. The packages are improving in quality and lowering in price, but a good package will still cost you from 50 to 500 dollars. This is much less than paying someone to build your site, but is still an expensive option. Carefully research the pros and cons of individual software packages before you spend money on them.

The last option is building the website yourself. What do you need to build your own website? We'll assure you want the rest of the world to see your site, so you will need an Internet account capable of supporting a website, FTP software to transfer your website from your company to your Internet account, and a text editor. You also should have a Web browser installed, so you may view your creation.

You can use a Web search engine (used to locate information on the Internet) such as Google (http://www.google.com) or Yahoo! (http://www.yahoo.com) to locate free FTP software. Almost all computers come with a simple text editor already installed so you need not spend money on the editor (although you will probably want to purchase a quality word processing program in any case). Finally, most Internet service providers (ISPs) offer a Web page account at a price similar to maintaining an e-mail account. Also, many organizations with their own websites offer to host personal individual Web pages for free or for a nominal charge. For just a few dollars a month you can have your own website!

Building the site involves learning the basics of Hypertext Markup Language (HTML) programming. Actually, HTML is not a true programming language. A markup language is simply a collection of tags used to format text and images in different ways. It is similar to using <u>underline</u> or **Boldface** in a word processing document.

In the following example we guide you through the steps for building a simple Web page. We will focus on the steps for creating the actual file for your website and viewing it locally right off your computer's hard drive. We will not cover how to transfer the file to your Internet Account, as that can be done in a variety of ways.[1] This example assumes that you are using *Windows*.

**Step 1: Content**

Decide on the content of your website. It sounds obvious, but quite a few people run out and try to build a website before thinking about what should be on it. Ask yourself a few questions first: What information do I want on this site? Who do I want to look at it? How professional does it need to be? If you just want a site on the Web for your friends to look at then you probably don't need to think too deeply about content. But if you want your site to be worth visiting and revising, you must carefully choose the contents of your site. If you want sports fans to view your page, then think about what content they would find useful or interesting. If you want gardeners to visit your site, you might provide a list of green thumb tips. Remember, once you build your website and upload it to the Internet server, anyone on the Internet anywhere in the world can view it simply by entering its unique Web address, or URL.[2]

**Step 2: Open Your Text Editor**

Double-click on your text editor and if it does not have a new file open already then choose File|New from the menu bar.

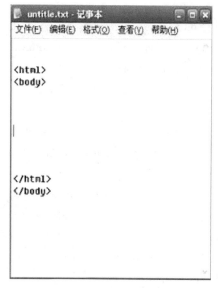

Figure 16-1

**Step 3: The Basics**

All HTML files need to have the following two tags: html and body. (A tag indicates the specifications applied to the following text, similar to style sheet tags in word processing and page layout programs.) Tags in HTML are bracketed as follows: 〈html〉 〈body〉. Most copy within HTML requires an opening and closing tag. For example, the body tag would be 〈body〉to open and 〈/body〉 to close. Begin your document as shown in Figure 16-1.

The space between your 〈body〉 and 〈/body〉 tags is where you will do almost all your work. The space between your 〈html〉 and 〈body〉 tags is reversed for formatting the background, selecting the colors, and adding a title.

Choose File|Save and name your document "howto. html" (do not type the quotation marks). Make sure you know where you saved it. Your file is now ready to be viewed on the Web! Of course at this point, nothing will show up, so we will add more HTML to test your page. (Note: You do not need to space out the HTML tags. However it is a good idea to insert spaces so that as your HTML document grows it will remain easily readable.)

**Step 4: Title and Basic Text**

Add the following lines to your text:

1. Add this between your 〈html〉 and 〈body〉 tags:

〈head〉〈title〉This is my first webpage〈/title〉〈/head〉 This demonstrates an important point: tags within HTML can be nested, on inside the other. Make sure you order the tags properly. For example, 〈head〉〈title〉〈/head〉〈/title〉 is not valid HTML; you must close the title before you close the head. The 〈head〉 tag is used to place to place information in the heading of your browser and ⟨title⟩ is used to place a title in the heading of the browser.

2. Add this between your ⟨body⟩ and ⟨/body⟩ tags:

⟨h1⟩Hello⟨/h1⟩⟨h2⟩welcome⟨/h2⟩⟨h3⟩to my first website⟨/h3⟩⟨font size = 2⟩How do⟨/font⟩⟨font size = 4⟩you like⟨/font⟩⟨font size = 7⟩it?⟨/font⟩

⟨hx⟩⟨/hx⟩ stands for "heading" and can be between 1 and 6 size. The tag ⟨font size = x⟩⟨/font⟩ is an adjustable font size between 1 and 7.

3. Open your browser and choose File | Open File in Internet Explorer and choose "howto.html." You should have something as Figure 16-2 shows.

Do you notice any differences between headings and font sizes? You should see the following: Headings get smaller as you increase towards 6 and font sizes get larger as you increase towards 7. The heading tag (⟨hx⟩) automatically sends the cursor to the next line when you close the tag (⟨hx⟩). To keep your document readable, space out the heading and font size statements in your document now.

Figure 16-2

**Step 5: Break Lines and Images**

Let's add a simple break and an image. The tag ⟨hr⟩ does not need a closing tag. The ⟨hr⟩ creates a line on the screen and positions your cursor below the line. The ⟨hr⟩ is typically used to denote a new section or signify some sort of major change.

The code *img* stands for image, and *src* stands for source. These are used in combination to tell your browser where to get your image from. The source can be from other directions or websites (make sure you have permission to link to the image or use it), but in our example the image will be in the same directory as howto.html file. Note: You must have a GIF or JPEG (specific image format used by HTML browsers) files in the same directory as howto.html in order for the image to appear in this example. If necessary, place such a file now before continuing.

Add the following to your text editor below the heading and font size section:

⟨hr⟩

⟨h3⟩My Picture Gallery⟨/h3⟩

⟨img src = "plannkis.gif"⟩

**Step 6: Links**

Finally, we will add both a link to another website and an e-mail link. Here is the generic formula for links:

⟨a href = "location"⟩link description seen on the webpage⟨/a⟩

The tag ⟨a⟩⟨/a⟩ stands for anchor and tells your browser you are creating a link. href =

"location" gives the browser the location of the webpage you are creating the link to. The location must be cited as a URL (uniform resource locator-the exact location of an object on the Internet, which in this case is a Web page).

1. Add the following in your text editor below the image section:

〈hr〉

〈h3〉My Links〈/h3〉

〈a href = http://www.northshore.net/homepages/plankisb/guide/index.html〉Effective website development〈/a〉

〈hr〉

〈a href = "mailto: plankisb@ northshore.net"〉Send mail to the author〈/a〉

2. Save your file again and open your browser again. Select File | Open to reopen howto.html, or if your browser was still on your page, just click the Reload or Refresh button. (Note: in order for the links to work you must be connected to the Internet and have your e-mail set up in your browser for the e-mail link.) Note also that the links provided here should be valid. (However, if they are not, ask your instructor for a link to the school's website.)

This example has illustrated the use of only a few HTML tags and what they can do. We hope that this has been a fun experience. Enjoy!

## New Words

last resort　　1. 最后的依靠,最后的贷款者 2. 最后的补救办法
the pros and cons　　赞成与反对的票数;赞成与反对的理由;赞成与反对者
nominal　*adj.* 1. 名义上的,有名无实的 2.（金额）很少的;象征性的
green thumb　*n.* 有特殊园艺才能
style sheet　　样式表
page layout　*n.* 页面
bracketed　*adj.* 相等的
nested　*adj.* 嵌套的
anchor　*n.* 锚

## Notes

[1]　We will not cover how to transfer the file to your Internet Account, as that can be done in a variety of ways.

译文:对于如何从个人计算机向网站上传文件的操作,我们在这里不做介绍,因为它有很多不同的实现方式。

- how to transfer the file to your Internet Account 是宾语从句,用来解释谓语 cover。
- as that can be done in a variety of ways 是连词 as 引导的原因状语从句。
- transfer to 移动到

[2] Remember, once you build your website and upload it to the Internet server, anyone on the Internet anywhere in the world can view it simply by entering its unique Web address, or URL.

**译文**:记住,一旦网站建成,上传到网络服务器上,世界上任何一个地方的人都可以通过输入网址或 URL 来访问它。

◆ once you build your website and upload it to the Internet server 是由连词 once 引导的时间状语从句。

◆ anywhere in the world 是由 anywhere 引导的地点状语从句。

## Selected Translation

## Text A

### 创建 Web 页面

制作网页或网站(由相互关联的多个网页组成)有三种方法:第一种是雇佣别人为你创建网站;第二种是购买软件包来创建网站;第三种方法是自己动手创建网站。

第一种方法通常是昂贵的。个性化网页设计的收费高达每小时 150 美元甚至更多。不仅如此,与网页设计师签约,意味着你对网站的内容和设计失去了一定的控制权。出于上述原因,尽量不要采用这种方法。正如你将要了解到的,基本的网页设计是很容易的,而且花费很低。

第二种方法是购买软件包来协助进行网站创建。目前流行的软件包括 Macromedia Dreamweaver™ 和 Adobe PageMill™。不过,像所有的计算机技术一样,网页创作软件也在不断升级。购买前,可以咨询懂软件的朋友或者计算机商店销售助理,了解软件的最新版本。这些软件包质量在不断提高,而价格在不断降低,但即使这样,好的软件包的价格也要 50—500 美元。这个价格比雇佣别人创建网站便宜了很多。但是,仍然是一个比较昂贵的选择。在购买软件之前,要注意了解各种软件包的优缺点。

第三种方法是自己动手创建网站。怎样建立自己的网站呢?我们假定你希望网上所有的人都能访问你的网站,那么,首先,你需要申请一个网络账号,以支持网站的运行;其次,你需要 FTP 软件,用于从你的计算机向网络账号上传网页;第三,你需要一个文本编辑器,来编辑网页信息。最后,你还需要安装一个网页浏览器,这样你可以浏览自己创作的网页了。

你可以使用 Google(http://www.google.com)或 Yahoo!(http://www.yahoo.com)等搜索引擎(用于寻找网上的信息)来寻找免费的 FTP 软件。几乎所有的计算机都自带一个简单的文本编辑器,因此,你不需要花钱单独购买(虽然你可能打算买一个高质量的文字处理软件)。最后,很多拥有网站的机构也向个人提供网页服务,完全免费或者只收取象征性的费用。每个月只需要几美元,你就可以拥有自己的网站!

创建网站需要学习 HTML(超文本标记语言)的基础知识。事实上,HTML 不能算是一种真正的编程语言,它只是一种标记语言(Markup Language),通过标签以不同的方式定义文本和图片的显示格式。它类似于文字处理软件中所使用的"下划线"和"加粗"等功能。

在下面的例子中,我们将引导你一步一步地创建简单的网页。我们主要介绍创建网站文件以及从本机浏览网站文件的主要步骤。对于如何从个人计算机向网站上传文件的操作,由于有很多不同的实现方式,我们在这里不做介绍。另外,我们假定你使用的是 Windows 操作系统。

### 步骤 1:内容

决定网站的内容。这一条看似显而易见,但确实有一些人在建网站的时候完全没有考虑要在网站上放哪些内容。先问自己这几个问题:我想通过网站提供什么信息?我希望谁来看我的网站?我的网站应该有多专业化?如果你只是想建一个网站给朋友看,就不需要对内容进行太深入的思考。但是,如果你希望用户经常访问你的网站,就需要仔细地选择网站的内容。如果你希望体育爱好者访问你的网站,那么应该考虑他们觉得什么样的内容有用或者有趣。如果你希望园艺师来访问你的网站,可以考虑提供一系列的园艺窍门。记住,一旦网站建成,上传到网络服务器上,世界上任何一个地方的人都可以通过输入网址或 URL 来访问它。

### 步骤 2:打开文本编辑器

双击,打开文本编辑器。如果系统没有自动打开一个新的空白文件,请从菜单中选择"文件|新建"命令。

### 步骤 3:HTML 基础知识

所有的 HTML 文件都需要下面的两个标签:html 和 body。(标签指定了跟在后面的文字的显示格式,这类似于文字处理中的样式表标签和页面排版软件当中的格式标签。) HTML 的标签需要用尖括号括起来,比如:〈html〉和〈body〉。HTML 当中的多数标签都有开始和结束。例如,body 标签应该以〈body〉标签开始,以〈/body〉结束。按照图 16-1 所示,开始设计你的文档。

剩下的工作主要是在〈body〉和〈/body〉标签之间的空白处完成。〈html〉和〈body〉之间的空白用于设定背景、选择颜色和添加标题。

选择"文件"菜单的"保存"选项,将你的文档命名为"howto.html"(输入文件名的时候不要输入引号)。一定要记住文档保存的目录。现在,可以在网上浏览这个页面了!当然,此时,页面上什么都没有,我们要逐渐加入更多的内容来测试你的页面。(注意:你不需要把标签分隔开来,但是,在文档中分隔标签是一个好主意,当 HTML 文档变得越来越长的时候,分隔标签可以提高文档的可读性。)

### 步骤 4:标题和文本

在文档中,加入下面的几行:

1. 在你的〈html〉和〈body〉标签之间加入:

〈head〉〈title〉This is my first webpage〈/title〉〈/head〉

这体现了 HTML 最重要的特点:标签可以嵌套。请保证标签顺序的正确性。例如,〈head〉〈title〉〈/head〉〈/title〉就是一个无效的 HTML 标签。你必须先结束 title 标签,然后才能结束 head 标签。Head 标签用于在浏览器的标题栏添加信息,title 标签用于在浏览器的标题栏添加标题。

2. 在你的〈body〉和〈/body〉标签之间添加：

〈h1〉Hello〈/h1〉〈h2〉welcome〈/h2〉〈h3〉to my first website〈/h3〉〈font size = 2〉How do〈/font〉〈font size = 4〉you like〈/font〉〈font size = 7〉it?〈/font〉

〈hx〉〈/hx〉表示标题，数值可以从 1 到 6。标记〈font size = ×〉〈/font〉可以调整字号，取值为 1 和 7。

3. 打开你的浏览器，在 Internet Explorer 浏览器中，选择"文件"菜单中的"打开"选项；然后，选择"howto.html"。你将看到视图 16-2。

你是否注意到了标题和字号的不同？你应该注意到这个现象：随着你将 hx 数字向 6 增加，标题的字会变小；而将 font size 向 7 增大，字号就变大。在你结束标题（〈/hx〉）时，鼠标被自动移至下一行。为了保持文档的可读性，在你的 HTML 文档中，隔开标题指令和字号大小调整指令。

**步骤 5：分割线和图片**

让我们加入一条分隔线和一张图片。〈hr〉标签不需要结束，它在屏幕上创建了一条直线，并且将你的鼠标移到直线下方。〈hr〉标签多用于表示一个新的段落或者表示重要的改变。

标签 img 表示图片，src 表示来源。它们合起来告诉浏览器从哪里得到图片。图片可以来自其他的目录或者是网站（必须要经过同意才能链接到别人的图片或者使用别人的图片），不过，在我们的例子里，图片和 howto.html 在同一个目录下。请将一个 GIF 或者 JPEG 格式（网页浏览器可以识别的图片格式）的图片和 howto.html 保存在同一个目录下，以便在网页上显示这个图片。需要的话，先把图片放好，再进行下面的操作。

在文本编辑器中，将下列代码添加在标题指令和文字大小调整指令的后面：

〈hr〉

〈h3〉My Picture Gallery〈/h3〉

〈img src = "plannkis.gif"〉

**步骤 6：链接**

最后，我们将加入一个连到其他网站和一个邮件地址的链接。以下是链接的代码格式：

〈a href = "location"〉link description seen on the webpage〈/a〉

标签〈a〉与〈/a〉表示锚，告诉浏览器你正在创建一个链接。href = "location"告诉浏览器你正在创建的链接地址，该地址必须是一个网页地址 URL（某一个物体在因特网上的确切位置，这里表示网页）

1. 在你的文本编辑器里，将下列代码添加在图片部分的后面：

〈hr〉

〈h3〉My Links〈/h3〉

〈a href = "http://www.northshore.net/homepages/plankisb/guide/index.html"〉Effective website development〈/a〉

〈hr〉

〈a href = "mailto: plankisb@ northshore.net"〉Send mail to the author〈/a〉

2. 再次保存你的文件,并重新打开浏览器。选择"文件|打开"菜单命令,重新打开howto.html,或者,如果你的浏览器没有关掉,点击刷新或者重载按钮即可。(为了保证可以点开上面的链接,你的计算机需要连接到因特网上,并且能够从浏览器中启动你的邮件账号。)还要注意的是:这里的链接应该是有效的。(不过,如果它们无效,可以向教师要一个学校网站的网址。)

上述的例子只展示了一部分 HTML 标签的用法。我们希望这对于你来说是一个有趣的经历!祝愉快!

## Exercises

**1. Short Answers:**

(1) What are the three approaches in creating a web page or a website? Which is the best?

(2) What do you need if you build your own web page?

(3) What are the steps to create a web page? Please try them out in your computer.

# 科技论文的结构与写作初步(Ⅱ)

下面我们以研究论文为主,简述科技论文的结构与规范。研究论文的一般结构如下:

```
标题(Title)
摘要(Abstract)
关键词(Keywords)
正文
    引言(Introduction)
    主体(Body)
    结论(Conclusion)
致谢(Acknowledgment)
参考文献(Reference)
```

## 一、标题

标题是论文特定内容最恰当、最简明的逻辑组合,即应"以最少数量的单词来充分表述论文的内容"。标题主要有两个作用:(1)吸引读者,题名相当于论文的"标签"(label),读者通常根据标题来考虑是否需要阅读摘要或全文,因此,标题表达不当,就会失去其应有的作用,使读者错过阅读论文的机会。(2)帮助文献追踪或检索。文献检索系统多以题名中的主题词为线索,因而标题必须准确地反映论文的核心内容,否则就有可能产生漏检与错误。因此,不恰当的标题很可能会导致该论文的"丢失",从而失去科技论文本身的意义与潜在价值。

1. 基本要求

（1）准确（Accuracy）。

标题要准确地反映论文的内容，不能过于空泛和一般化，也不宜过于繁琐。为确保标题的含义准确，应尽量避免使用非定量的、含义不明的词，并确保用词的专业性与专指性。

（2）简洁（Brevity）

标题的用词应该简短明了，以最少的文字概括尽可能多的内容。题名最好不超过12个单词，或100个英文字符；若能用一行文字表达，则尽量不用2行（超过2行可能会削弱读者的印象）。当然，在撰写题名时不能因为追求形式上的简短而忽视对论文内容的反映。题名过于简短，常起不到帮助读者理解论文的作用。另外，还要注意避免题名中词意上的重叠；在内容层次很多的情况下，如果难以简短化，最好采用主、副题名相结合的方法。

（3）清楚（Clarity）

标题要清晰地反映文章的具体内容和特色，明确表明研究工作的独到之处，力求简洁有效、重点突出。为使表达直接、清楚，能引起读者的注意，应尽可能将表达核心内容的主题词放在标题开头。题名中应慎重使用缩略语，尤其对于有多个解释的缩略语，应严加限制，必要时应在括号中注明全称。可以使用那些得到科技界公认的缩略语，不过这种使用应得到相应期刊读者群的认可。

2. 标题的结构

（1）标题的构成

标题常分为词组型标题、动宾型标题、陈述句标题、问句型标题以及主副标题等几种。标题通常由名词、分词与动名词等短语所构成。即使确实需要用一个句子来表达标题，标题通常也不应由陈述句构成。一般认为，陈述句容易使标题具有判断式的语意。有时可以用问句作为标题，尤其是在评论论文中，使用具有探讨性的疑问句标题显得比较生动，易引起读者的兴趣，生动且切题。

（2）标题的句法规则

由于标题比句子简短，且无需主、谓、宾，因此词序显得尤为重要。题名最好由最能反映论文核心内容的主题词扩展而成，如果词语间的修饰关系使用不当，就会影响读者正确理解标题的真实含意。例，Cars blamed for pollution by scientist（科学家造成的污染归罪于汽车）这一标题表意不正确，正确的写法应为 Cars blamed by scientist for pollution（科学家将污染归罪于汽车）。

（3）标题中介词的用法

"with"是标题中常用到的介词。一般而言，汉语中是以名词作形容词的，英语中用对应的名词作形容词就不适合。如当名词用作形容词来修饰另一个名词时，如果前者是后者的一部分或者是后者所具有的性质、特点时，常需要用由前置词"with + 名词"组成的前置词短语作形容词放在所要修饰的名词之后。如"具中国特色的新型机器"应译为"New types of machines with the Chinese characteristics"而不用"Chinese characteristics machines"。

在标题中,常常会遇到"××的××",此处"的"在英语有两个前置词相对应,即"of"和"for"。其中"of"主要表示所有关系,"for"主要表示目的、用途。如:A design method of sliding mode robust controller for uncertain system is presented(提出了一种针对不确定系统的滑模鲁棒控制器设计方法)。

(4)题名中单词的大小写

题名中字母主要有全大写、首字母大写、每个实词首字母大写等三种形式。作者应遵循相应期刊的习惯,专有名词首字母、首字母缩略词、德语名词首字母与句号后单词的首字母等一般情况下均应大写。

3. 实例分析

根据上述结构与特征,下面以实例形式简要分析论文标题的命名。

(1)翻译标题"中国远程教育技术发展"。较为合理的翻译为:Technical Progress of Distance Education in China。分析:这是一种偏正结构多词组的标题,作者按词组的组成关系翻译了(Distance Education)远程教育,重点强调技术进步。该标题重点突出,内容准确、清晰,且相当简洁。

(2)翻译标题"关于教育技术课程改革的几个问题"。原译为:Some Problems on Curriculum Reform of Educational Technology。分析:problems 与 with 属习惯搭配,有"对于"之意,此外,"Reform"应变为复数 Reforms。改译:Some problems with curriculum reforms on Educational Technology。

(3)翻译标题"立足科研和教学实际提高教学质量"。原译为:Basing on science and research and teaching,raising teaching quality。分析:应用 based 而非"basing";此外,结构不合理。改译:Raising teaching quality based on scientific research and teaching quality.

(4)翻译标题"基于网络的自适应学习系统研究"。较为合理的翻译为:The research of Web-based Adaptive Learning system。分析:作者按词组的组成关系翻译了(Web-based Adaptive Learning system)基于网络的自适应学习系统,重点强调对其所作的研究。该标题重点突出,内容准确、清晰,且相当简洁。

(5)翻译标题"绩效技术及其应用研究"。较为合理的翻译为:Performance Technology and Its Application Research。分析:作者直接按标题的顺序来翻译绩效技术(Performance Technology)和应用研究(Application Research),然后用 and 表示两者之间的并列关系,而 its 则限制了 Application Research。该标题一目了然,准确清晰。

(6)翻译标题"Instructional Transaction Theory: An Instructional Design Model based on Knowledge Objects"。较为准确的翻译为:教学事务理论———一种基于知识目标的教学设计模型。Instructional Transaction Theory 作为论文的研究重点应放在开头,紧接着冒号后解释 Instructional Transaction Theory 的类型,该标题内容准确,结构清晰。

(7)翻译标题"Instructional System Design (ISD): Using the ADDIE Model"。较为准确的翻译为:使用 ADDIE 模型的教学系统设计(ISD)。Instructional System Design (ISD) 作为文章的研究内容放在了开头,而冒号后则介绍了采用怎样的模型来进行教学系统设计(Using the ADDIE Model),该标题内容简洁、准确。

(8)翻译标题"How do instructional designers use automated instructional design tool?"。

较为准确的翻译为:教学系统设计者们怎样利用教学设计自动化工具?此标题用提问的方式来吸引读者的兴趣,并以此来说明此论文的研究内容:怎样利用教学设计自动化工具。该标题既生动又简洁,且结构清晰。

总之,科技论文标题撰写的 ABC 是 Accuracy(准确)、Brevity(简洁)与 Clarity(清楚),此外,要特别注意中英文句法的正确性,尤其是动词分词和介词的使用。对于题名的长度、缩写与字母的大小写等细节,应注意参考相关期刊的"读者须知"及其近期发表的论文。

### 二、摘要

摘要是全文的精华,是对一项科学研究工作的研究目的、方法和研究结果的概括与总结。摘要写得好与坏直接关系到论文是否被录用。一般来说,摘要必须回答"研究什么"、"怎么研究"、"得到了什么结果"、"结果说明了什么"等问题。此外,简短精练是其主要特点,只需简明扼要地概括了目的、方法、结果和结论即可。

1. 基本要求

摘要首先必须符合格式规范。第二,语言必须规范通顺、准确得体,用词要确切、恰如其分,而且要避免非通用的符号、缩略语、生偏词。另外,摘要的语气要客观,不要言过其实。

有相当数量的作者和审稿人认为,科技论文的撰写应使用第三人称、过去时和被动语态。但调查表明,科技论文中被动语态的使用在 1920—1970 年曾比较流行,但由于主动语态的表达更为准确,且更易阅读,因而目前大多数期刊都提倡使用主动态。国际知名科技期刊"Nature","Cell"等尤其如此,其中第一人称和主动语态的使用十分普遍。

(1)时态以简练为佳。

一般现在时:用于说明研究目的、叙述研究内容、描述结果、得出结论、提出建议或讨论等;公认的事实、自然规律、永恒真理等也要用一般现在时。

一般过去时:用于叙述过去某一时刻的发现、某一研究过程(实验、观察、调查、医疗等过程)。用一般过去时描述的发现、现象,往往尚不能确认为自然规律、永恒真理,只是当时的情况;所描述的研究过程也明显带有过去时间的痕迹。

现在完成时把过去发生的或过去已完成的事情与现在联系起来,而过去完成时可用来表示过去某一时间以前已经完成的事情,或在一个过去事情完成之前就已完成的另一过去行为。一般较少使用。

(2)语态要合适

采用何种语态,既要考虑摘要的特点,又要满足表达的需要。一篇摘要很短,尽量不要随便混用,更不要在一个句子里混用。

主动语态:摘要中谓语动词采用主动语态,有助于文字简洁、表达有力。

被动语态:以前强调多用被动语态,理由是科技论文主要是说明事实经过,至于那件事是谁做的,无需一一证明。为强调动作的承受者,最好采用被动语态;被动者无关紧要,也必须用被强调的事物做主语。

英文摘要的人称:原来摘要的首句多用第三人称 This paper... 等开头,现在倾向于采用更简洁的被动语态或原形动词开头。如:To describe..., To study..., To investigate..., To assess..., To determine...,行文时最好不用第一人称。

(3) 注意事项

冠词:主要是定冠词 the 易被漏用。the 用于表示整个群体、分类、时间、地名以及独一无二的事物、形容词最高级等较易掌握,用于特指时常被漏用。这里有个原则,即当我们用 the 时,听者或读者已经明确我们所指的是什么。

数词:避免用阿拉伯数字作首词。

单复数:一些名词单复数形式不易辨认,从而造成谓语形式出错。

使用短句:长句容易造成语义不清,但要避免单调和重复。

2. 内容与结构

从结构与内容来看,摘要一般都包括:

(1) 目的(objectives,purposes):包括研究背景、范围、内容、要解决的问题及解决这一问题的重要性和意义。

一般有"论文导向"与"研究导向"两类:论文导向多使用现在式,如 This paper presents...;研究导向则使用过去式,如 This study investigated...。

(2) 方法(methods and materials):包括材料、手段和过程。

介绍研究或试验过程时,常用词汇有:test, study, investigate, examine, experiment, discuss, consider, analyze, analysis 等。

说明研究或试验方法 常用词汇有:measure, estimate, calculate 等。

介绍应用、用途时,常用词汇有:use, apply, application 等。

(3) 结论(conclusions):主要结论,研究的价值和意义等。

介绍结论常用词汇有:summary, introduce, conclude 等;展示研究结果常用词汇有:show, result, present 等;陈述论文的论点和作者的观点常用词汇有:suggest, report, present, explain, expect, describe 等;阐明论证常用词汇有:support, provide, indicate, identify, find, demonstrate, confirm, clarify 等;推荐和建议常用词汇有:suggest, suggestion, recommend, recommendation, propose, necessity, necessary, expect 等。

另外,在摘要中不要用公式、参考文献等。要始终记住一点:Abstract 是一个独立的部分;换句话说,别人不看你的文章,只看你的 Abstract 就能了解你的研究工作。

3. 实例分析

根据上述内容与要求,下面以实例形式加以说明:

(1) The purpose of this study was to investigate the use of an automated design tool by non-designers, novice designers, and expert designers. A talk-aloud protocol, attitude survey, performance assessment, and direct observation were used to gather data. While the expert designers used the tool, they used it as a word processor with a rich database of instructional strategies. The novice designers relied on the tool for advice, guidance, and assistance in completing all the design tasks. Non-designers used the tool for learning about design.

The novice designer is likely to gain more benefits from using the tool than a naive or expert designer. Novice designers can use the tool to reinforce their prior knowledge as well as filling in any gaps in the knowledge of the design process. Based on this study, we might expect the use of an automated tool to diminish as the designer gains experience. Non-designers should probably be trained on instructional design tasks prior to exposure to automated instructional design tools.

分析:第一段第一句话指出了研究目的,即调查非设计者、新手设计者和专家设计者对教学设计自动化工具的使用,然后说明了此调查所收集的数据,即:"只管说"协议、态度调查、绩效评估和直接观察。接着将专家设计者、新手设计者和非设计者使用教学设计自动化工具的方式进行对比说明:专家设计者把工具当作有丰富教学策略资源的文字处理器,新手设计者主要依赖工具获得咨询、指导和帮助,以此来完成所有的设计任务,而非设计者则只是用来学习设计。第二段介绍了通过调查这些设计者对教学设计自动化工具的使用,发现新手设计者比另外的二者能获得更多的好处:既加强他们的先前知识,同时也填补设计过程中不知道的知识。最后作者给出了结论:由于设计者所获得的经验在不断增多,那么教学设计自动化工具可能会减少使用,而且,非设计者很可能必须在接触教学设计自动化工具前接收教学设计任务的训练。

(2) 翻译文摘:建构主义被当成一种最科学、最时兴的观点在国内传播和推广,它反映了时代精神的要求,具有先进性,然而对建构主义理论的理解和运用,常常会出现偏差。因此,本文对建构主义运用中存在的问题进行了辨析,目的在于使人们更科学、合理地理解和运用建构主义,促进教育教学改革。

分析:本摘要第一句介绍建构主义,然后一个"然而"引出了该论文的研究原因,因此,根据中文习惯可以将摘要翻译成:Constructivism serves as one of the most scientific and fashionable view to disseminate and promote in China. It reflects the spirit of the times with an advanced nature. However, there're often deviations in the comprehension and utilization。接下来,本摘要介绍了该论文的内容及目的,我们可以采用两种方式进行翻译:

采用主动语态:This paper analyzes the problems in the utilization of constructivism and its goal is to make people understand and apply constructivism more scientificly and rationally and to promote educational reform.

采用被动语态:The problems in the utilization of constructivism are analyzed in this paper and the goal of this paper is to make people understand and apply constructivism more scientificly and rationally and to promote educational reform.

这里采用主动语态更合适一些,因为采用主动语态能使整个句子更简洁;此外,"被当成"利用词汇"serve as"而不是"treat as"较为准确。

在英文摘要的撰写中,还应注意以下几点:

(1) 力求简捷。如:at a temperature of 250℃ to 300℃→at 250 to 300℃;at a high pressure of 2 kPa→at 2 kPa;has been found to increase→increased;from the experimental results, it can be concluded that→the results show。

(2) 能用名词作定语的尽量不用动名词作定语,能用形容词作定语的尽量不用名词作定语。如 measuring accuracy→measurement accuracy;experiment results→experimental results。

（3）可直接用名词或名词短语作定语的情况下，要少用 of 句型。如 accuracy of measurement→measurement accuracy；structure of crystal→crystal structure。

（4）可用动词的情况下尽量避免用动词的名词形式。如 Measurement of thickness of plastic sheet was made→Thickness of plastic sheet was measured。

（5）一个名词不宜用多个前置形容词来修饰，可改用复合词，兼用后置定语。如 thermal oxidation apparent activation energy→Apparent active energy of thermo-oxidation。

（6）描述作者的工作一般用过去时态（因为工作是在过去做的），但陈述这些工作所得出的结论时，应该用现在时态。

（7）一般应使用动词的主动语态，如 B is exceeded by A→A exceeds B。

（8）尽量用短句。

## 三、主体

科技论文是集假说、数据和结论为一体的概括性描述，而论文的主体则是对研究工作进行具体描述。论文主体的撰写一般始于论文提纲。论文提纲是一篇论文的行文计划，是论文目的、假说、内容与结论最清楚的表述形式。

论文提纲主要解决三个问题：A. 为什么我要做这件工作，主要的目的和假设是什么？B. 我的研究方法与结果是什么？C. 这一结果意味着什么？意义何在？提纲本身应该文字简练、思路完整。如果提纲准备充分，那么正文组织起来就更容易。

一般论文提纲与相对应的主体部分包括相关研究简介（Introduction）、研究方法或者系统制作（Methods）、实验与讨论（Experiment & Discussion）与结论（Conclusion）几个部分。

**基本结构及其要求**

（1）Introduction

Introduction 是本项研究的导读，主要包括：谁做了什么、做得怎么样、我们做了哪些工作、做得怎样。Introduction 要体现出一篇论文的初衷和创新要素。外刊论文对于 Introduction 的要求是非常高的，可以毫不夸张地说，写出一个好的 Introduction 就相当于文章成功了一半。

要写好一个 Introduction，最重要的是要保持层次感和逻辑性。

首先，要阐述自己的研究领域，尽量简洁；

其次，相关工作的总结回顾，要把该领域内的过去和现在的状况全面地概括总结出来，不能有丝毫的遗漏，特别是要概括出最新的进展和过去经典文献的引用，否则，很可能意味着你做得不够深入或者全面；

再次，分析过去研究的局限性，并且阐明自己研究的创新点。阐述局限性时要客观公正、实事求是。在阐述自己的创新点时，要紧紧地围绕过去研究的缺陷性来描述，完整而清晰地描述自己的解决思路。中文文章的特点是要求有创新性，而英文文章的特点恰恰相反：深入系统地解决一到两个问题就算相当不错了。

最后，在 Introduction 的结尾总结论文的研究内容。

（2）Methods

Methods部分是描述论文的实践过程，应该按照逻辑思维规律来组织结构，包含材料、内容、概念、判断、推理、最终形成观点。通常按照研究对象可分为：以系统为主的研究论文与以方法研究为主的论文。以系统为主的研究论文主要介绍系统的设计或制作；以方法研究为主的论文主要介绍某种研究方法，一般包括实验方法与理论推理两种。由于研究对象千差万别，Methods部分很难形成统一的模式，但是它们的主要构件一般包括：

- 研究目的

研究目的是正文的开篇，要写得简明扼要、重点突出。先介绍为什么要进行这个研究，通过研究要达到什么目的。如果课题涉及面较广，论文只拟写其某一方面，那么研究目的部分就要写清本文着重探索哪一方面的问题。另外还要交代探索原因、效果或方法。

- 研究方法

科研课题从开始到成果的全过程，都要运用实验材料、设备以及观察方法。因此，应说明所选用的材料、设备和实验的方法，以便他人据此重复验证。

- 研究过程

研究过程主要说明研究的技术路线以及具体操作步骤。对于实验型研究，主要说明试验条件、实验设备和操作过程；对于理论性研究，主要说明问题的假设、推理工具与推理过程，力求使研究具有严谨的科学性、逻辑性。

- 实验结果或仿真结果分析与讨论

该部分是整篇论文的心脏部分。一切实验成败由此判断，一切推理由此导出，一切议论由此引出。因此，应该充分表达，并且采用表格、图解、照片等附件。要尽量压缩众所周知的评论，突出本研究的新发现以及经过证实的新观点、新见解。这一部分一般应包括：主要原理或概念、实验条件；本研究的结果与他人研究结果的相同或差异；解释因果关系，论证其必然性；提出本研究所存在的问题或尚需探索的问题。

此外，Methods撰写中特别要注意表述的完整性和科学性。

（3）Conclusion

该部分是整个研究的总结，是全篇论文的归宿，具有画龙点睛的作用。一般说来，读者选读某篇论文时，常常是先看标题、摘要、前言，再看结论，然后才能决定阅读与否。因此，结论写作也是很重要的。撰写结论时，不仅要对研究的全过程、实验的结果、数据等进行进一步的综合分析，准确反映客观事物的本质及其规律，而且，对论证的材料、选用的实例、语言表达的概括性、科学性和逻辑性等方方面面，也都要一一进行总判断、总推理、总评价。同时，撰写时，不是简单复述前面论述的结果，而是要与引言相呼应，与正文其他部分相联系。总之，结论要有说服力，恰如其分。语言要准确、鲜明。结论中，凡归结为一个认识、肯定一种观点、否定一种意见，都要有事实、有根据，不能想当然，不能含糊其辞，不能用"大概"、"可能"、"或许"等词语。如果论文得不出结论，也不要硬写。凡不写结论的论文，可对实验结果进行一番深入的讨论。

此外，论文在内容上，要思路清晰、层次分明、逻辑性强；在文字表述上，要语句通顺、通俗易懂、文字简练准确;特别要强调的是,表格与图像图形信息能够达到文字描述所不易达到的效果。表格的优点是能够清晰地展示文章的第一手结果,便于后人在研究时进行引用和对比;图的优点在于能够将数据的变化趋势灵活地表现出来,表达上更为直接和富于感染力。总体上来说,图表应该结合使用,取长补短,使结果的展现更加丰富。

## 四、其他

### 1. Order of Authors and Affiliation

科技论文的作者在享受科技成果和荣誉的同时也应承担相应的责任。严谨的科学工作者并不会无原则地分享成果和荣誉。要成为一篇论文的作者,必须对论文的思想和写作有实质性的贡献。只要你的名字在论文作者中,你就要对整篇文章负全部责任。实际上,很多著名学者事后往往会后悔成为某些论文的作者;当导师和研究生合作的论文出现问题时,导师无论怎样辩白都是十分无力的。国内学生与导师尤其要注意这个问题。

科技论文作者的署名顺序也需特别注意,许多著名学者也会因为科技论文的署名问题导致合作关系破灭。通常,署名顺序取决于学科领域与学会的惯例,如在医学界,署名顺序一般根据作者的资历来决定,第一作者一般是实验室主任或者是课题负责人;又如某些领域,作者的署名往往根据作者姓氏顺序来决定。

一般认为文章的成果是属于通讯作者的,说明思路是通讯作者的;而第一作者是最主要的参与者,应该说,通讯作者多数情况下和第一作者是同一个人。通讯作者的另一个好处是能和外界建立更广泛的联系,这会大大地提高他(她)在科学界的地位。

现在,大多数作者建议按照作者的贡献来确定作者的署名顺序,因为这样比较公平,也符合 IEEE 与 IEE 的惯例。为了避免出现争议,建议慷慨分享成果和荣誉。从长期合作的角度出发,某一篇论文的署名顺序并不重要。

大家知道,中国人人名与外国人人名顺序也有差异,中国人姓在前,名在后;而外国人名在前,姓在后。如中文名字曹晓红,则英文应写成 Xiaohong Cao;有些外国学者了解中国人的姓氏习惯,又有可能把本已经正确的英文名字 Xiaohong Cao 理解成 Xiaohong 为姓氏、Cao 为名字。鉴于这一点,更多学者建议采用 Xiao-hong Cao 这样的写法。

通常,如果有多个作者,则应在作者姓名的右上角用阿拉伯数字标明作者所在的单位。由于各国各单位对成果的归属都有较严格的控制,因此,不要使用几个大写字母所组成的完全缩写或简称,单位内部级别按照从小到大的顺序。如:

Xiao-hua Xia[1], Alan S. I. Zinober[2]

[1] Department of Educational Technology, University of Pretoria, South Africa

[2] Department of Applied Mathematics, The University of Sheffield, Sheffield S10 2TN, UK

### 2. Keywords

关键词(Keywords)是论文的文献检索标识,是表达文献主体概念的自然语言词汇。列出关键词有助于读者理解全文,同时便于查阅和检索。

按照 GB7713-87 规定:关键词一般使用名词形式,词数为 3—6 个,以显著的字符另起一行,排在摘要的下方。关键词的选用要语义准确,能概括出论文所要论述的主要内容或中心,要尽可能避免词汇的语义过宽或过窄。

3. Acknowledgement

通常,Acknowledge 包含两个主要的内容:第一是表明研究的基金来源,如中国的国家自然科学基金(Nature Science Foundation of China,NSFC)等。写基金的时候一般都要标注清楚基金号(Grant Number),只有这样才算是该项基金的研究成果;第二是对参与人员(没有列在作者中的研究人员)和单位表示感谢,有时候还要添加上对编辑(editor)和匿名审稿人(anonymous reviewers)的感谢,这是一种基本的礼貌。

下面给出几个例子:
- This work is supported by Bogazici University Research Fund (Project No: 99A202).
- This project is supported by Perkins Engines, TRW and EPSRC Grant Reference GR/L42018. The invaluable assistance of our colleague Mr. John Twiddle during the data capture phase of this work is gratefully acknowledged.
- Financial support for the present work was granted by the Iranian Telecommunication Research Center under grant number T500/10177. The authors, hereby, gratefully acknowledge this support.
- We would like to thank an anonymous reviewer for assistance with the proof of Theorem 1. This research was partially supported by the Engineering and Physical Sciences Research Council (EPSRC), United Kingdom, by Grant GR/S41050/01, and partially supported by the RSA-China Scientific Agreement.

下面给出几个中国基金项目的翻译:
- 国家自然科学基金:Chinese National Natural Science Foundation.
- 国家"863 计划"(国家高技术研究发展计划项目):Chinese National Programs for High Technology Research and Development
- 国家"973 项目"(国家基础研究发展规划项目):Key Project of Chinese National Programs for Fundamental Research
- 国家"十五"重点科技攻关项目:The 10th Five Years Key Programs for Science and Technology Development
- 国家杰出青年科学基金:National Science Foundation for Distinguished Young Scholars

4. Reference

References 的重点在于格式。不同的杂志对于参考文献的格式要求不一样。作者一般要注意以下几个问题。

作者:有的是简写在前,有的简写在后,有的简写有点,有的简写没有点。

文章:有的要加上引号,有的没有引号;

文章的期刊:有的要简写,有的要全称,有的要斜体,有的则不需要;

文章年和期卷号的顺序:有的是年在前,有的是年在后;

文献的排列顺序：有的是按照字母的顺序，有的则是按照在论文中出现的顺序用阿拉伯数字排序。

下面给出实例如下：

• Tao, C. W., Chan, M.-L., & Lee, T.-T. (2003). Adaptive fuzzy sliding mode controller for linear systems with mismatched time-varying uncertainties. *IEEE Transactions on Systems, Man, and Cybernetics—Part B: Cybernetics*, 33(2), 283—293.

• Harb A. Nonlinear chaos control in a permanent magnet reluctance machine. Chaos, Solitons & Fractals 2004;19(5):1217—24.

• B. K. Yoo, W. C. Ham, Adaptive control of robot manipulator using fuzzy compensator, IEEE Trans. Fuzzy Systems 8 (2000) 186.

以上是一般科技论文参考文献的格式。请注意：在不同的格式中有些年代写在前面，有些在后面；有些作者写完后用"，"，有些则用"."；有些把页码写全，如283—293，有些只写初始页码，如283。

• A. J. Koivo, Fundamentals for Control of Robotic Manipulators, *Wiley, New York*, 1989.

参考书籍的格式，一般会写明出版社、地点、年代以及版本号。

• Silpa-Anan C, Brinsmead T, Abdallah S, Zelinsky A. Preliminary experiments in visual servo control for autonomous underwater vehicle. IEEE/RSJ international conference on intelligent robotics and systems (IROS); 2001. Available from: http://www.syseng.anu.edu.au/rsl/.

有些参考文献是通过网络获取的，通常也应该注明。

此外，有些杂志在标注所引用的论文时，还特别要注明文献类别，如专著 monograph(M)、论文集 conference(C)、期刊 journal(J)、学位论文 doctrinal(D)、报告 report(R)、标准 standard(S)与专利 patent(P)，具体可以参考中华人民共和国国家标准 UDC 025.32 与 GB 7714-87。

5. Supplement

前面已经谈到，适当的表格与图像图形信息能够达到文字描述所不易达到的效果，使表达更为直接和富于感染力。一般来说，表格与图像图形应该出现在正文引用部分的适当位置。有时，为了文章的简洁清晰，作者常常把复杂的表述放在文章结尾处 Supplement 中，如某定理的公式证明、某方法的详细描述等。

# Part 6　Network Education

## Unit 17　Distance Education

▲ **Knowledge Objectives**

When you have completed this unit, you will be able to:

◆ Know about Distance Education, the key players in it and the ways Distance Education is delivered

◆ State the four generations of Distance Education and the comparison of the characteristics of delivery technologies

◆ Understand "the 4-Square Map of Groupware Options" that was developed by Johansen et. al. in 1991

◆ State the content of future research of Distance Education

▲ **Professional Terms**

| | |
|---|---|
| distance education | 远程教育 |
| audioconferencing | 电话会议 |
| slide | 幻灯片 |
| moving images | 动态影像 |
| computer-assisted instruction (CAI) | 计算机辅助教育 |
| computer-managed instruction (CMI) | 计算机管理教学 |
| computer-mediated education (CME) | 计算机媒体教育 |
| computer application | 计算机应用 |
| study guide | 学习指导书 |
| visually oriented | 视觉导向 |
| courseware | 课件 |
| correspondence education | 函授教育 |
| computer managed learning (CML) | 计算机管理学习 |
| computer assisted learning (CAL) | 计算机辅助学习 |
| audio-teleconferencing | 声音电传会议 |
| audiographic communication systems | 视讯图像通信系统 |
| interactive multimedia (IMM) | 交互式媒体 |
| on-campus education | 在校教育 |

| computer mediated communication (CMC) | 计算机媒介通信 |
| asynchronous communication | 异步通信 |
| Integrated Services Digital Network (ISDN) | 综合服务数字网络 |
| integrated telecommunication systems | 综合电信系统 |
| groupware | 组件,群件 |

# Text A

## Distance Education: An Overview[①]

### What is Distance Education?

Figure 17-1  The Continuing and Distance Education programs providing for distance learners

Within a context of rapid technological change and shifting market conditions, the American education system is challenged with providing increased educational opportunities without increased budgets. Many educational institutions are answering this challenge by developing distance education programs. (Figure 17-1) At its most basic level, distance education takes place when a teacher and student(s) are separated by physical distance, and technology (i.e., voice, video, data, and print), often in concert with face-to-face communication, is used to bridge the instructional gap.[1] These types of programs can provide adults with a second chance at a college education, reach those disadvantaged by limited time, distance or physical disability, and update the knowledge base of workers at their places of employment.

### Is Distance Education Effective?

Many educators ask if distant students learn as much as students receiving traditional face-to-face instruction. Research comparing distance education to traditional face-to-face instruction indicates that teaching and studying at a distance can be as effective as traditional instruction, when the method and technologies used are appropriate to the instructional tasks, there is student-to-student interaction, and when there is timely teacher-to-student feedback.[2]

### How is Distance Education Delivered?

A wide range of technological options are available to the distance educator. They fall into four major categories:

 Voice—Instructional audio tools include the interactive technologies of telephone,

---

① http://www.uidaho.edu/eo/dist1.html

audioconferencing (Figure 17-2), and short-wave radio. Passive (i.e., one-way) audio tools include tapes and radio.

Figure 17-2  The Audio conferencing using the special conference phone that automatically adapts to each meeting environment, providing high fidelity voice clarity for all participants

Video—Instructional video tools include still images such as slides, pre-produced moving images (e.g., videotape [Figure 17-3], film), and real-time moving images combined with audioconferencing (one-way or two-way video with two-way audio).

Data—Computers send and receive information electronically. For this reason, the term "data" is used to describe this broad category of instructional tools. Computer applications for distance education are varied and include:

Figure 17-3  An example of video tapes

- Computer-assisted instruction (CAI)—uses the computer as a self-contained teaching machine to present individual lessons.
- Computer-managed instruction (CMI)—uses the computer to organize instruction and track student records and progress. The instruction itself need not be delivered via a computer, although CAI is often combined with CMI.
- Computer-mediated education (CME)—describes computer applications that facilitate the delivery of instruction. Examples include electronic mail, fax, real-time computer conferencing, and World-Wide Web applications.

Print—is a foundational element of distance education programs and the basis from which all other delivery systems have evolved. Various print formats are available including: textbooks, study guides, workbooks, course syllabi (Figure 17-4), and case studies.

**Which Technology is Best?**

Although technology plays a key role in the delivery of distance education, educators must remain focused on instructional outcomes, not the technology of delivery. The key to effective distance education is focusing on the needs of the learners, the requirements of the content, and the constraints faced by the teacher, before selecting a delivery system. Typically, this systematic approach will result in a mix of media, each serving a specific purpose. For example:

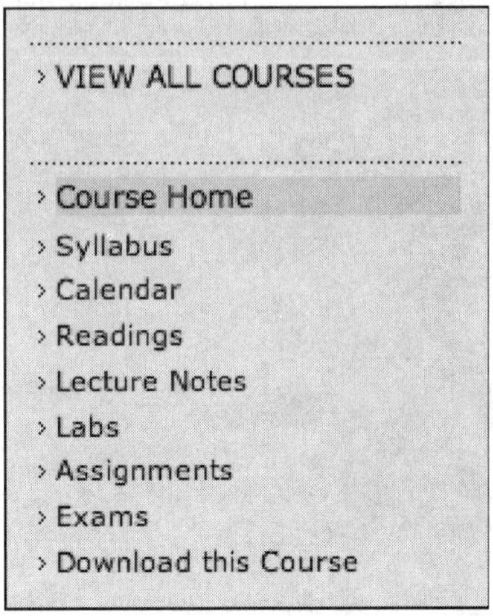

• A strong print component can provide much of the basic instructional content in the form of a course text, as well as readings, the syllabus, and day-to-day schedule.

• Interactive audio or video conferencing can provide real time face-to-face (or voice-to-voice) interaction. This is also an excellent and cost-effective way to incorporate guest speakers and content experts.

• Computer conferencing (Figure 17-5) or electronic mail can be used to send messages, assignment feedback, and other targeted communication to one or more class members. It can also be used to increase interaction among students.

Figure 17-4 Course syllabi typically contain information such as the course description and objectives, as well as textbooks used in the course, a calendar of lectures and homework, collaboration guidelines, and grading criteria.

Figure 17-5 Computer conferencing—attendees can see the visual presentation and enjoy 2-way communication.

Figure 17-6 An example of fax, which allows you to transmit pieces of paper to someone else instantly

• Pre-recorded video tapes can be used to present class lectures and visually oriented content.

• Fax (Figure 17-6) can be used to distribute assignments, last minute announcements, to receive student assignments, and to provide timely feedback.

Using this integrated approach, the educator's task is to carefully select among the technological options. The goal is to build a mix of instructional media, meeting the needs of the learner in a manner that is instructionally effective and economically prudent.

## Effective Distance Education

Without exception, effective distance education programs begin with careful planning and a focused understanding of course requirements and student needs. Appropriate technology can only be selected once these elements are understood in detail. There is no mystery to the way effective distance education programs develop. They don't happen spontaneously; they evolve through the hard work and dedicated efforts of many individuals and organizations. In fact, successful distance education programs rely on the consistent and integrated efforts of students, faculty, facilitators, support staff, and administrators.

## Key Players in Distance Education

The following briefly describes the roles of these key players in the distance education enterprise and the challenges they face.

**Students**—Meeting the instructional needs of students is the cornerstone of every effective distance education program, and the test by which all efforts in the field are judged. Regardless of the educational context, the primary role of the student is to learn. This is a daunting task under the best of circumstances, requiring motivation, planning, and an ability to analyze and apply the instructional content being taught. When instruction is delivered at a distance, additional challenges result because students are often separated from others sharing their backgrounds and interests, have few if any opportunities to interact with teachers outside of class, and must rely on technical linkages to bridge the gap separating class participants. [3]

**Faculty**—The success of any distance education effort rests squarely on the shoulders of the faculty. In a traditional classroom setting (Figure 17-7), the instructor's responsibility includes assembling course content and developing an understanding of student needs. Special challenges confront those teaching at a distance. For example, the instructor must:

Figure 17-7 A traditional classroom setting is often set with the desks in rows and teachers instructing in the front of learners.

- Develop an understanding of the characteristics and needs of distant students with little first-hand experience and limited, if any, face-to-face contact.
- Adapt teaching styles taking into consideration the needs and expectations of multiple,

often diverse, audiences.

• Develop a working understanding of delivery technology, while remaining focused on their teaching role.

• Function effectively as a skilled facilitator as well as content provider.

**Facilitators**—The instructor often finds it beneficial to rely on a site facilitator to act as a bridge between the students and the instructor. To be effective, a facilitator must understand the students being served and the instructor's expectations. Most importantly, the facilitator must be willing to follow the directive established by the teacher. Where budget and logistics permit, the role of on-site facilitators has increased even in classes in which they have little, if any, content expertise. At a minimum, they set up equipment, collect assignments, proctor tests, and act as the instructor's on-site eyes and ears.

**Support Staff**—These individuals are the silent heroes of the distance education enterprise and ensure that the myriad details required for program success are dealt with effectively. Most successful distance education programs consolidate support service functions to include student registration, materials duplication and distribution, textbook ordering, securing of copyright clearances, facilities scheduling, processing grade reports, managing technical resources, etc. Support personnel are truly the glue that keeps the distance education effort together and on track.

**Administrators**—Although administrators are typically influential in planning an institution's distance education program, they often lose contact or relinquish control to technical managers once the program is operational. Effective distance education administrators are more than idea people. They are consensus builders, decision makers, and referees. They work closely with technical and support service personnel, ensuring that technological resources are effectively deployed to further the institution's academic mission. Most importantly, they maintain an academic focus, realizing that meeting the instructional needs of distant students is their ultimate responsibility.

## Text B

### Distance Education, Face to Face Teaching and Technology[①]

Although Moses is regarded by many as the first external student, it was not until print technology replaced tablets of stone (Figure 17-8) as the medium of instruction that correspondence education became an accepted part of mass public education systems.[4] The Correspondence Model, regarded generally as the first generation of distance education, has since been subsumed by the second generation Multi-media Model of distance education, which entails the use of highly-developed and refined teaching-learning resources, including printed study

---

① http://www.usq.edu.au/users/taylorj/readings/4thgen.htm

guides, selected readings, videotapes, audiotapes (Figure 17-9), and computer-based courseware, including computer managed learning (CML), computer assisted learning (CAL), and interactive video (disk and tape).[5] While many institutions have evolved from using the Correspondence Model to the Multi-media Model, another significant trend is to move towards the third generation Telelearning Model of distance education. This third generation of distance education is based on the use of information technologies, including audio-teleconferencing, audiographic communication systems, video conferencing and broadcast television/radio with attendant audio-teleconferencing. The emerging fourth generation of distance education, the Flexible Learning Model, promises to combine the benefits of high quality CD-ROM based interactive multimedia (IMM), with the enhanced interactivity and access to an increasingly extensive range of teaching-learning resources offered by connection to the Internet. While distance educators continue to eagerly experiment with all four generations of technological development, on-campus education could perhaps be justifiably characterised as still leaning heavily on the first generation of technology (ie print). This point is not meant to devalue the potential for face to face teaching to enhance learning, but such interactivity is only one aspect of the interaction required for effective learning.

Figure 17-8  Tablets of stone, once as the medium of instruction

Figure 17-9  audiotape

As Bates has highlighted, there are two very different types of interactivity in learning: social and individual. Social interaction between learners and teachers needs to be balanced with the individual student's interaction with teaching-learning resources, including textbooks, study guides, audiotapes, videotapes and computer assisted learning programs. He argues that the view that students in conventional institutions are engaged for the greater part of their time in meaningful, face to face interaction is a myth, and that: "for both conventional and distance education students, by far the largest part of their studying is done alone, interacting with textbooks and other learning media."[6] One of the strengths of the Multi-media Model of distance education is that it has concentrated efforts on improving the quality of the student's individual

Figure 17-10  Audio-teleconferencing, which has a speakerphone including a programmable Digital Signal Processor (DSP) for receiving a conference audio signal

interaction with learning materials, such as specially designed printed materials, audiotapes, videotapes and computer-based learning packages, aimed at teaching concepts and cognitive skills associated with clearly defined objectives in the context of a coherent curriculum. Distance educators have also recognized the need to provide opportunities for social interaction to support effective learning and have therefore tried to simulate face to face communication through the development of instructional systems based on technologies such as audio-teleconferencing (Figure 17-10), audiographic communication systems, videoconferencing (Figure 17-11) and computer mediated communication (CMC) that can support contiguous two-way communication between students and teachers. Alternatively, residential school's local tutors have been used to provide for the social interaction that can facilitate effective learning. It is worth noting that the necessary balance between social and individual interactivity will vary from course to course and will be a function of such variables as the type of subject matter, the specific objectives of the course and the structure and quality of the learning materials, and not least the student target audience.[7]

Figure 17-11  They're conducting a videoteleconference at the office.

Because the clientele for distance education consists largely of part-time students in full-time employment, distance educators have had to provide teaching-learning resources (printed study guides, audiotapes, videotapes, computer-based courseware, etc.) of high quality that could be used at a time and in a place convenient to each student. In effect, these "flexible access" technologies allow the student to turn the teacher on, or off, at will as lifestyle permits. Similarly, access to the Internet facilitates is also interactively, without sacrificing the benefits of flexible access, since it can be used to support asynchronous communication. Such flexibility has a major pedagogical benefit—it allows students to progress at their own pace. Thus varying rates of individual progression can be accommodated, unlike typical conventional educational practices where the whole class tends to progress at the same pace in synchronisation with the delivery of information through mass lectures and tutorials. Some of the characteristics of the various models of distance education that are relevant to the quality of teaching and learning are summarised in Table 1.

Table 1  Models of Distance Education: A Conceptual Framework

| Models of Distance Education and Associated Delivery Technologies | Characteristics of Delivery Technologies | | | |
|---|---|---|---|---|
| | Flexible Access | Flexible Student Progression | Highly Refined Materials | Advanced Interactive Delivery |
| **First Generation—The Correspondence Model** | | | | |
| ● Print | Yes | Yes | Yes | No |
| **Second Generation—The Multimedia Model** | | | | |
| ● Print | Yes | Yes | Yes | No |
| ● Audiotape | Yes | Yes | Yes | No |
| ● Videotape | Yes | Yes | Yes | No |
| ● Computer-based learning (e.g. CML/CAL) | Yes | Yes | Yes | Yes |
| ● Interactive video (disk and tape) | Yes | Yes | Yes | Yes |
| ● Interactive multimedia (IMM) | Yes | Yes | Yes | Yes |
| **Third Generation—The Telelearning Model** | | | | |
| ● Audioteleconferencing | No | No | No | Yes |
| ● Videoconferencing | No | No | No | Yes |
| ● Audiographic Communication (e.g. Smart 2000) | No | No | Yes | Yes |
| ● Broadcast TV/Radio + Audioteleconferencing | No | No | Yes | Yes |
| **Fourth Generation—The Flexible Learning Model** | | | | |
| ● Interactive multimedia (IMM) | Yes | Yes | Yes | Yes |
| ● Computer mediated communication (CMC) (e.g. Email, CoSy etc.) | Yes | Yes | No | Yes |

# Text C

## Distance Learning Technologies[①]

Until the advent of telecommunications technologies, distance educators were hard pressed to provide for two-way real time interaction, or time-delayed interaction between students and the instructor or among peers. In the correspondence model of distance education, which emphasized learner independence, the main instructional medium was print and it was usually delivered using the postal service. Interaction between the student and the instructor usually took the form of correspondence of self-assessment exercises that the student completed and sent to

---

① http://seamonkey.ed.asu.edu/~mcisaac/dechapter/

the instructor for feedback. Formal group work or collaborative learning was very rare in distance education even though attempts have been made to facilitate group activities at local study centers. Also, traditionally, distance education courses were designed with a heavy emphasis on learner independence and were usually self-contained. With the development of synchronous (two-way, real time interactive technologies) such as audio teleconferencing, audio graphics conferencing and videoconferencing it is now possible to link learners and instructors who are geographically separated for real time interaction. However, the type of interaction that takes place is usually on a one-to-one basis, between one learner and another and between one learner and the instructor at one particular time. These technologies are not very suitable for promoting cooperative learning between groups of learners located at different sites. Also, the synchronous nature of these technologies may not be suitable or convenient for many distance learners.

The asynchronous (time-delayed) feature of computer-mediated communications (CMC), on the other hand, offers an advantage because the CMC class is open 24 hours a day, seven days a week to accommodate the time schedules of distance learners. Although CMC systems may be either synchronous (real-time), or asynchronous (time-delayed), it is asynchronous CMC, because of it's time independent feature that is an important medium for facilitating cooperative group work among distance learners.

Current developments in digital communications and the convergence of telecommunications technologies exemplified by international standards such as ISDN (Integrated Services Digital Network), make available audio, video, graphic and data communication through an ordinary telephone line on a desk top workstation (Figure 17-12). Therefore, as we look at distance learning technologies today and look to the future, it is important to think in terms of integrated telecommunication systems rather than simply video vs. audio, vs. data systems. More and more institutions that teach at a distance are moving toward multi-media systems integrating a combination of technologies both synchronous and asynchronous that meets learner's needs. Therefore, while in the 1970's and 1980's many distance education institutions throughout the world used print as a major delivery medium, by the year 2000 many institutions will probably have adopted telecommunications-based systems (Figure 17-13) for the delivery of distance education. This does not necessarily mean that print will no longer be used in distance education. It is more likely that print will be used as a supplementary medium in most telecommunications-based systems, and better ways of communicating information through print will be investigated and incorporated into the design of study guides and other print-based media. [8]

Figure 17-12  A desktop workstation enables audio, video, graphic and data communication through an ordinary telephone line.

Figure 17-13  The telecommunication facility providing the wireless communications

In order to describe the technologies used in distance education we have selected "The 4-Square Map of Groupware Options" (Figure 17-14) that was developed by Johansen et. al. which is based on recent research in groupware. This model seemed most suitable to our purpose because we see distance education moving from highly individualized forms of instruction as in correspondence education, to formats that encourage teaching students as a group and collaborative learning among peers. The 4-Square Map of Groupware Option model is premised on two basic configurations that teams must cope with as they work: time and place. Teams or groups of people who work together on a common goal deal with their work in the same place at the same time as in face-to-face meetings, and sometimes they must work apart in different places and at different times as in the use of asynchronous computer conferencing. They also need to handle two other variations: being in different places at the same time as in the use of telephones for an audio teleconference, and at the same place at different times as in workplaces, study centers (Figure 17-15) or laboratories (Figure 17-16). Based on these configurations, the four square model classifies four types of technologies that support the group process: 1. Same Time/Same Place, 2. Different Time/Different Place, 3. Same Time/Different Place, and 4. Same Place/Different Time. These four categories are used for describing technologies that currently support distance teaching and learning.

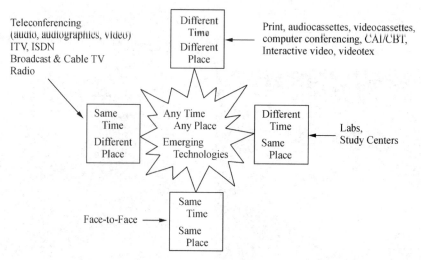

Figure 17-14  The Four Square Map of Distance Education Technology Options

Figure 17-15  Study center, in which Instructors and student tutors are available to answer questions, encourage, and support students

Figure 17-16  laboratory

## Text D

## Summary and Recommendations for the Future of Distance Education[①]

Distance education programs will continue to grow both in the United States and abroad. One of the reasons for this growth is related to the ever growing global need for an educated workforce combined with financial constraints of established educational systems. Distance education offers life-long learning potential to working adults and will play a significant part in educating societies around the world. Distance education will become of far greater importance in the United States in the years ahead because it is so cost efficient and because it allows for independent learning by working adults. If society is to cope with this growing need for an educated workforce, distance education must continue to make its place in the educational community.

Although distance education has been difficult to establish in a number of European countries, influential networks are being established to facilitate future growth. The European Association of Distance Teaching Universities (EADTU) have combined with Eurostep (which organizes educational television across Europe using satellite) and the Budapest Platform (providing satellite television to central and eastern countries) to develop a system of distance education programs throughout Europe. Distance education programs will become major components facilitating economic progress throughout the world.

Future research should focus on establishing theoretical frameworks as a basis for research, and should examine the interactions of technology with teaching and learning. Researchers should address issues of achievement, motivation, attrition, and control.

Distance education is no longer viewed as a marginal educational activity. Instead, it is regarded internationally as a viable and cost effective way of providing individualized instruction. Recent developments in technology are erasing the lines between traditional and distance learners as more students have the opportunity to work with multimedia designed for individual and interactive learning. Print, once was the primary method of instructional delivery, is now taking a backseat to modern interactive technologies.

The content of future research should:
- Move beyond media comparison studies
- Examine the characteristics of the distance learner and investigate the collaborative effects of media attributes and cognition
- Explore the relationship between media and the socio-cultural construction of knowledge
- Identify course design elements effective in interactive learning systems

---

[①] http://seamonkey.ed.asu.edu/~mcisaac/dechapter/

- Contribute to a shared international research database
- Examine the cultural effects of technology and courseware transfer in distance education programs

Research methodologies should:
- Avoid micro-analyses
- Progress beyond early descriptive studies
- Generate a substantive research base by conducting longitudinal and collaborative studies
- Identify and develop appropriate conceptual frameworks from related disciplines such as cognitive psychology, social learning theory, critical theory, communication theory and social science theories
- Conduct thorough qualitative studies which identify the combination of personal, social and educational elements that create a successful environment for the independent learner

Combine qualitative and experimental methodologies, where appropriate, to enrich research findings. Technology may be driving the rapid rise in popularity of distance education, but it is the well designed instructional situation which allows the learner to interact with the technology in the construction of knowledge. It is the effective interaction of instructor, student and delivery system that affords distance education its prominence within the educational community. Distance education can offer the opportunity for a research based and practical integration of technology, instruction and instructor, and create a successful educational package.

## New Words

self-contained   *adj.* 设备齐全的,独立的,沉默寡言的
syllabus   *n.* 教学大纲;课程提纲
cost-effective   *adj.* 有成本效益的,划算的
incorporate   *vt.* 1. 包含,加上,吸收 2. 把……合并,使并入 3. 组成公司
prudent   *adj.* 审慎的;有先见之明的;判断力强的
consistent   *adj.* 1. 一贯的,始终如一的 2. 一致的,符合的
facilitator   *n.* 推进者,促进者,协助者
daunting   *adj.* 使人畏缩的
logistics   后勤学,后勤
proctor   *n.* (大学的)学监,监考人
myriad   *adj.* 无数的 *n.* 无数,极大数量
consolidate   *vt. & vi.* 1. (使)巩固;(使)加强 2. (使)合并
duplication   *n.* 复制,重复
relinquish   *vt.* 1. 交出,让给 2. 放弃
deploy   *vt.* (尤指军事行动)使……展开;施展;部署
subsume   *vt.* 归入,包括

contiguous　*adj.* 接触的,邻近的,共同的

clientele　*n.* 委托人

advent　*n.* 出现,到来

attrition　*n.* 消耗;消磨,磨损

marginal　*adj.* 1. 在页边的 2. 不重要的,微小的,少量的 3. 仅以微弱多数票获胜的

viable　*adj.* 1. 切实可行的;可实施的 2. 能自行生产发育的

backseat　*n.* 后座,次要位置

longitudinal　*adj.* 经度的,纵向的

## Notes

[1] At its most basic level, distance education takes place when a teacher and student (s) are separated by physical distance, and technology (i.e., voice, video, data, and print), often in concert with face-to-face communication, is used to bridge the instructional gap.

**译文:**远程教育基本上是由于老师和学生的实际距离太远而引起的,而像音频、视频、数据和印刷物等技术通常作为面对面交流的补充被用来弥补教育上的不足。

• when a teacher and student(s) are separated 是时间状语从句,由连词 when 引导,用来修饰主句的谓语。

• 由 when 引导的状语从句中有两个主语,分别为 a teacher and student(s) 和 technology。

• in concert with 和……相呼应(合作)

[2] Research comparing distance education to traditional face-to-face instruction indicates that teaching and studying at a distance can be as effective as traditional instruction, when the method and technologies used are appropriate to the instructional tasks, there is student-to-student interaction, and when there is timely teacher-to-student feedback.

**译文:**远程教育和传统的面对面授课之间的比较研究表明,当远程教育所使用的方法和技术与教学任务相适应后出现了学生之间的互动,并且当学生和老师之间存在及时的反馈的话,远程教学可以像传统教学一样有效。

• comparing distance education to traditional face-to-face instruction 是现在分词做后置定语,用来修饰主语 research。

• when the method and technologies used are appropriate to the instructional tasks, there is student-to-student interaction, and when there is timely teacher-to-student feedback 是由 when 引导的时间状语从句,用来修饰主句的谓语,第二个 when 同样如此。

• at a distance 在远处

• appropriate to 适合于,与……相适应

[3] When instruction is delivered at a distance, additional challenges result because students are often separated from others sharing their backgrounds and interests, have few if any opportunities to interact with teachers outside of class, and must rely on technical linkages

to bridge the gap separating class participants.

**译文**：以远程的方式进行教学会产生一些额外的困难，因为学生通常并没有共享他们的背景和兴趣，很少有机会在课外与老师交流，而且必须依赖技术来消弭分散的课程参与者之间的距离。

- When instruction is delivered at a distance 是由 when 引导的时间状语从句，用来修饰主句的谓语。
- because students are often separated from others 是由 because 引导的原因状语从句，用来修饰主句的谓语。
- sharing their backgrounds and interests 是现在分词做后置定语，用来修饰限定先行词 others。
- if any 如果真有的话
- interact with 与……相互作用，与……相互影响
- rely on 依靠

[4] Although Moses is regarded by many as the first external student, it was not until print technology replaced tablets of stone as the medium of instruction that correspondence education became an accepted part of mass public education systems.

**译文**：虽然摩西被许多人认为是第一个函授学生，但是直到印刷技术取代小石板作为教学媒介时，函授教育才成为可被接受的大规模公共教育系统一部分。

- Although Moses is regarded by many as the first external student 是由 although 引导的让步状语从句。
- it was not until...that 这句话中，that 连接词引导的主语从句置于句末，用 it 充当形式主语。not until 直到……才……
- regard as 把……认作

[5] The Correspondence Model, regarded generally as the first generation of distance education, has since been subsumed by the second generation Multi-media Model of distance education, which entails the use of highly-developed and refined teaching-learning resources, including printed study guides, selected readings, videotapes, audiotapes, and computer-based courseware, including computer managed learning (CML), computer assisted learning (CAL), and interactive video (disk and tape).

**译文**：从那以后，函授模型——普遍认为是远程教育的第一代模型——才被纳入第二代远程教育多媒体模型之中。它需要使用高度发展的和精良的教学资源，包括学习指导书打印版、名篇选读、录像带、录音磁带和基于计算机的课件，而这种课件又包括计算机管理学习（CML）、计算机辅助学习（CAL）和交互式视频（光盘和磁带）。

- regarded generally as the first generation of distance education 是过去分词做后置定语，用来修饰先行词 the Correspondence Model 的。
- which entails the use of highly-developed and refined teaching-learning resources 是由 which 引导的非限制性定语从句，用来修饰先行词 the second generation Multi-media Model of distance education。

[6]　He argues that the view that students in conventional institutions are engaged for the greater part of their time in meaningful, face to face interaction is a myth, and that: "for both conventional and distance education students, by far the largest part of their studying is done alone, interacting with textbooks and other learning media."

**译文**:他辩论道,在传统教学制度下,学生们更多的时间都是花在有意义的、面对面的交互上,这种观点是不准确的,并且"对于传统的和远程教育的学生而言,到目前为止他们绝大部分学习都是单独完成的,只与教科书和其他学习媒体交互而已"也不正确。

- that the view that students in conventional institutions are engaged for the greater part of their time in meaningful, face to face interaction is a myth 是由 that 引导的宾语从句。其中,第二个 that 引导的是定语从句,用来修饰限定先行词 view 的,其主语的结构为 the view... is a myth。
- engage for 允诺;保证

[7]　It is worth noting that the necessary balance between social and individual interactivity will vary from course to course and will be a function of such variables as the type of subject matter, the specific objectives of the course and the structure and quality of the learning materials, and not least the student target audience.

**译文**:值得注意的是,社会和个人之间交互性的必然平衡随课程的不同而不同,并且此平衡将会以教材、课程的具体目标、学习教材的结构与质量,特别是以学生为目标受众来作为这个可变因素的函数。

- it 是该长句的形式主语,而 that 引导的主语从句置于句末,这样能保证整个句子的平衡。
- vary from... to 不同
- not least 尤其是,特别是

[8]　It is more likely that print will be used as a supplementary medium in most telecommunications-based systems, and better ways of communicating information through print will be investigated and incorporated into the design of study guides and other print-based media.

**译文**:打印机将更有可能在大部分基于电信的系统中被用作补充媒体,而且通过打印而传递信息的这些较好的方式将被探索并被并入学习指导书和其他基于打印的媒体的设计中去。

- that print will be used as a supplementary medium in most telecommunications-based systems 是由 that 引导的主语从句并置于句末,用 it 充当形式主语。
- it is likely that... 可能会
- incorporate into 使成为……的一部分

## Selected Translation

## Text A

### 远程教育综览

**什么是远程教育？**

在科学技术发展迅猛和市场千变万化的背景下，美国教育系统所面临的挑战就是，要在不增加预算的前提下提供与日俱增的教育机会。许多教育机构通过开发远程教育项目来回应这种挑战。远程教育基本上是由于老师和学生的实际距离太远而引起的，而像音频、视频、数据和印刷物等技术通常作为面对面交流的补充被用来弥补教育上的不足的。这些类型的项目可以再次为成人提供受大学教育的机会，可以帮助那些为时间和距离所限或者身体残疾的人获取知识，也可以在工作的地方更新员工的知识库。

**远程教育有效吗？**

许多教育者都怀疑远程的学生是否能学到和传统的面对面教导的学生一样多的东西。远程教育和传统的面对面授课之间的比较研究表明，当远程教育所使用的方法和技术与教学任务相适应后出现了学生之间的互动，并且如果学生和老师之间存在及时的反馈的话，远程教学可以像传统教学一样有效。

**远程教育怎样被传递？**

远程教育有很大范围的技术选择。它们可以分成四个主要范畴：

音频——教学音频工具包括电话、电话会议和短波无线电广播这样的交互技术。被动的（例如单向的）音频工具包括录音磁带和收音机。

视频——教学视频工具包括类似于幻灯片、预先制作的活动图片（例如电影、录像磁带等）这样的静止图像以及与电话会议结合的实时活动影像。

数据——电脑发送和接收电子信息。因为这个原因，"数据"这个术语被用来描述教学工具这种宽广的类别。电脑在远程教育方面的应用各不相同，它包括：

- 计算机辅助教育（CAI）——将电脑作为一种独立的教学机器来显示单独的课程。
- 计算机管理教学（CMI）——通过电脑来组织教学并记录学生的进展。虽然CAI通常都与CMI结合起来，但是教学本身并不需要通过电脑传递。
- 计算机媒体教育（CME）——描述有利于教学传递的计算机应用，例子包括电子邮件、传真、实时电脑会议和万维网应用。

印刷物——是远程教育项目的基础元素，也是所有其他传递系统演变的基础。现有的各种印刷物版式包括教科书、学习指导书、工作手册、课程表和案例研究。

**哪种技术是最好的？**

虽然技术在远程教育传递的过程中扮演着关键角色，但是教育家们仍然必须关注教学成果，而不是传递的技术。有效的远程教育的关键是在选择某种传递系统前，致力于学习者的需要、对内容的要求和教师所面临的限制条件。这种系统观点将典型地导致媒体结合，每种媒体都有其特定的目的。比如：

- 一个功能强大的打印设备能够以教科书以及阅读物、教学大纲和日常时间表的形式提供许多基础教学内容。

- 交互式音频会议或视频会议能够提供实时的面对面(或声音对声音)的交流。这同样是一个将特邀发言人和内容专家结合进来的非常棒并且划算的方式。
- 电脑会议或电子邮件能够用来发送消息、任务反馈以及与班上其他一个或多个成员进行其他的定向交流。这同样能够增加学生间的交互。
- 预录录像磁带能够用来展现课堂讲课和视觉导向内容。
- 传真能够被用来发放任务、紧急公告,能接收学生的任务,并提供及时的反馈。

通过使用这种综合方式,教育家们的任务就是在这些可选技术里仔细挑选。其目的就是为了制造一个混合的教学媒体以便能以某种方式满足学习者在教学上有效且节省开支的需求。

**有效的远程教育**

有效的远程教育项目都毫无例外地是从谨慎规划和对课程要求及学生需求的深度理解开始的。仅仅当这些技术元素被详细理解时适当的技术才能被挑选出来。有效的远程教育项目的开发方式并不神秘,它们并不是自发发生的,而是通过许多个人和组织的艰辛工作和专心致志的努力发展而来的。事实上,远程教育项目的成功取决于学生、教职员、协助商、教学辅助人员和管理者相互协调的一致努力。

**远程教育中的关键角色**

下面简要地描述这些关键角色在远程教育项目中所起的作用以及他们所面对的挑战。

学生——满足学生的教学需求是每个有效的远程教育项目的基础,并且是评判该领域里所有努力的试金石。不管教育环境怎样,学生最根本的任务就是学习。但是在最好的环境下这也是十分艰难的任务,因为它要求学生有自我激励、规划和分析、应用被教内容的能力。以远程的方式进行教学会产生一些额外的困难,因为学生通常并没有共享他们的背景和兴趣,很少有机会在课外与老师交流,而且必须依赖技术来消弭分散的课程参与者之间的距离。

教职人员——任何一个远程教育的成功都直接取决于教职人员。在传统的教室背景下,教师的职责就在于组织课程内容以及理解学生的需求。而远程教学就面临着特殊的挑战。例如,教师必须:

- 在第一手经验非常少、面对面的交流极其有限的情况下,去理解远程学生的特点和需求。
- 改变教学风格,顾及许多不同的听众的需求和期望。
- 在仍然致力于他们的教学角色的同时,开发对传输技术的有效的理解。
- 有效地担任起熟练的协助商和内容供应者。

协助商——教师往往觉得倚重网站来实现学生和教师之间的交流是很有利的。为了有效,协助商必须理解被服务的学生和教师的期望。更重要的是,协助商必须乐于听从老师的指示。在预算和后勤允许的情况下,现场协助者在课堂上的人数也会增加,即使是在只有微乎其微的专业知识的情况下。至少,他们会建立设备、收集任务、监考测试,并充当教师的现场耳目。

教学辅助人员——这些人是远程教育事业的幕后英雄,他们保证了项目成功所需的大量细节能够被有效处理。大部分成功的远程教育项目都将辅助性服务功能与学生注册、文件复制及发放、教材预订、保证著作权的出清、利于行程安排、处理成绩单、管理技术资源等等合并起来。教学辅助人员的确是维持远程教育并且随时跟踪远程教育的黏合剂。

　　管理者——虽然管理者通常能影响教师的远程教育项目的规划,但是一旦这个项目运转起来,他们往往与技术管理人员失去联系或放弃对技术管理人员的控制。有效的远程教育管理者不仅仅只是出主意的人,他们是将意见统一起来的人,是决策者和仲裁人。他们与技术人员以及提供教学辅助的服务人员密切联系,保证技术资源的有效实施,进而推进教育机构的学术使命。更重要的是,他们持久地关注学术,能够意识到满足远程学生的教学需要是他们最终的责任。

## Exercises

**1. Please Explain the Following Professional Terms：**

a) computer-assisted instruction (CAI)

b) computer-managed instruction (CMI)

c) computer-mediated education (CME)

d) interactive multimedia (IMM)

e) computer mediated communication (CMC)

f) Integrated Services Digital Network (ISDN)

**2. Short Answers：**

(1) How is distance education delivered and who are the key players in distance education?

(2) What are the four models of distance education and what are the characteristics that are relevant to the quality of teaching and learning?

(3) What are the four types of technologies that support the group process in "the 4-Square Map of Groupware Options" that was developed by Johansen et. al. in 1991?

(4) Can you state what the future researches of distance education are according to the text?

# 投稿指南（Ⅰ）

### 一、如何选题

　　科技论文是科学工作者对创造性成果进行理论分析和科学总结的文字表达形式。科技论文的关键点是创新,如何寻找新意则需要在选题上下工夫。

　　随着科技的进步与发展,像牛顿、爱因斯坦、爱迪生那样依靠灵感与天才寻找原始火花已经非常困难了。因此许多人在确定一个新颖的选题之后,常常会到杂志上去寻找灵感。在他们看来,似乎这就是创新。显然,这样写出的文章难有创新性,因为科学研究并没有终南捷径,不花几年甚至十几年的苦功是很难真正收获创造性成果的。如果这时匆匆忙忙写文章,退稿率会很高。

一般而言,研究者应多与导师讨论,听取导师的看法,不要一味地标新立异,不要在大方向上偏离导师的研究方向,只有这样才能得到导师的指导和帮助。一般而言,我们建议大家:

- 按导师指导的方向大量阅读,增加自己的知识储备,了解本学科、本方向的研究历史与现状,明确过去已经进行了哪些研究,有什么成果,哪些问题尚未得到解决。要泛读和精读相结合,合理搭配,节约宝贵的时间。
- 研究领域不要太泛,要选几个自己感兴趣的领域深挖,逐步从广泛性中找出特殊性,即先广再博。
- 善于总结。注意将平常的思考记录下来,尤其是要将突然来临、转瞬即逝的灵感记录下来。
- 勤于思考。一旦发现问题,要抛开对权威刊物的迷信,抛开原定的结论,穷追下去;应该充分运用自己的思考力,通过分析、综合、演绎、归纳、分类、组合、加减、反逆、类推等等,对文献资料进行积极的加工。这是一种创造性的工作,缺少它就得不到新的题目。
- 在确定选题之前,要了解选题是否具有新意和价值。通常我们要通过检索来证实这个想法是否具有创新性。此外,还要注意这个选题的现实意义或者长远意义。
- 可行性论证,这包括对方法、材料、资金、设备等进行可行性论证。

一旦创新性与可行性得到初步保证,那么我们就得到了一个不错的选题,从而有可能得到一份很有分量的研究结论。

## 二、投稿过程与投稿信(COVER LETTER)

1. 投稿过程

写论文的真正意义在于与别人分享你的知识而获得一种成就感,尽管大多数人写科技论文的直接目的是为了获得某种荣誉,如晋职、晋级、获得学位等,但目标却是一致的,即将论文刊出。正确的投稿将有助于科技论文的发表,投稿中一般应该注意以下问题:

(1)正确选择期刊:首先要掂量一下自己论文的分量,想想在哪个杂志上发表最合适。由于期刊种类繁多,即使在同一学科也有许多期刊,且各个期刊的办刊宗旨、专业范围、主题分配、栏目设置及各种类型文章发表的比例均不相同。因此,选择一本恰当的期刊并非易事。然而,选择期刊是论文得以发表的一个极其重要的环节。选择期刊应考虑的因素有:

- 论文主题是否在刊物的征稿范围内。投稿论文可能极为优秀,但如果不适合于该刊物,则不可能在该刊物上发表。
- 期刊的声望。期刊的学术水平高,其声望就高。当然期刊声望越高,被引用的可能性就越大,影响力就越大。
- 期刊的审稿周期。一般而言,期刊声望越大审稿周期就越长。当然,期刊又分为一般期刊、快报（Letters）等（如 IEEE Communication Letters，Physics Review Letters 等），通常快报的效率较高。

（2）认真阅读投稿须知。确定期刊后，要阅读投稿须知，认真浏览目录，以确定该刊物是否能发表你的文章及发表的比例有多大。一般应该注意：

- 注意栏目设置，确定拟投稿件的栏目。
- 了解稿件的撰写要求。
- 根据刊登文章的投稿日期、接收日期以及见刊日期，估算发表周期，以便出现问题时能及时与编辑沟通。

（3）正式投稿：一般来说，投稿程序分以下三步进行：

- 准备投稿信（cover letter or submission letter）
- 投稿及其包装：目前投稿更多地提倡网络在线投稿，无能是网络投稿还是邮寄投稿，一般要把稿件及其拟投期刊所需的伴随资料一并寄出，它们一般包括：投稿信、刊物要求的稿件（包括文题页、文摘页、正文、致谢、参考文献、图注、表及图）、版权转让声明、作者地址等。有些还需要提供程序、图片等。
- 稿件追踪：如果投稿两周仍无任何有关稿件收到的信息，也可打电话、发 e-mail 或写信给编辑部核实稿件是否收到。

2. 投稿信（COVER LETTER）

向国外期刊投稿时，除了文章正文外，还需要写一封投稿信。一封好的投稿信可以起到很好的作用，就好比求职时的自荐信一样，如果能吸引编辑的注意，你就成功了一半。

投稿信的内容主要目的是希望编辑详细了解文章的主要内容，因而要突出文章的创新性价值，还有你为什么要发表这篇文章，还可以简要指出目前该领域的发展方向。此外，要特别注意用语恰当与格式规范等。

实例1：

Dear Dr：

Enclosed are three copies of a manuscript by XXXXX, XXXXX, and XXXXX titled "XXXXXXXXXXXXXXXXXXXXXX". It is submitted to be considered for publications a "Original Article" in your journal. This paper is neither the entire paper nor any part of its content has been published or has been accepted elsewhere. It is not being submitted to any other journal. We believe the paper may be of particular interest to the readers of your journal because XXXXXXXXXXXXXXXXXXXXXXX.

Correspondence and phone calls about the paper should be directed to XXXXXXX at the following address, phone and fax number, and e-mail address：

Department of XXXXXXXXX，
Tsinghua University，
Beijing，10084，
P. R. China
Tel：XXXXXX

Fax：XXXXX

E-mai：XXXXX

实例2：

Dear Prof. XXX：

    I want to submit our manuscript with title "XXXXXXXXX" for publication in "XXXXXXXXX". It is not being submitted to any other journal or is under consideration for publication elsewhere.

    The authors claim that none of the material in the paper has been published or is under consideration for publication elsewhere.

    I am the corresponding author and further information is as follows：

Address：Department of XXXXX,

Huazhong Normal University,

Wuhan, HuBei, 430079,

P. R. China.

Tel：XXXXXXX

Fax：XXXXXXX

E-mail：qushaocheng@mail.ccnu.edu.cn

Thanks very much for your attention to our paper.

Sincerely yours,

Shao-cheng Qu

### 三、审稿过程以及与编辑的沟通

1. 审稿过程

一般来说，在不同领域，审稿的过程可能不太一样，大致过程是初选、送审、修改和终审。我们一般要了解以下基本步骤与内容：

（1）编辑内部审查：一般包括论文文字、格式的审查与论文题材方面的检查，这种审查通常是编辑部内部的专家进行的。由于一些重要期刊投稿众多，许多好的中文期刊内部审查拒稿率达到60%；投稿英文期刊时如果英文表达不好，那么拒稿率也会相当高。如果论文形式不合格，无论你论文内容多么好，都有可能直接被拒绝，因为你的稿件根本没有到真正的专家的手中。此外，如果编辑觉得论文题材不适合本刊物，也会回信退稿。

（2）正式审稿：编辑会挑选2—5名同行对论文的创新性和正确性进行审查。有些期刊采取匿名审稿，有些公开审稿。国内审稿一般有少量审稿费，国外评审是自愿花时间评阅论文。由于评阅人一般已经在本领域建立了地位，比较忙，因此评审时间较长，投稿者应能理解这一点。审稿期间，作者一般应耐心等待。除按收稿通知建议时间与编辑联系外，一般应给评审4—6个月时间。若仍无消息，可以与编辑联系，催促他们一下。

（3）评审内容：主要包括论文内容的创新性；采用理论、方法和数据的正确性；对论文的表述方法、写作缺陷等提出批评。

（4）评审结果一般有以下情况：

- 接收（Accepted or without minor revision）：如果出现这种情况，作者会收到最终稿的指南，有时需要补充提供数字文件等。
- 修改后可接收（Conditional acceptance upon satisfactory revision）：如果出现这种情况，应按照评审意见修改论文，将修改部分单独写成报告提供给编辑。一般来说编辑比评审者更具有同情心，因而最终都能接受修改后的论文。
- 可以修改后再投：这种情况要分析评审意见，如果编辑希望继续修改提高，那么撰稿人就不要轻易放弃，因为修改后被接收的机会还是很大。对于高质量的杂志，多数论文第一次投稿时都会因这种情况而退回来。作者应根据评审意见认真修改。当然也可以提出不修改某些部分的理由。
- 拒绝：这种情况应根据评审意见修改文稿，然后投往其他刊物。千万不要与编辑较劲，甚至指责漫骂编辑，这样会对你所在学校甚至国家的类似投稿带来不好的影响。

（5）论文发表：收到印刷编辑寄回的校样后，应尽快订正，尽快寄还给印刷编辑。寄校样时，出版商会要求填写版权转让书（Transfer of Copy Right），并告知支付版面费的办法和订购单行本的方法。许多刊物不收版面费，但对特殊印刷品（如彩版印刷品）收费。有的超过定额免费页数的页面还可能按页面收费。不少收版面费的刊物费用都挺高，不过作者可以写信给出版商说明自己的情况，申请免费。

总之，作者对审查意见首先应高度重视，考虑审稿人为什么要提出这些建议。审稿人毕竟是一个旁观者，他的意见总有一定的道理。有的作者觉得审稿人没有读懂自己的文章，拒绝修改，这当然不好。当然，尽管审稿人是同领域的专家，但隔行如隔山，因此审稿人提出一些并不十分中肯的意见也不奇怪。好在评审人一般都在三个人以上，这至少最小化了由个人偏见而产生的不公正现象。

2. 与编辑的沟通

在投稿期间，为及时了解稿件信息，与编辑进行沟通是免不了的；作者要认真对待评阅人的审稿意见，因而与评阅人进行沟通也是必要的。

与编辑进行沟通，主要是询问稿件状况。下面给出了几个例子。

例1：

Dear Editor,

I want to know if you have received our manuscript with the title "XXXXXXXX" for submission in "XXXXXXXX". We submit our manuscript from e-mail：XXXXXXXX on Friday, 27, Feb., but we cannot receive the reply. Thank you for your kindly consideration of this request.

Sincerely yours：

XXXXXXXXX

例2：

Dear Editor,

I'm not sure if it is the right time to contact you again to inquire about the status of my submitted manuscript(Paper ID：XXXXXXXXX; Title of Paper：XXXXXXXXXXXX) although nearly one month have passed since I contacted you last time. I would be greatly appreciated if you could spend some of your time checking the status for me.

Best regards,

XXXX

例 3：

Dear Editor,

Thanks for your reply for time and patient. We have sent many dates and figures to you according to reviews. We want to know if you have received it.

Please contact us, if you have any question.

We are looking forward to hearing from your letters.

由于同行评审是匿名的，评审人的批评通常是直率、无情的，因此有些学者认为论文被要求修改或者被拒绝很丢面子，甚至认为这些批评是人身攻击。事实上，事情可能没有那么复杂。作者的主要目的是发表论文，因而按照审稿人的意见修改论文显得尤为必要；如果对自己的论文很有信心，认为评审人的意见是错误的，这时候一定要讲究策略。一般而言，要对每一个审稿人的意见加以逐个回答，如果可能的话，应该在回复中附上审稿人提出的意见，这样可以简化审稿人的二审工作，也能显示作者的真诚以及对审稿人工作的尊重。

根据审稿人意见完成论文修改之后，作者还应该写一封信对责任编辑表示感谢，同时表明你已经考虑了每一位审稿人的意见。绝对不能对审稿人写了很长的解释，但对论文本身却没有多少修改。一般而言，评阅人对按照他们的建议所付出的努力及其有条有理的修改工作会留下深刻的印象，这样你的工作得到评阅人承认的可能性就非常大了。

Dear Editor,

We have revised the manuscript according to reviews and your comments. Our point-to-point response attached below. At the same time, we would like to thank you and anonymous reviewers for your kindly patience and constructive suggestions, which are very important information to revise this paper.

With my king regards,

Faithfully yours, XXXX

## Unit 18 Online Learning

▲ Knowledge Objectives

When you have completed this unit, you will be able to:

• Understand the definition of Online Learning given in text A

• State the educational benefits of Online Learning

• Understand the reasons why evaluating Online Learning and the contents of measuring it in detail

## Professional Terms

| | |
|---|---|
| online learning | 在线学习 |
| discussion boards | 讨论板,讨论区社群群组 |
| java applets | java 小应用程序 |
| return on investment (ROI) | 投资报酬率,投资收益率 |
| labour savings | 省工 |

## Text A

### A Brief Introduction of Online Learning①

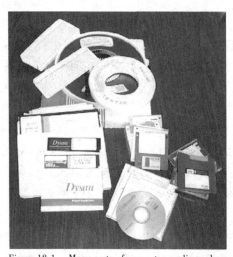

Figure 18-1  Many sorts of computer media such as floppy disks, disks and so on

There is ongoing debate about whether it is the use of a particular delivery technology or the design of the instruction that improves learning. It has long been recognized that specialized delivery technologies can provide efficient and timely access to learning materials; however, Clark has claimed that technologies are merely vehicles that deliver instruction, but do not themselves influence student achievement. As Clark notes, meta-analysis studies on media research have shown that students gain significant learning benefits when learning from audio-visual or computer media (Figure 18-1), as opposed to conventional instruction; however, the same studies suggest that the reason for those benefits is not the medium of instruction, but the instructional strategies built into the learning materials.[1] Similarly, Schramm suggested that learning is influenced more by the content and instructional strategy in the learning materials than by the type of technology used to deliver instruction.

According to Bonk and Reynolds, to promote higher-order thinking on the Web, online learning must create challenging activities that enable learners to link new information to old, acquire meaningful knowledge, and use their metacognitive abilities; hence, it is the instructional strategy and not the technology that influences the quality of learning. Kozma argues that the particular attributes of the computer are needed to bring real-life models and simulations to the learner; thus, the medium does influence learning. However, it is not the computer per se that makes students learn, but the design of the real-life models and simulations, and the students' interaction with those models and simulations. The computer is merely the vehicle that

---

① http://cde.athabascau.ca/online_book/pdf/TPOL_book.pdf

provides the processing capability and delivers the instruction to learners. Kozma is correct in his claim, but learners will not learn from the simulations if the simulations are not developed using sound design principles.

Online learning allows for flexibility of access, from anywhere and usually at anytime—essentially, it allows participants to collapse time and space—however, the learning materials must be designed properly to engage the learner and promote learning. According to Rossett, online learning has many promises, but it takes commitment and resources, and it must be done right. "Doing it right" means that online learning materials must be designed properly, with the learners and learning in focus, and that adequate support must be provided. Ring and Mathieux suggest that online learning should have high authenticity (i.e., students should learn in the context of the workplace), high interactivity, and high collaboration.

Different terminologies have been used for online learning, a fact that makes it difficult to develop a generic definition. Terms that are commonly used include e-learning, Internet learning, distributed learning, networked learning, telelearning, virtual learning, computer-assisted learning, Web-based learning, and distance learning. All of these terms imply that the learner is at a distance from the tutor or instructor, that the learner uses some form of technology (usually a computer) to access the learning materials, that the learner uses technology to interact with the tutor or instructor and other learners, and that some form of support is provided to learners. (Figure 18-2) This paper will use the

Figure 18-2 Online Learning is revolutionizing traditional education and is finally going mainstream.

term "online learning" throughout. There are many definitions of online learning in the literature, definitions that reflect the diversity of practice and associated technologies. Carliner defines online learning as educational material that is presented on a computer. Khan defines online instruction as an innovative approach for delivering instruction to a remote audience, using the Web as the medium. However, online learning involves more than just the presentation and delivery of the materials using the Web: the learner and the learning process should be the focus of online learning. As a result, the author defines online learning as the use of the Internet to access learning materials; to interact with the content, instructor, and other learners; and to obtain support during the learning process, in order to acquire knowledge, to construct personal meaning, and to grow from the learning experience.[2]

## Text B

## Educational Benefits of Online Learning[①]

According to CCA consulting, nearly 50% of higher education institutions currently engage in some type of online learning. Academic and professional organizations agree that using web-based learning environments can offer sound pedagogical benefits.

According to researchers from Cornell University, "the web provides significant new functionality in transmitting information to the student and providing forums for exchange. The web is revolutionizing some areas of study through increased opportunities for learning and alternative formats for information."

The goal of this tip sheet is to explain the educational advantages that arise when supplementing a course with web-based tools. These include:

- Enhancing student-to-student and faculty-to-student communication.
- Enabling student-centered teaching approaches.
- Providing 24/7 (24 hours a day, 7 days a week) accessibility to course materials.
- Providing just-in-time methods to assess and evaluate student progress.
- Reducing "administrivia" around course management.

### Enhancing student-to-student and faculty-to-student communication

Web-based education tools provide many ways to increase communication between class members and faculty, including discussion boards (Figure 18-3), chats, and e-mails. Researchers have found that adding these elements to a course increases student motivation and participation in class discussions and projects. Students are "more willing to participate [due to] a measure of anonymity, which serves as a motivator... people feel more empowered. They are daring and confrontational regarding the expression of ideas..."

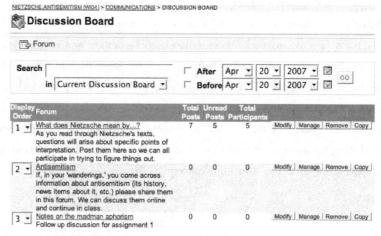

Figure 18-3  The Discussion Board is a communication tool that can be used to enhance a course web site.

---

① http://www.uth.tmc.edu/med/administration/edu_programs/ep/blackboard/text/Online_Learning_Benefits.pdf

### Students share perspectives

Online forums, like Blackboard's Discussion Board and Chat, provide public areas to post information. Each student can view another student's answers and learn through the exposure to different perspectives. This benefits students because they can combine new opinions with their own, and develop a solid foundation for learning. Research supports that "as learners become aware of the variations in interpretation and construction of meaning among a range of people [they] construct an individual meaning..."

### Students experience a sense of equality

Another benefit to using web-based communication tools is to give all students a reinforced sense of equality. Each individual has the same opportunity to "speak up" by posting messages without typical distractions such as seating arrangements, volume of student voices, and gender biases. Shy and anxious students feel more comfortable expressing ideas and backing up facts when posting online instead of speaking in a lecture room. Studies prove that online discussions provoke more confrontational and direct communication between students.

### Instructors are more accessible

Online communication also benefits students by providing additional layer of instructor accessibility. Students in courses that are supplemented by products like Blackboard no longer have to worry if they cannot make an instructor's regular office hours, as they still have the ability to submit inquiries via e-mail at any time. [3] This is good for the instructor too, as they can respond at his/her convenience instead of being tied to a desk or office. This is particularly helpful when a student's schedule conflicts with office hours or if a question arises at the spur of the moment. (Figure 18-4)

Figure 18-4　Instructors are more accessible and you can learn anywhere and anytime.

For example: A Blackboard course web site is supplementing an on-campus math course. On a Sunday night, a student is reviewing an assignment, thinks of a question, and e-mails it to the instructor. The instructor reads the e-mail Monday morning, looks up the answer, brings up the relevant information to the class during the Monday lecture, and the entire class benefits. If the student waited until office hours on Tuesday, perhaps the integration into the lecture would not have occurred, or maybe if the student asked the question during class on Monday, the instructor would not have had the time to frame the question correctly.

### Enabling student-centered teaching approaches

Every student has a unique learning style. Some students are visual learners; some learn better when they "learn by doing." Web-based learning environments permit the instructor to build one course, yet implement a variety of resources, so students can utilize materials in whichever way works best for them.

For example: Instructors can use Blackboard's Course Documents and Course Information areas to post all sorts of support documents for students, including handouts (Figure 18-5), audio clips, java applets, reserved readings, and lecture notes. (Figure 18-6) If this information is available to the students, they can access content and review it at a self-determined pace. This provides increased opportunities for students to view and review course elements without creating an additional drain on TAs or instructors.

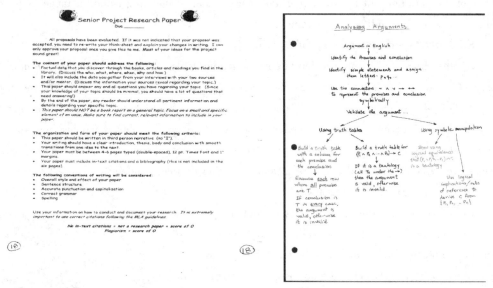

Figure 18-5　An example of handout　　　　Figure 18-6　An example of lecture notes

### Accommodate different learning styles

An instructor can also present these materials in many formats to accommodate different types of learning styles. For example, if an instructor puts both lecture notes and slides online, both visual and auditory learners benefit. Students who prefer to focus on "listening" and "watching" during lecture do not have to worry that they are missing important concepts while scrambling to take copious notes. They can focus on understanding the material and concepts as they are presented. Students with attention difficulties or those who get overwhelmed by organizational tasks also benefit, because materials provided show how the instructor has grouped and prepared materials in the handouts, and indicate what items are most important.

### Provide opportunities for exploration

Instructors can also provide increased opportunity for student exploration and activity learning by putting related web sites into Blackboard's External Links feature. When instructors reference these types of web sites, content reinforcement is provided as students can see how course material is utilized in "real world" situations.

### Encourage additional rehearsal time

Additional benefits for those who "learn by doing" occur when students participate in online discussions, as students are exposed to an extra period of information rehearsal. Typically, students rehearse information when they study for exams or complete assignments. However, they also rehearse information when formulating thoughts into sentences and typing those thoughts into the computer. When instructors post discussion questions or short essay assignments in the online portion of a course, students must attend to and reflect on the subject matter before responding. This results in reflection and articulation of content, as the very process of reporting and writing about what they have learned engages students in an active learning experience.[4]

### Providing 24/7 accessibility to course materials

Some students work best in the morning, some in the evening. Some students commute to campus and others take night classes. Scheduling time for homework and group projects can be difficult depending on each student's course, job, and personal responsibilities.

### Continual access to materials

When course content and activities are provided online, students no longer need to worry about accessing course materials. Students can complete assignments during their most productive times. Busy students can choose to download readings or take practice exams whenever it is most convenient, in the evening after kids are put to bed, or at 4am during a bout of insomnia. Continual access to course documents also insures students can obtain materials at any time, removing the opportunity for frustrations such as "The library was closed," "All the copies of reserve readings were checked out," or "I missed that handout during your lecture."

For Example: Anna is a commuting student who takes courses in addition to working and handling family responsibilities. A guest speaker for her astronomy section is scheduled to speak, but at a different time than the usual class session. Because the course is supplemented with an online component, the professor coordinates a live chat session with the guest speaker. Anna attends the lecture by logging in and even asking questions from home.

### Remove reliance on physical attendance

In traditional education, students working on group projects must coordinate schedules. In distance learning environments, this may not even be possible, forcing participants to work independently. When web-based collaborative tools are available, coordination is no longer an issue. Providing a project team with asynchronous discussions and file uploads, students can work in groups without the constraints of meeting together at a certain date, time, and location. (Figure 18-7)

Figure 18-7 Remove reliance on physical attendance by web-based communications.

For example: One student group has a member named George who works nights. Unfortunately George can't make the scheduled group meetings. When using the group communication tools in Blackboard, George can complete his part of the assignment and post it in the group File Transfer Area. This way, even if he is not physically present at the meeting, group members can access and edit his work.

## Providing just-in-time methods to assess and evaluate student progress

Learner assessments are essential in education. Tests and surveys inform the instructor whether teaching methods and course structures are successful. These assessments also determine if student progress is satisfactory. Online assessment tools provide instructors with many ways to build, distribute, and compile information quickly and easily.

For example: An instructor assigns students to watch a political debate on television at 8pm on Sunday night. He wants to assess students' opinion of the issue to discuss during Monday's lecture. The instructor creates a short poll using Blackboard's Quiz/Survey engine. After the show, students log in and complete the survey. The results are tallied automatically and available for the instructor in plenty of time for lecture.

### Adds pedagogical benefits

Web-based testing features also have pedagogical benefits. From the student viewpoint, frequent assessment provides concept reinforcement and increases motivation. Instructors can post practice exams and end-of-chapter reviews without worrying about finding the time and resources to analyze results. Students can access these assessments at any time, privately and in the comfort of their home. Since grading is computerized, students receive immediate feedback. This may also help students who suffer from test anxiety relax and minimize embarrassment for those that do poorly. (Figure 18-8)

Figure 18-8  Adds pedagogical benefits by assessing students anywhere and anytime.

### Reducing amount of faculty time spent on "administrivia"

In addition to the pedagogical benefits of online learning, there are also several time and money saving advantages. Students can save and print items as needed when provided with handouts and readings online. The direct result is a reduced institutional expense for both the cost and time associated with copying, collating, and distributing these materials. Instructors can also use E-mail to send messages directly to students or the Announcements feature to communicate with the entire class. Not only does this insure that students receive the materials, but it is also environmentally appealing, as it drastically reduces paper waste.

## Utilize time efficiently

The time saving elements introduced by web-based education tools like Blackboard apply to both the instructor and the student. Students benefit because they have immediate access to course materials at any location. They do not have to spend time walking across campus to the instructor's office or searching for a reading in the library. Instructors can minimize time spent in office hours, and address student concerns online instead.

## Maximize the classroom experience

Instructors working with tools like Blackboard no longer have to spend valuable classroom time dealing with "administrivia." The 15 minutes at the start of each class typically spent distributing handouts, collecting assignments, and making announcements (Figure 18-9) can be utilized for teaching when administrative tasks are managed through online tools.

Figure 18-9  Making announcements—an example of spending time dealing with "administrivia"

## Reduce faculty workload

Instructors and TAs can also save time using products like Blackboard. When the Quiz/Survey generator is used to deliver tests, all the grading and analysis is automated. Time previously spent correcting, formulating statistical deviations, and analyzing specific questions can be used for other things. Even student records can be exported directly into spreadsheets for turnover to the registrar.

# Text C

## Evaluating Online Learning[①]

There are many good reasons for measuring the success of your online learning programme. Here are four:

☆ **To validate training as a business tool**

Training is one of many actions that an organization can take to improve its performance

---

① http://www.fastrak-consulting.co.uk/tactix/Features/evaluate/evaluate.htm#Contents

and profitability. Only if training is properly evaluated can it be compared against these other methods and can you expect it, therefore, to be selected either in preference to or in combination with other methods.

☆ **To justify the costs incurred in training**

We all know that when money is tight, training budgets are amongst the first to be sacrificed. Only by thorough, quantitative analysis can training departments make the case necessary to resist these cuts.

☆ **To help improve the design of training**

Training programmes should be continuously improved to provide better value and increased benefits for an organization. Without formal evaluation, the basis for changes can only be subjective.

☆ **To help in selecting training methods**

These days there are many alternative approaches available to training departments, including a variety of classroom, on-job and self-study methods. Using comparative evaluation techniques, organizations can make rational decisions about the methods to employ.

**What are we measuring?**

With evaluation, as in life, there are many ways of measuring success. When you set your life goals—for health, wealth, fame or happiness (and all those unprintable ones that don't quite fit into this list)—you also determine your criteria for success. And so with evaluation. What you measure is a factor of your original goals.

The form of evaluation that we undertake is determined by the criteria that we choose, or are told to use, to measure success. The following four levels of evaluation were defined by Kirkpatrick back in 1975:

**Level 1: Reactions**

Reactions are what you measure with the "happy sheet". Reactions are important because, if learners react negatively to your courses, they are less likely to transfer what they learned to their work and more likely to give bad reports to their peers, leading in turn to lower numbers.

**Level 2: Learning**

Learning, in terms of new or improved skills, knowledge and attitudes, is the primary aim of a training event. Learning can be measured objectively using a test or exam or some form of assessed exercise. If a learner has to achieve a certain level of learning to obtain a "pass mark", then the number of passes may be used as an evaluation measure. Another important aspect of learning is the degree of retention—how much of the learning has stuck after the course is over.

**Level 3: Application**

If a learner has learned something from a course, you hope that this will be reflected in their behaviors on the job. If a learner employs what they have learned appropriately, then their work behaviors will meet desired criteria. Behaviors can be measured through observation or, in some cases, through some automated means. To assess behaviors change requires that the measurements are taken before and after the training.

**Level 4: Business results**

If, as a result of training, learners are using appropriate behaviors on the job, then you would expect that to have a positive impact on performance. A wide variety of indicators can be employed to measure the impact of training on performance—numbers of complaints, sales made, output per hour and so on. It is hard to be sure that it is training that has made the difference without making comparisons to a control group—a group of employees who have not been through the training.

Recently, attention has focused on the financial implications of training and, consequently, a fifth level has been defined:

**Level 5: Return on investment**

Return on investment (ROI) is a measure of the monetary benefits obtained by an organization over a specified time period in return for a given investment in a training programme. Looking at it another way, ROI is the extent to which the benefits (outputs) of training exceed the costs.

But leaving aside the five levels of Kirkpatrick and Phillips, in the real world we are measured in other ways as well:

● **Numbers**

One way of measuring the success of training is the good old "bums on seats". Although by no means a true measure of the effectiveness of training, learner numbers do reflect the fact that the training is addressing a need and that the design and methodology is meeting expectations. (Figure 18-10)

Figure 18-10 Learner numbers in training

● **Direct cost**

Direct costs are those costs that are incurred directly as a result of a training programme—external design and development, consultancy fees, travel expenses and so on. If the programme did not take place, these costs would not be incurred. Many organizations only ever take direct costs into consideration when measuring training costs.

● **Indirect cost**

Indirect costs are costs that may or may not be directly associated with a training event, but which would have been incurred anyway, whether or not the training took place. Examples are salaries of in-house tutors and learners and the costs of rooms and equipment. Any analysis of the true costs of training will include both direct and indirect costs.

● **Efficiency**

Efficiency is a measure of the amount of learning achieved relative to the amount of effort put in. In practical terms this means the amount of time it takes to complete a piece of training. Efficiency has a direct relation to cost—the more efficient a training method is, the less it will cost.

● **Performance to schedule**

Sometimes with a training programme, "time is of the essence"—the training needs to be completed by a given date if a particular business objective is to be achieved. In these situations, the extent to which a training programme performs to schedule is a critical measure of success.

● **Income received**

If you are a training provider operating externally to a client organization, then income received is a vital measure of your success. It's the financial equivalent of "bums on seats"—the more courses you run or places you fill, the greater the benefit. Some internal training providers may also cross-charge their clients, although, because this correspondingly increases the cost to the organization, this would not be regarded as a benefit when assessing return on investment.

● **The extent to which learners mix**

A justification often made for training, particularly group events, is that it provides an opportunity for learners who work in different departments or regions to interact with each other, share experiences and make contacts. Because this is a valued outcome of training, it needs to be considered when comparing training methods. Similarly, some training may be regarded as a perk, a benefit of some value, even if this is not directly related to learning. (Figure 18-11)

Figure 18-11  Interactions in different departments to share experiences and make contacts

## ◆ Measuring reactions

Reactions are the first level of measurement in Kirkpatrick's four-step approach. Although sometimes disregarded, reactions are important because, if students react negatively to your courses, they are less likely to transfer what they learned to their work and more likely to give bad reports to their peers, leading in turn to lower student numbers. [5]

Here are probably the most common methods of measuring reactions:

### Questionnaire

The reactions questionnaire, often called a "happy sheet" because of the way it captures end-of-course euphoria, is almost ubiquitous with classroom courses. Of course, there's no reason why it has to be given out at the end of the course—a more considered opinion may be obtainable some days or even weeks after the course has finished.

### Observation

A good trainer or tutor will be able to detect the reactions of learners by observing their behaviors and their comments. This method can generate useful feedback, but not in an objective or structured fashion.

### Meetings

Another way to look at reactions is to hold a group meeting with all the learners on the course. This way issues that are brought up can be debated and suggestions found for making improvements in the future. (Figure 18-12)

### Interviews

It would also be possible to measure reactions through one-to-one interviews with learners. The best results will be obtained by structured interviews that work methodically through the key issues.

Figure 18-12　Debate issues and make suggestions in a group meeting.

The online environment also provides many opportunities for measuring reactions:

### Chat

Chat programs are the equivalent of the group discussion in a classroom. They can be used to gain feedback from a group of learners or for a one-to-one.

### Email

Email provides the asynchronous alternative to chat. Learners can use email to submit their comments directly to the tutor or to debate issues in a discussion forum.

### Online questionnaires

Web page forms can be used in much the same way as paper happy sheets. In fact, they have quite an advantage, in that the results can be automatically stored in a file on the web server, for analysis by a spreadsheet or database program. With a little programming, you can even have the analysis performed automatically.

### ♦ Measuring learning

Learning is the primary objective of any training event and, as such, must be measured if you are to know whether the event has been successful. The techniques that you use to measure learning depend to a large extent on the type of learning that the course has been designed to achieve. One way of looking at types of learning is in terms of the three learning domains.

**Cognitive**

The cognitive domain includes all knowledge and those skills that require thought rather than practical action. There are many ways of testing for cognitive learning:

- essays
- written or verbal tests
- problem-solving exercises
- interviews

**Affective**

The affective domain is concerned with attitudes and emotions. This is a harder area to test for learning, but there are some options:

- attitude surveys or questionnaires
- interviews
- group meetings

**Psychomotor**

The psychomotor domain covers all practical skills. There's usually only one way to test for practical skills and that's to have them performed, although in certain circumstances they can be simulated (many pilots only ever get to use a flight simulator before flying a new plane for real [Figure 18-13]).

Figure 18-13　An example of Microsoft Flight Simulator

Many, but certainly not all types of learning can be assessed online:

**Cognitive**

Online methods include:

- submission of essays as email attachments
- on-screen tests
- problem-solving exercises
- assessment using one-to-one chat

**Affective**

In this domain, online methods include:
- questionnaires using web page forms
- one-to-one chat
- group chat

**Psychomotor**

The psychomotor domain is not well suited to online measurement, unless the subject happens to be use of the mouse or keyboard. (Figure 18-14)

Figure 18-14   An example of mouse and keyboard

◆ **Measuring application**

Although the primary purpose of training is to bring about learning, not much money would be made available for training if that was as far as it went. Sponsors of training need to know that what is learned as a result of training will be applied back on the job with some effect, hopefully positive. In fact, as the sponsors, they have a *right* to know this.

At level 3, we are measuring the extent to which new knowledge, skills and attitudes are translated into new job behaviors—in other words, the extent to which learning is being applied.

Unfortunately, there are many reasons why learning does not get applied:
- it is forgotten
- it is discouraged
- it is not reinforced
- there is no opportunity to apply it
- when applied, it doesn't work

If any of these are the case, then you need to know about it. You may be able to revise the course or introduce new follow-up procedures that will help cure the problem.

So how can we measure the extent to which learning is applied?

**Observation**

Tutors, coaches or the learner's supervisor can watch out for the way in which learning is being applied. They can also provide positive reinforcement where the results are successful and constructive feedback and encouragement where they are not.

**Questionnaires**

A more structured approach is to have the learner's peers, subordinates or supervisor complete a questionnaire (Figure 18-15), listing the desired behaviors and asking for feedback on the extent to which they are in evidence.

**Automatically**

In some job positions, where the learner is working with electronic equipment, it may be possible for evidence of behaviors to be gathered automatically.

Figure 18-15 Filling in questionnaire

**Self-reporting**

Learners will know better than anyone whether they are applying their new learning. You may ask learners to keep counts of what they do, complete checklists or questionnaires.

◆ **Measuring business results**

The real benefits of training can not be measured in terms of learner reactions, nor the amount of learning that has been achieved; not even the extent to which behaviors may have changed. The real benefits come from improved performance—traditionally the hardest training outcome to forecast or measure.

So, what do when the going gets tough? Back away and focus our evaluation efforts on easier measures? No, we do the very best we can, because all other measures fail to reflect the hard reality that training must pay off in measurable business results.

If it is any comfort, trainers are not alone in finding it difficult to calculate the benefits of what they do. Is it any easier to measure the benefits obtained from launching a new product, running an advertising campaign, initiating a research programme or changing the pay and benefits policy?

Let's look at some of the major categories of benefits:

**Labour savings**

Labour savings occur where, as a result of the training, less effort is needed to achieve current levels of output. We have to assume that savings are realised by a reduction in the amount of labour applied to a particular job, not by utilizing the newly available time to achieve further output on the same job.

Labour savings will only be realised if the labour applied to a job can really be reduced, whether this comes as a result of transfers of staff to new positions, re-allocations of work or redundancies. If the time savings simply result in slacker, then there is no saving.

Examples of labour savings include:
- reduced duplication of effort
- less time spent correcting mistakes
- faster access to information

**Productivity increases**

Productivity increases occur where, as a result of training, additional output can be achieved with the same level of effort. This implies that the organization requires or desires more output in the area in question. If it does not, then it might be better to express the benefit as a cost saving.

Examples of productivity increases include:
- improved methodologies reducing the effort required
- higher levels of skill leading to faster work
- higher levels of motivation leading to increased effort

**Other cost savings**

Cost savings can be achieved in a variety of ways, not just through savings in labour. Examples include:
- fewer machine breakdowns
- lower staff turnover
- a reduction in bad debts

**Obtaining measures**

Level 4 measures are the key performance indicators of the organization and, as such, you will probably find that the relevant data is already available. However, you may need to work hard to gain access to it in the form you need.

◆ **Measuring return on investment**

At level 5 we measure the financial impact of the business results realised at level 4. The most popular way of expressing this impact is as a return on investment (ROI).

ROI is calculated as follows:

$$\% \text{ROI} = \frac{\text{benefits} \times 100}{\text{costs}}$$

ROI relates to a specified period of time, typically a year or two years. First you measure all of the costs associated with the particular training programme over this period:
- analysis, design and development costs
- promotional costs
- admin costs
- tutor costs
- learner costs (time, expenses, lost productivity)

- equipment and facilities costs
- evaluation costs

Then you measure the financial benefits obtained over the same period:

- labour savings
- productivity increases
- cost savings

Then you can calculate the ROI.

Let's imagine you have been running an online management training programme and want to calculate the ROI over the first year. You measure the costs as \$100,000 and the benefits as \$130,000. Your ROI is $130,000/100,000 \times 100$, or $130\%$.

◆ **Measuring before and after**

To measure the effect of training, you need to take each indicator in turn and generate before and after data—what the level was before the training and what it was afterwards. The difference between the two provides an indication of the effect of the training.

For example, sales in a certain region may be \$10m a month leading up to a training programme and \$12m a month after. The 20% increase in productivity could be attributed to the training and entered into the ROI analysis.

**Control groups**

It is not always so clear cut that training has been the cause of a change in a performance indicator. Say that a number of measures were taken simultaneously to cure a problem. How do you know which of the measures was responsible for any positive results? Similarly, at the same time as a training programme is run, there may be a completely unexpected downturn in a market, meaning that performance actually goes down after the training. How can you separate the effect of the training from the effect of the downturn?

In these situations, the interaction between these variables can be significantly reduced by the use of a control group. A control group is a subset of the target population that does not receive the training. By comparing the results of those who have received the training with those of the control group, you can separate the effect of the training on performance.

For example, here are some statistics for a particular performance indicator:

|  | **Before** | **After** | **Change** |
| --- | --- | --- | --- |
| Group receiving training | 10 | 16 | +60% |
| Control group | 10 | 12 | +20% |
| Effect of training |  |  | +40% |

It can be seen from this table that performance has raised by 20% even without training. The increase in performance that can be attributed to the training is therefore 40%.

**Where next?**

Sometimes it seems that evaluation is becoming a show of machismo. "What level is your company up to? Oh dear, you mean you're still using happy sheets? We've just graduated to level 5. Soon we'll be measuring the effects of our training on the global economy."

It's true to say that evaluation does get trickier the more you move up the levels. It's also true to say that financial impact is an increasingly important issue. Remember that *all* levels of evaluation are important for different reasons, but that the only ones that count are those where you can produce valid, reliable results. Get evaluating—you may even find that your online learning's been a success.

## New Words

  meta-analysis 元分析,后设分析
  audio-visual *adj.* 视听的
  metacognitive *adj.* 认知的 *n.* 元认知
  per se *adv.* 本身,本质上
  authenticity *n.* 确实性,真实性
  terminology *n.* 1. 专门用语,术语 2. 术语的正确使用,术语用法
  administrivia *n.* 1. 每天重复性的电子信件 2. 新闻 3. 摘要等的处理工作
  confrontational *adj.* 挑衅的,对抗的
  spur *n.* 1. 马刺 2. 激励因素;刺激,鞭策 *vt.* 1. 以马刺策(马)使其快跑 2. 激励
  scramble *vt.* 混杂,把……搅乱
  copious *adj.* 丰富的
  rehearsal *n.* 练习,排练,排演
  articulation *n.* 清晰度;咬合;关节
  bout *n.* 1. 比赛,较量,回合 2. 一段(工作),一次(训练),一场(疾病)
  insomnia *n.* 〈医〉失眠(症)
  tally *n.* 账;记录;比分;得分 *vt.* & *vi.* (使)符合;(使)吻合
  collate *vt.* 校对,整理
  spreadsheet *n.* 电子制表软件,电子数据表
  slacker *n.* 逃避工作的人;偷懒的人
  self-determined *adj.* 自主的,自决的
  ubiquitous *adj.* 普遍存在;无处不在的

## Notes

[1] As Clark notes, meta-analysis studies on media research have shown that students gain significant learning benefits when learning from audio-visual or computer media, as opposed to conventional instruction; however, the same studies suggest that the reason for those benefits is not the medium of instruction, but the instructional strategies built into the learning materials.

**译文:** 正如 Clark 所说,有关媒体研究的元分析研究已经显示,当从音频—视频或计

算机媒体学习而不是从传统教学学习时,学生获得了显著的学习帮助。但是,同样的研究表明,这些帮助的原因并不是教学媒体,而是建构在学习资料中的教学策略。

- as Clark notes 是由 as 引导的方式状语从句。
- that students gain significant learning benefits 是由 that 引导的宾语从句,用来解释说明 show。
- when learning from audio-visual or computer media 是由 when 引导的时间状语从句。
- that the reason for those benefits is not the medium of instruction, but the instructional strategies built into the learning materials 是由 that 引导的宾语从句,用来解释说明 suggest。
- as opposed to 与……相反

[2] As a result, the author defines online learning as the use of the Internet to access learning materials; to interact with the content, instructor, and other learners; and to obtain support during the learning process, in order to acquire knowledge, to construct personal meaning, and to grow from the learning experience.

**译文**:因此,作者将在线学习定义为:使用因特网来获得学习资料,与教学内容、教师和其他学生交流,在学习过程中获得支持以便能获取知识,构建个人的理解并从学习经验中成长。

- define... as 定义为,解释为
- interact with 1. 与……相互作用,与……相互影响 2. 与……相互配合
- 四个 to 都表示目的。

[3] Students in courses that are supplemented by products like Blackboard no longer have to worry if they cannot make an instructor's regular office hours, as they still have the ability to submit inquiries via e-mail at any time.

**译文**:在有如黑板这种设施的课程里,学生不必再为他们是否能在教师正常办公时间去而烦恼了,因为他们仍然能随时通过发送电子邮件来询问问题。

- that are supplemented by products like Blackboard 是由 that 引导的定语从句,用来修饰限定先行词 courses 的。
- supplemented by 通过……增补(补充)
- if they cannot make an instructor's regular office hours 是由 if 引导的宾语从句。
- regular office hours 正常办公时间
- at any time 在任何时候,随时

[4] This results in reflection and articulation of content, as the very process of reporting and writing about what they have learned engages students in an active learning experience.

**译文**:这(指学生必须登陆课程的在线部分并在回答问题之前思考相关教学内容)使学生能思考和表达课程内容,因为学生们对所学内容进行报道和写作的这一过程使他们处在一个活跃的学习体验中。

- result in 引起,导致;以……为结局
- as the very process of reporting and writing about what they have learned engages students in an active learning experience 是由 as 引导的原因状语从句。

- engage in 参加；从事；忙于

[5] Although sometimes disregarded, reactions are important because, if students react negatively to your courses, they are less likely to transfer what they learned to their work and more likely to give bad reports to their peers, leading in turn to lower student numbers.

**译文：**虽然有时学习者的反应被忽视,但这种反应其实是很重要的,因为如果学生对你的课程反应消极的话,他们不可能将所学的东西运用到工作中去,而是很有可能对他们周围的人给予坏的报道,这又将导致更少的学生数量。

- although sometimes disregarded 是过去分词作后置定语,修饰限定 reactions。
- if students react negatively to your courses 是由 if 引导的条件状语从句。
- what they learned 是由 what 引导的宾语从句,用来解释说明 transfer。
- leading in turn to lower student numbers 是现在分词做状语。
- react to 对……作出反应（评价,应答）
- transfer to 移动到,调至,转移到
- lead to 导致,引起
- in turn 依次,轮流地

## Selected Translation

## Text A

### 在线学习简述

关于是使用某种特别的传输技术还是使用教学设计改进了学习的争论与日俱增。人们已经认识到专门的传输技术能为学习教材提供高效、及时的入口。但是,Clark 在 1983 年声称,技术仅仅是传输教学的手段而已,它们本身并没有影响学生的成绩。正如克拉克所说,有关媒体研究的元分析研究已经显示,当从音频—视频或计算机媒体学习而不是从传统教学学习时,学生获得了显著的学习帮助。但是,同样的研究表明,这些帮助的原因并不是教学媒体,而是建构在学习资料中的教学策略。同样地,Schramm 表示,学习更大程度上被学习资料中的内容和教学策略,而不是被用来传输教学的技术类型所影响。

根据 Bonk 和 Reynolds,为了促进对网络的更高考虑,在线学习必须创造有挑战性的活动,这种活动能使学生将新旧信息连接在一起,能获得有意义的知识,并且能应用他们的元认知能力。因此,是教学策略而非传输技术在影响学习的质量。Kozma 辩论道,需要电脑的某种特定属性将现实模型及仿真物呈现给学生,因此媒体的确影响了学习。然而,在本质上并不是电脑使学生学习,而是所设计的现实模型及仿真物以及学生与这些模型及仿真物的交互使学生学习。电脑仅仅是提供处理能力并且传输教学给学生的手段。Kozma 的主张是正确的,但是如果仿真物没有用声音设计原理来开发的话,学生将不会从仿真物中学到东西。

进入在线学习非常灵活,在任何地方并且通常在任何时间都可以。本质上,在线学习能使参与者打破时空限制,然而,必须合理设计学习资料以吸引学生并促进学习。根

据 Rossett,在线学习前途远大,但是它需要大量的工作和资源,而且必须做好。"做好"意味着必须合理设计在线学习资料,以学生和学习为中心,而且必须提供足够的帮助。Ring 与 Athieux 认为,在线学习必须有较高的真实性(例如学生必须在上课的环境下学习)、较高的交互性和较高的合作。

有许多不同的术语被用来指代在线学习,这个事实使得开发出一个通用的定义很难。通常被使用的术语就有电子化学习、因特网学习、分布式学习、网络化学习和远程学习。所有这些术语都意味着学生与导师或教师离得远,学生使用一些技术(通常是电脑)来获得学习教材,学生通过传输技术来与辅导老师或教师以及其他学生进行交流,以及学生获得了某种形式的支持。这篇文章将通篇使用"在线学习"。在文献资料里在线学习有很多定义,这些定义折射出实践和相关技术的多样性。Carliner 将在线学习定义成展示在电脑上的教学资料。Khan 将在线教学定义为通过使用网络这种媒介来传输教学到远程听众的创新方法。然而,在线学习不仅仅是通过网络来进行教材的展示和传递:学生和学习的过程必须是在线学习的中心。因此,作者将在线学习定义为:使用因特网来获得学习资料,与教学内容、教师和其他学生交流,在学习过程中获得支持以便能获取知识,构建个人的理解并从学习经验中成长。

## Exercises

**1. Short Answers:**

(1) What's the author's definition of Online Learning according to text A?

(2) What are the educational advantages that arise when supplementing a course with web-based tools?

(3) What are the reasons for measuring the success of online learning programme?

(4) What are the four levels of evaluation defined by Kirkpatrick in 1975 and what is the fifth level defined by Phillips in 1997?

**2. Calculation:**

Given that

$$\% \text{ROI} = \frac{\text{benefits} \times 100}{\text{costs}}$$

then, if you have been running an online management training programme and you measure the costs as \$100,000 and the benefits as \$120,000, what is your ROI?

# 投稿指南(Ⅱ)

## 一、如何修改论文

不管在哪里,稿件的评审都不可能是百分之百地公平。丘吉尔有一句名言:同行评审(peer review)是最坏的体系。一般说来,作者拿出的初稿都不是尽善尽美的,有必要进行认真的修改和润色,这正如唐朝人李沂所说:"能改则瑕可为瑜,瓦砾可为珠玉。"下面介绍几种常用的改稿方法。

其一，诵读法。初稿写成后要诵读几遍，一边读，一边思考，并把文气不接、语意不顺的地方随手改过来。叶圣陶先生十分推崇这种"诵读法"；鲁迅先生写完文章后，总要先读读，"自己觉得拗口的，就增删几个字，一定要它读得顺口。"可见，诵读法实在是一种简便易行、效果显著的方法。

其二，比较法。比较是认识事物的有效方法。把自己的初稿和同类文章中的优秀范文对照、比较，反复揣摩，分析得失，然后加以修改。这是初学者最需要掌握的。

其三，旁正法。"三人行，必有我师焉"，修改稿件时多听取各方面的意见，扬长避短，去粗取精，是大有益处的。作者必须高度重视修改这一环中，通过反复推敲、加工，使文稿从内容到形式都达到精粹、完美的高度。

## 二、如何做学术报告（How to Give a Technical Talk）

进行学术报告对一个学者是至关重要的，它不仅展示了你的研究成果，同时也锻炼了你把握事情的能力。通常中国留学生遇到的最苦闷的事情就是做报告（Presentation），这当然是中西教育上的差异造成的。目前，许多高校教学中正在积极鼓励做报告。

好的论文并不等于好的报告。要做好报告，准备充分是关键。一般应考虑以下因素：

- 好的报告工具，如 PPT。
- 清晰的报告结构。
- 适当的字体。
- 得体的姿势与肢体语言，包括手势、语调等。
- 适中的语速。
- 掌握好时间。

必须要记住，报告人感兴趣的内容听众不一定感兴趣，报告人的任务是让听众对所讲的内容感兴趣，因而以听众为中心的报告风格非常值得提倡。

下面是一段有关注意力与时间关系图的论述：

The average attendee of a conference is by all means willing to listen to you, but he is also easily distracted. You should realize that only a minor part of the people have come specifically to listen to your talk. The rest is there for a variety of reasons, to wait for the next speaker, or to get a general impression of the field, or whatever. Figure 18-16 illustrates how the average audience pays attention during a typical presentation of, let's say, 30 minutes. Almost everyone listens in the beginning, but halfway the attention may well have dropped to around 10% — 20% of what it was at the start. At the end, many people start to listen again, particularly if you announce your conclusions, because they hope to take something away from the presentation.

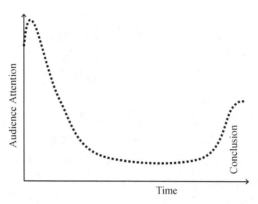

Figure 18-16  Typical attention the audience pays to an average presentation

下是文章（Figure 18-17）与报告（Figure 18-18）结构安排上的区别。

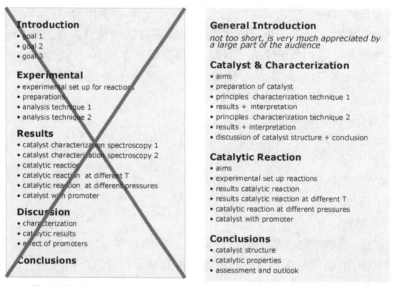

Figure 18-17　Article structure not recommended for talks

Figure 18-18　Presentation structure

### 三、科技论文中常见的错误

科技论文是一种专门的文体，由于许多科技论文都由英文写成，加之很多国内学者没有海外求学经历，因而想写出一篇准确规范的英文科技论文还是有相当的难度，正如Felicia Brittman 所言，即使以英语为母语的学生要写出一篇规范的科技论文也需要半年到一年的训练时间。下面是 Felicia Brittman 总结出的中国学生撰写科技论文时的常见错误。

• The single most common habit is the omission of articles a, an, and the.

• Very long sentences are especially common in Chinese-English writing because the writers often translate directly from Chinese to English. A example as follows:

Too long: The clear height of the case is 6.15 meters; the thickness of the roof is 0.85

meters; the thickness of the bottom is 0.90 meters, the overall width is 26.6 meters, the overall length of the axial cord is 304.5 meters, the length of the jacking section is about 148.8 meters; the weight of the case is about 24127 tons.

Modification:

- Case clearance height 6.15 meters
- Roof thickness 0.85 meters
- Bottom thickness 0.90 meters
- Overall width 26.6 meters
- Overall length of the axial cord 304.5 meters
- Length of the jacking section 148.8 meters (approx.)
- Weight of the case 24127 tons (approx.)

• Prefacing the main idea of a sentence by stating the purpose, location or reason first.

Incorrect: For the application in automobile interiors, this paper studies the nesting optimization problem in leather manufacturing.

Correct: This paper studies the nesting optimization problem in leather manufacturing for application in automobile interiors.

• Tendency of placing phrases which indicate time at the beginning of a sentence

Incorrect: When $U$ is taken as the control parameter, the BDs for $\Delta = 0.0, 0.001, 0.005$ are shown in Fig. 8.

Correct: Figure 8 shows the BDs for $\Delta = 0.0, 0.001$, and $0.005$ when $U$ is taken as the control parameter.

• Place the most important subject at the beginning of the sentence for emphasis.

Incorrect: Based on the triangulation structure built from unorganized points or a CAD model, the extended STL format is described in this section.

Correct: The extended STL format is described in this section based on the triangulation structure built from unorganized points or a CAD model.

• Avoid redundancy in the following types of phrases frequently used by Chinese English writers

| Instead of | Say |
|---|---|
| Research work | Research or work |
| Limit condition | Limit or condition |
| Layout scheme | Layout or scheme |
| Arrangement plan | Arrangement or plan |
| Output performance | Output or performance |
| Simulation results | Simulation or results |
| Application results | Application or results |
| Knowledge information | Knowledge or information |

• Certain words demand that the noun they modify is plural. These include different, various, and number words.

| Don't write | Instead write |
| --- | --- |
| Different node | Different nodes |
| Various method | Various methods |
| Two advantage | Two advantages |
| Fifteen thermocouple | Fifteen thermocouples |

# Part 7　The Evaluation of Educational Technology

## Unit 19　The Evaluation of Learning Source and Learning Process

▲ **Knowledge Objectives**

When you have completed this unit, you will be able to:
- Know a bit of history and context of evaluation
- State the two kinds of evaluation and identify the differences between them
- Understanding the educational framework advocated by Alessi and Trollip and know the three basic methods of evaluating the design qualities and their respective processes
- Be familiar with the evaluation for distance education

▲ **Professional Terms**

| | |
|---|---|
| summative evaluation | 总结性评价 |
| formative evaluation | 形成性评价 |
| conceptual framework | 构思范围,概念范围,基本概念 |
| distance education | 远程教育 |
| quantitative evaluation | 定量评价 |
| qualitative evaluation | 定性评价 |

## Text A

### The History and Context of Evaluation[①]

Evaluation, like the urban poor, grew up in the projects-large government structures aimed at concentrating limited resources on seemingly unlimited problems.[1] House has insightfully reviewed the emergence of evaluation as a profession under the tutelage and hegemony of government. Regardless of political-economic system, the dominant motif of modern government worldwide is planning. That means assessing needs, identifying solutions, targeting populations, setting goals, procuring resources, implementing programs, and, of course, evaluating results. It's all very logical and rational.

---

① http://www.abrasco.org.br/GTs/GT%20Promocao/develomental%20evaluation_patton.pdf

Of course, imperfections exist: inadequately assessed needs; fuzzy and conflicting goals; poorly defined targets; insufficient resources; and sloppy implementation. But those are precisely the problems evaluations expose. The logic remains intact.

Within this logic, we've distinguished two kinds of evaluations: summative and formative. Summative evaluations judge merit and worth: the extent to which desired goals have been attained; whether measured outcomes can be attributed to observed interventions; and the conditions under which goals were attained that would affect generalizability and therefore intervention dissemination.[2] Formative evaluations help programs get ready for summative evaluation by improving program processes and providing feedback about strengths and weaknesses that appear to affect goal attainment.

Striven's original distinction between formative and summative in curriculum evaluation made it clear that the purpose of formative evaluation was to get ready for summative evaluation. Over time, the meaning of formative evaluation has been enlarged to include any evaluation whose primary purpose is program improvement, where improvement means a higher degree of goal attainment.[3]

# Text B

## Three Basic Methods of Learning Evaluation[①]

Holistic conceptual frameworks for educational evaluation have been developed over many years. These frameworks are designed for use with traditional forms of educational delivery and require large resources over considerable periods of time to implement. Other, less comprehensive and less expensive evaluation frameworks have also been devised. For example, Alessi and Trollip advocate three basic methods of evaluating the design qualities of any course:

- review of subject matter by experts and instructional designers to assess the content, appearance, and evidence of good instructional practices
- feedback from students involved in a pilot offer of the course
- validation of the instructional effectiveness by students in a mainstream (normal) class

The first of Alessi and Trollip's methods can also be referred to as a quality review process consisting of seven parts:

- language and grammar
- surface features of the displays
- questions and menus
- other issues of pedagogy
- invisible functions of the lesson
- subject matter

---

① http://www.ncver.edu.au/research/proj/nr8007.pdf

- offline materials (Figure 19-1)

Alessi and Trollip have designed a quality review checklist to guide such evaluations. The checklist itemises different features of the lessons that need deliberate decisions. Considerations relating to "language and grammar" include features such as reading level, cultural bias, technical terms and jargon spelling, grammar and punctuation and spacing. Displays, presentation modes, text quality, input, notes to indicate the end of the lesson form aspects relating to "surface features". The section on "questions and menus" include menus, questions, how to answer questions, format of feedback, and quality feedback. "Issues of pedagogy" relates to considerations about learner types, facilitation methods, types of resources, student control, motivation, interactions, and animation and graphics. Records and data, security and accessibility, too much data and restarting are classed as "invisible functions of the lesson". The "subject matter" features concentrate on goals and objectives, information, content emphasis and organization. "Offline materials" relates to printed manuals (Figure 19-1), general advice about the operation of learning systems, lesson content, auxiliary materials and other resources.

Figure 19-1　Printed manuals and books as offline materials

The second method of evaluation, pilot testing, according to Alessi and Trollip (1991) is a seven-step process:
- selecting helpers (for example, students)
- explaining the procedures to them
- determining their prior knowledge
- observing them during the learning sessions
- interviewing them afterwards
- assessing their learning
- revising the lesson

The third of the processes advocated by Alessi and Trollip involves validation of the lessons to check instructional effectiveness. This is done by delivering the course in a natural instructional setting. Summative evaluation procedures for a thorough treatment are recommended for this stage of evaluation. Two key areas that need to be assessed are students' "achievements—to ensure that they have learnt what was intended—and assessment of attitudes towards the course.[4] The Alessi and Trollip approach, however, does not make explicit any relying view of what constitutes good teaching and learning practice, leaving the basis of the evaluation hidden from scrutiny. Other authors have also advocated approaches where the views of teaching and learning remain undeclared. For example, Eisenberg and Johnson provide a checklist, named the "big six skills approach to information problem solving", that lists major

Figure 19-2  Web-based learners on campus

skills important for a range of learning tasks. The skills are task definition, information-seeking strategies, location and access, use of information, synthesis and evaluation. According to Eisenberg and Johnson, these skills are required for learning using computers and hence have relevance for web-based learners (Figure 19-2). No doubt these skills are important for carrying out a range of learning tasks. However, they are eclectic criteria not based on a coherent body of research as to what constitutes good teaching and learning practice.[5]

## Text C

## Evaluation for Distance Education①

Effective teachers use a variety of means, some formal and others informal, to determine how much and how well their students are learning. For example, to formally evaluate student learning, most teachers use quizzes, tests, examinations (Figure 19-3), term papers, lab reports, and homework. These formal evaluation techniques help the instructor to evaluate student achievement and assign grades.

Figure 19-3  An examination is taken at an examination hall.

To evaluate classroom learning informally, teachers also use a variety of techniques. For example, teachers pose questions, listen carefully to student questions and comments, and monitor body language and facial expressions. Informal, often implicit evaluations permit the teacher to make adjustments in their teaching: to slow down or review material in response to questions, confusion, and misunderstandings; or to move on when student performance exceeds expectations.

When teaching at a distance, educators must address a different teaching challenge than when teaching in a traditional classroom. For example, instructors no longer have:

- A traditional, familiar classroom.
- A relatively homogeneous group of students.

---

① http://www.uidaho.edu/eo/dist4.html

- Face-to-face feedback during class (e. g. students' questions, comments, body language, and facial expressions).
- Total control over the distance delivery system.
- Convenient opportunities to talk to students individually.

For these reasons, distance educators may find it useful to not only formally evaluate students through testing and homework, but to use a more informal approach in collecting data to determine:

- Student comfort with the method used to deliver the distant instruction.
- Appropriateness of assignments.
- Clarity of course content.
- If class time is well spent.
- Teaching effectiveness.
- How a course can be improved.

Evaluation can be either formative, summative, or a combination of both.

**Formative evaluation:**

- Is an on-going process to be considered at all stages of instruction?
- Will enable the instructor to improve the course as he/she proceeds.
- Facilitates course and content adaptation.
- Will identify major gaps in the instructional plan or the need for minor adjustments.

Some strategies that educators can use to collect formative data from their distant students include:

- Post cards—provide each student with prestamped and preaddressed postcards. On a weekly basis, have students use the postcards to share their concerns or respond to questions during the last three to five minutes of class. (Figure 19-4)

Figure 19-4 Students use the postcards to share their concerns or respond to questions.

- Electronic mail—Can be a very effective way for instructors and students to communicate. Another plus, while the instructor is eliciting information about classroom learning, students become familiar with the use of electronic mail, a valuable skill.

- Telephone—Call students often. Ask them open ended questions (e. g., "What snags did you run into on the second writing assignment?") to let students voice their concerns. Follow with probes (e. g., "Then, will you need more information sources?"). Set phone-in office hours but be sure to welcome calls at other times. (Figure 19-5)

Figure 19-5 Ask students open ended questions through telephone.

**Summative evaluation:**

- Assesses overall effectiveness of the finished product or course.
- Can be a springboard in developing a revision plan.
- Can be a baseline of information for designing a new plan, program, or course.
- Will not help current students since it is conducted upon course completion.

Some questions that educators may want to ask students when collecting summative data include:

- List five weaknesses of the course.
- List three (or five) strengths of the course.
- If you were teaching the course, what would you do differently?
- Student background information: age, level in school, number of distance delivered courses taken prior to this one.
- What would you recommend to a friend planning to take this course?
- What did you think would be covered in this course but was not?
- Would you recommend this course to a friend? Why or why not?

Within the context of formative and summative evaluation, data may be collected through quantitative and qualitative methods.

**Quantitative evaluation:**

- Involves asking questions which can be statistically tabulated and analyzed, frequently using a scale, check list, or yes/no responses.
- Limits students to responding to the categories made available to them.
- Needs a large student sample for relevant statistical analyses.

Quantitative methods may be most useful for gathering information on large numbers of respondents for whom more in-depth, personalized approaches are not feasible. However, they do have some significant drawbacks:

- Many distance education courses have relatively small class sizes with students from various backgrounds. These small, stratified populations typically defy relevant statistical analysis.
- Quantitative surveys typically result in a rate of return of under 50 percent. A low rate of return often suggests that only those feeling very positively or negatively about the course responded to the evaluation.
- By definition and design, forced choice surveys offer respondents a limited number of possible response options. Therefore, fresh insights and unique perspectives falling outside the provided response categories go unreported.
- The cumbersome and often tedious nature of quantitative data collection can discourage formative evaluation, and often results in an over-reliance on summative evaluation.
- Statistical analysis often results in an illusion of precision that may be far from reality.

**Qualitative evaluation:**

- Is typically more subjective.
- Involves gathering a wider range and depth of information.
- Is more difficult to tabulate into neat categories.
- Will be less affected by typical small class size.
- Is a more flexible and dynamic method.
- Is not limited to pre-conceived topic of inquiry.
- Allows for student output of topics.

Can use:

• Open ended questioning—with respondents asked to identify course strengths and weaknesses, suggest changes, explore attitudes towards distance delivery methods, etc.

• Participant observation—with the distance educator observing group dynamics and behavior while participating in the class as an observer, asking occasional questions, and seeking insights regarding the process of distance education.

Figure 19-6  Interactive Television classes are classes that are aired at one campus and sent electronically to other campuses.

• Non-participant observation—with the distance educator observing a course (e.g., an audioconference, interactive television class [Figure 19-6], etc.) without actually participating or asking questions.

• Content analysis—with the evaluator using predetermined criteria to review course documents including the syllabus and instructional materials as well as student assignments and course-related planning documents.

• Interviews—with a facilitator or specially trained individual collecting evaluative data through one-on-one and small-group interviews with students. (Figure 19-7)

Figure 19-7  Collecting evaluative data through small-group interviews with students

**What to Evaluate**

Consider the following areas:

• Use of technology—familiarity, concerns, problems, positive aspects, attitude toward technology.

• Class formats—effectiveness of lecture, discussion, question and answer; quality of questions or problems raised in class; encouragement given students to express themselves.

• Class atmosphere—conduciveness to student learning.

• Quantity and quality of interaction with other students and with instructor.

• Course content—relevancy, adequate body of knowledge, organization.

• Assignments—usefulness, degree of difficulty and time required timeliness of feedback, readability level of print materials.

• Tests—frequency, relevancy, sufficient review, difficulty, feedback.

• Support services—facilitator, technology, library services, instructor availability.

• Student achievement—adequacy, appropriateness, timeliness, student involvement.

• Student attitude—attendance, assignments submitted, class participation.

• Instructor—contribution as discussion leader, effectiveness, organization, preparation, enthusiasm, openness to student views.

**Evaluation Tips**

• Check out and adapt already published questionnaires; there's no need to re-invent the wheel.

• Draft and revise questions; change if necessary.

• Make use of follow-up probes.

• Alternate between instruction and interaction.

• Sequence your questions for best effect—go ahead and ask for suggestions for improvement before asking for what is good. This will help convey sincerity for seeking improvements.

• Place open ended questions after quick answer questions. This gives students built-in thinking time.

• On summative evaluation, assure anonymity. This can be accomplished by having all questionnaires sent to a neutral site where they would be removed from their envelopes and forwarded to the instructor without a postmark.

• Establish rapport by being interested and supportive. Withhold judgmental responses.

• Adapt to the student in degree of formality and pace of communication.

• Use evaluation as a method for understanding teaching and learning.

Try to get both positive and negative feedback. It is important not only to know what is not working, but also what is working.

# New Words

tutelage    *n.*  指导

hegemony  n. 统治;势力范围
motif  n. 1.（文艺作品等的）主题,中心思想;基本模式 2. 基本图案,基本色彩
procure  vt. （努力）取得,（设法）获得
implement  vt. 使生效,贯彻,执行 n. 工具,器具,用具
dissemination  n. 分发
holistic  adj. 整体的,全盘的,整体主义的
pilot  n. 1. 飞行员,宇航员 2. 引航员;舵手 vt. 1. 驾驶 2. 带领,指引,引导 3. 试验,试用 adj. 实验性的;引导的
jargon  n. 行话;黑话;隐语
pedagogy  n. 教育学,教学法
facilitation  n. 简易化,助长
animation  n. 1. 兴奋,生气,活跃 2. 卡通[动画]片的制作
auxiliary  adj. 辅助的,补充的;备用的
scrutiny  n. 细看,细查;监视
eclectic  adj. （人）兼收并蓄的;（方法、思想等）折中的;从不同来源选辑的
elicit  vt. 引出,探出
snag  n. 1.（尤指潜伏的）困难,（未料到的）障碍 2. 尖利的突出物 3. 被刮破或钩坏的裂口
springboard  n. 跳板
tabulate  vi. 制表,列表显示,把……列为表格
stratify  vt. （使）分层,成层
cumbersome  adj. 沉重的,笨重的,转动不灵的
syllabus  n. 教学大纲;课程提纲

## Notes

[1] Evaluation, like the urban poor, grew up in the projects-large government structures aimed at concentrating limited resources on seemingly unlimited problems.

**译文：**就像城市的贫民一样,评价体系在庞大的政府结构下逐渐演变,旨在将有限的资源集中在看似无限的问题上。

◆ aimed at concentrating limited resources on seemingly unlimited problems 是过去分词做后置定语,用来修饰限定 government structures。

◆ aim at （以……）瞄准;针对,以……为目标;计划,打算

◆ concentrate on 专心于,把思想集中于;将……集中于……

[2] Summative evaluations judge merit and worth: the extent to which desired goals have been attained; whether measured outcomes can be attributed to observed interventions; and the conditions under which goals were attained that would affect generalizability and therefore intervention dissemination.

**译文：**总结性评价判断优点和价值:多大程度上达到了预期的目标,测量的结果是否

可以归因于观察干预,以及达到所预期的能够影响普遍性进而消除干涉因素的目标的条件。

• to which desired goals have been attained 作为 extent 的定语从句,用来解释说明 extent,其中介词 to 在定语从句中需提前。

• under which goals were attained 作为 conditions 的定语从句,用来解释说明 conditions,其中介词 under 在定语从句中需提前,而 that 从句又作为 conditions 的定语从句来进一步解释 conditions。

• attribute to 把某事归因于某人(某事)

[3] Over time, the meaning of formative evaluation has been enlarged to include any evaluation whose primary purpose is program improvement, where improvement means a higher degree of goal attainment.

**译文**:时至今日,形成性评价的意义已经扩大到包含任何一种首要目标为改进程序的评价,在这里改进意味着更大程度地达到目标。

• whose primary purpose is program improvement 作为 any evaluation 的定语从句,用来解释说明 any evaluation,其中 where improvement means a higher degree of goal attainment 是状语从句,由 where 引导。

[4] Two key areas that need to be assessed are students' achievements—to ensure that they have learnt what was intended—and assessment of attitudes towards the course.

**译文**:两个需要被评估的领域是学生的成绩——为了确保他们已经学会了预置的内容——以及学生对于课程的态度的评估。

• that need to be assessed are students' achievements 作为 areas 的定语从句,用来解释说明 areas,其中 to ensure that they have learnt what was intended 作为 students' achievements 的同位语,在这个同位语中,that 和 what 引导的从句分别作为 ensure 和 learnt 的宾语从句。

[5] However, they are eclectic criteria not based on a coherent body of research as to what constitutes good teaching and learning practice.

**译文**:尽管如此,他们还只是折中的标准,并没有基于研究的连贯体制——这种研究体制研究的是什么构成好的教学和学习实践。

• not based on a coherent body of research 是过去分词做定语,限定修饰 criteria。

• as to what constitutes good teaching and learning practice 作为 research 的定语从句,用来解释说明 research。

• as to 1. 至于,关于 2. 按着,根据

## Selected Translation

## Text A

### 评价的历史背景

就像城市的贫民一样,评价体系在庞大的政府结构下逐渐演变,旨在将有限的资源

集中在看似无限的问题上。豪斯具有洞察力地回顾了在现代政府的指导和统治下评价作为一种行业的出现。无论采取何种政治—经济体制,全世界范围内现代政府的指导思想是计划,这意味着评估需求、找出解决方法、瞄准对象、制定目标、获得资源、执行程序,当然还有评价结果。这都非常具有逻辑性和理性。

当然,有些地方还需要完善:需求评估不足、目标小而矛盾、目标不明确、资源不足,还有执行草率大意。但这些才是评价需要准确揭露的问题所在。整个逻辑性还是完整的。

在这个逻辑里,我们已经区分了评价的两种类型:总结性评价和形成性评价。总结性评价判断优点和价值:多大程度上达到了预期的目标、测量的结果是否可以归因于观察干预,以及达到所预期的能够影响普遍性进而消除干涉因素的目标的条件。形成性评价通过改进程序进程并且提供影响目标实现的优缺点的反馈来为总结性评价做准备工作。

斯屈芬对形成性和总结性在总课程评价里的独创性区别清晰地阐明了形成性评价的目标就是为总结性评价做准备。时至今日,形成性评价的意义已经扩大到包含任何一种首要目标为改进程序的评价,在这里改进意味着更大程度地达到目标。

## Exercises

**1. Please Explain the Following Professional Terms:**

(1) summative evaluation

(2) formative evaluation

(3) Quantitative evaluation

(4) Qualitative evaluation

(5) conceptual framework

**2. Short Answers:**

(1) What are the functions of summative evaluation and formative evaluation?

(2) Please state the three basic methods of evaluating the design qualities advocated by Alessi and Trollip.

(3) What are the subjects in summative evaluation of distance education?

# 应用文写作之一——信函

## 一、信函的基本原则和种类

一直以来,信函都是人们交际的一种重要的手段,即使在通信技术高度发达的今天,信函在社会交际和商业事务中仍然扮演着非常重要的作用,这是其他交际形式所无法取代的。信函具有独特的结构、格式和一些惯用的表达方式,掌握这些特点是十分重要的。信函的侧重点在于传递信息,表达情感,它要求内容简明扼要,条理清楚,表意准确,礼貌适度。随着时代的发展,写信的原则(Writing Principles)已从最原始的 3 个"C"(Conciseness、Clearness、Courtesy)发展到5个"C":Clearness(清晰)、Conciseness(简洁)、Correctness(正确)、Courtesy(礼貌)和Consideration(周到),继而到现在的7个"C",即在"5C"的基础上又增加了completeness(完整)和Concreteness(具体)。

具体来说,信函可以分为商业信函或公函(Business Letter or Official Correspondence)和个人信函(Private Letter)两种。商业信函一般谈论或处理重要事务,可能是推荐信、邀请信,或者询问、答复某事。个人信函一般比较随意,只需要满足以上的"5C"原则即可,我们在后面也将会以实例进行讲解。而如果是商业信函,在"5C"基础上我们还需要加上"完整"和"具体"的两个要求,因为商业信函精确的特点决定了它必须"完整"和"具体",完整而具体的书信更能达到预期的目的,更有助于建立友善的关系,还可以避免不必要的麻烦。

## 二、信封的写法

1. 邮票应该贴在信封右上角。
2. 寄信人的姓名、地址应该写在信封的左上角。
3. 收信人的姓名、地址应该写在信封的正中或右下角四分之一处。
4. 也有人喜欢把收件人的名字、地址写在信封正面中央,把寄件人的姓名、地址写在信封的反面。
5. 如果信是由第三者转交给收信人,则要在收信人姓名下面写明转交人的姓名,其前加(C/O = Care Of)。
6. 住址的写法与中文相反;英文住址原则上是由小至大,也就是说必须先写门牌号码、街路名称,再写城市、省(州)和邮政区号,最后一行则写上国家的名称。

## 三、信函的组成部分和格式

英语书信通常包括下面几个组成部分:信内地址、称呼、开头语、正文、结束语、签名、附件等。我们逐一来介绍。

1. 信内地址(Inside Address, Introductory Address)

信内地址即收信人的姓名和地址,写在信纸的左上角,从信纸的左边顶格开始写,低于写信人地址和发信日期一二行,也分并列式和斜列式两种,但应与信端(即信头)的书写格式保持一致。其次序是,先写收信人姓名、头衔和单位名称,占一二行,然后写地址,可占二至四行,例如:

(1) 并列式

Ms. Zhang
Wuhan University
Hongshan District, 430022
Wuhan
China

(2) 斜列式

Ms. Zhang
　Wuhan University

Hongshan District, 430022
　　Wuhan
　　　China

2. 称呼(Salutation)

称呼是收信人展开信后最先看到的文字,所以称呼也很有讲究。对收信人的称呼一般自成一行,写在低于信内地址一两行的地方。从信纸的左边顶格开始写,每个词的开头字母要大写。末尾处的符号,英国人用逗号,但美国和加拿大英语则多用冒号。称呼用语可视写信人与收信人的关系而定。

常用的收信人称呼有:先生 Mr.;夫人 Mrs.;小姐 Miss;夫人、小姐统称 Ms.;夫妇俩人用 Mr. and Mrs.。

3. 开头语(Initial Sentences)

开头语一般是一些寒暄语,用来引出正文。可以表示对对方的真挚的问候,也可以是表示对对方来信的感谢,还可以是对对方的想念之情。一些常用的开头语有:

- Many thanks for your last kind letter.
- I hope everything goes well.
- I miss you so much that...
- I beg to inform you that...
- I have the pleasure to tell you that...
- I regret to inform you that...
- I feel indebted for the kind note which you sent me on Saturday.
- I am going to answer your letter immediately and with pleasure.
- I am sorry that I have delayed answering your letter of recent date.

4. 信的正文(Body of the letter)

信的正文每段第一行应往右缩进约四五个字母。在写事务性信件时,正文一般开门见山,内容简单明了,条理清楚、易读、语气要自然诚恳。在写私人信件时,信写好之后若有什么遗漏,可用 P.S. 表示补叙。

5. 结束语(Complimentary Close)

结束语是指写信人的结尾套语。结束语一般低于正文一二行,可写在左边,也可以从信纸的中间或偏右的地方开始写。第一个词的开头字母要大写,末尾用逗号。结束语视写信人与收信人的关系而定。例如,写给机关、团体或不相识的人的信,一般:Yours (very) truly, Yours (very) sincerely, Yours (very) respectfully, Yours appreciatively, Comradely yours 等等。

在欧洲的一些国家里,多把 Yours 放在 sincerely 等词的前面。在美国和加拿大等国,则多把 yours 放在 Sincerely 等词之后。Yours 一词有时也可省略。

6. 签名(Signature)

信末的签名一般低于结束语一二行,从信纸中间偏右的地方开始写。若写信人是女性,与收信人又不相识,则一般在署名前用括号注上 Miss、Mrs. 或 Ms.,以便对方回信时知道如何称呼。

7. 附件（Enclosure）

信件若有附件，应在左下角注明 Encls. 或 Enc.。若附件不止一个，则应写出 2（或 3,4,5 等）Encls.，例如：

Enc：Resume

Encls：Grade Certificate

## 四、范例

1. 祝贺信

在国际交往中，祝贺信使用场合很多。国家之间、团体之间以及个人之间常对一些值得庆祝的大事互致祝贺，这也是增进国家之间的关系、加强个人的友谊的一种方式。这类书信也有正式的和普通的两种。正式的祝贺主要用于政府间、官员间，普通的祝贺则多用于个人交往。前者用词拘谨，经常使用一些套语；后者用词亲切，不拘格式，但也有一些常用的词句。

（1）祝贺新年

Your Excellency Mr. Ambassador,

On the occasion of New Year, may my wife and I extend to you and your wife our sincere greetings, wishing you a happy New Year, your career success and your family happiness.

Minister of Foreign Affairs

（2）祝贺信常用套语

- On the occasion of..., I wish to extend to you our warm congratulation on behalf of... and in my own name.

值此……之际，我代表……，并以我个人的名义，向你致以热烈祝贺。

- As..., may I, on behalf of the Chinese people and Government, express to you and through you to the people and Government of your country the heartiest congratulations.

当……之时，我代表中国人民和政府，向你并通过你向你们的人民和政府表示衷心的祝贺。

- May the friendly relations and co-operation between China and Japan develop daily.

祝愿中日两国友好合作，关系日益发展。

- May your session be a complete success.

祝大会圆满成功。

2. 感谢信

感谢信在国际交往中是一种很常见的书信形式。按照西方的惯例，当收到邀请、接待，收到祝贺、慰问，接受礼品、帮助等等，都应该写信致谢，以示礼貌。感谢信没有固定格式。语言要求诚恳、适当，不宜过长。

（1）感谢招待：

Dear Minister,

I am writing this letter to thank you for your warm hospitality accorded to me and my delegation during our recent visit to your beautiful country. I would also like to thank you for your interesting discussion with me which I have found very informative and useful.

During the entire visit, my delegation and I were overwhelmed by the enthusiasm expressed by your business representatives on cooperation with China. I sincerely hope we could have more exchanges like this one when we would be able to continue our interesting discussion on possible ways to expand our bilateral economic and trade relations and bring our business people together.

I am looking forward to your early visit to China when I will be able to pay back some of the hospitality I received during my memorable stay in your beautiful country. With kind personal regards.

Faithfully yours,

Chao Cai

Minister of Economic Cooperation

（2）感谢讲学

Dear Mr. Brown：

I am writing on behalf of all members of our department to say how much we all enjoyed your excellent lecture on Tuesday. We have learned a lot about the changes in present-day Information Technology and are very grateful to you for coming to our university and giving us such an interesting and informative talk.

Thank you very much and we look forward to hearing from you again.

Yours sincerely,

（3）用于各种场合的感谢语：

- I can't sufficiently express my thanks for your thoughtful kindness.

对你给予我们的无微不至的关怀，我难以充分表达我的谢意。

- This is to thank you again for your wonderful hospitality.

再次感谢你的盛情款待。

- We acknowledge with gratitude your message of good wishes.

感谢你的良好的祝愿。

- Many thanks for the fine desk lamp that you send me, and I feel deeply moved by this token of your affection.

非常感谢你送给我的精致的台灯。这一友情的象征，使我深受感动。

3. 投诉信

投诉信一般是用来向被投诉单位的领导或者负责人提出交易过程中出现的失误，这些失误可能是服务的质量问题、态度问题，还有可能是所需商品没有及时达到，或者数量上或者质量上存在问题。当出现失误的时候，我们就可以写一封投诉信，向对方的负责人说明情况。

Dear Sir/Madam：

I am writing to you to complain about your hotel. I had a terrible stay in Room 3008 of your hotel from the 4th to the 16th of August 2006, when I came to Guangzhou on business.

Firstly, the air-conditioning in my room could not be turned down or switched off. When I asked the reception staff to do something about it, they laughed and told me it was better than being hot. I asked your front of house manager and she told me she would send someone to my room immediately. No one came. As a result, I was very cold every time I was in the room.

Secondly, I found the bathroom dirty and the hot water was always warm.

Thirdly, the noise at night was extremely loud and I found it difficult to sleep. I asked to change rooms, but was told it was impossible because the hotel was full.

I paid a lot for my stay in your hotel and expect much better service from such a well-known hotel. In future, I will not be staying at your hotel again and will inform my business associates of the terrible service. Wish your service can be improved.

4. 道歉信

在日常生活中难免会出现一些差错,因为失约、损坏了别人的东西等。在这种情况下,应及时写信表示道歉,以消除不必要的误会。写道歉信时应注意态度要诚恳,原委要解释清楚,措辞要委婉。

来看一个因未能及时还书致歉的例子。

Dear Miss Liu:

Excuse me for my long delaying in return to you your *Robinson Crusoe* which I read through with great interest. I had finished reading the book and was about to return it when my cousin came to see me. Never having seen the book, she was so interested in it that I had to retain it longer. However, I hope that in view of the additional delight thus afforded by your book, you will overlook my negligence in not returning it sooner.

Thank you again for the loan.

Sincerely yours,

\*\*\*\*\*\*\*\*

5. 申请信

申请信的篇幅一般不超过一页,其语气必须诚恳。申请信的正文一般由三至四个段落组成,内容大致如下:

(1) 说明向某单位申请工作的理由;例如见广告应征,熟人介绍,本人专业与该单位业务对口等。

(2) 概括本人的经历和特长,表明自己能够胜任此项工作。

(3) 希望聘方积极考虑和尽早答复;按西方惯例,录用前,聘方对申请人进行面试(interview),因此,申请信经常以要求安排面试结尾。

我们来看一个申请任汉语教师的例子。

Dear Dr Smith:

Mr. Liu Yang who has just returned to China from your university informed me that you are considering the possibility of offering a Chinese language course to your students in the next academic year and may have an opening for a teacher of the Chinese language. I'm very much interested in such a position.

I have been teaching Chinese literature and composition at college level since 2000. In the past six years, I have worked in summer programs, teaching the Chinese language and culture to students from English speaking countries. As a result, I have got to know well the common problems of these students and how to adapt teaching to achieve the best results.

With years of intensive English training, I have no difficulty conducting classed in English and feel quite comfortable working with American students.

I will be available after July 2006. Please feel free to contact me if you wish more information. Thank you very much for your consideration and I look forward to hearing from you.

Sincerely yours,<br>Liu Wei

## Unit 20    Educational Evaluation

### ▲ Knowledge Objectives

When you have completed this unit, you will be able to:

• State the four key paradigms given by Alexander and Hedberg with their advantages and disadvantages

• Know the two online projects-WIER and SNS, and understand the conclusion by the clustered study of them

• Tell the conception of CAA, including how CAA is used and what subjects are suitable for CAA

• Understand the advantages and limitations of CAA

### ▲ Professional Terms

| | |
|---|---|
| objective-based | 基于目标的 |
| decision-based | 基于决策的 |
| value-based | 基于价值的 |
| naturalistic approach | 自然主义方法 |
| macro analysis | 综合分析 |
| cognitive model | 认知模型 |
| subjective empirical analysis | 主观实证分析 |
| comparative analysis | 比较分析 |
| project implementation | 项目执行 |
| Computer-assisted Assessment (CAA) | 计算机辅助评价 |
| optical mark readers (OMRs) | 光学标记阅读器 |
| Computer Aided Learning (CAL) | 计算机辅助学习 |
| self-assessment | 自我评估 |
| information technology (IT) | 信息技术 |

Text A

# Educational Evaluation[①]

## Models of Educational Evaluation

Alexander and Hedberg summarise the representative approaches used in educational research over the past 50 years and give the following four key paradigms with their perceived advantages and disadvantages:

★ *Objective-based*: Evaluation as a process of determining the degree to which educational objectives are being achieved. This follows the scientific tradition and is straightforward to apply, but does not take account of unintended outcomes, and takes no account of students as individuals with all their differences.

★ *Decision-based*: Focuses on the decisions made during development and improvements that could be made. It is useful for programs with a large scope or multiple levels, but needs the co-operation of decision makers. It has proved difficult to put into practice and expensive to maintain.

★ *Value-based*: Evaluation is not only concerned with goals, but also whether the goals are worth achieving. Formative and summative evaluation is used, and the evaluator considers major effects, achievements and consequences of the program. This acknowledges the importance of unintended outcomes, and learners' perceptions of the learning experience, and evaluation can be made without the need to know about the objectives. Its perceived disadvantages are that it may leave important questions unanswered.

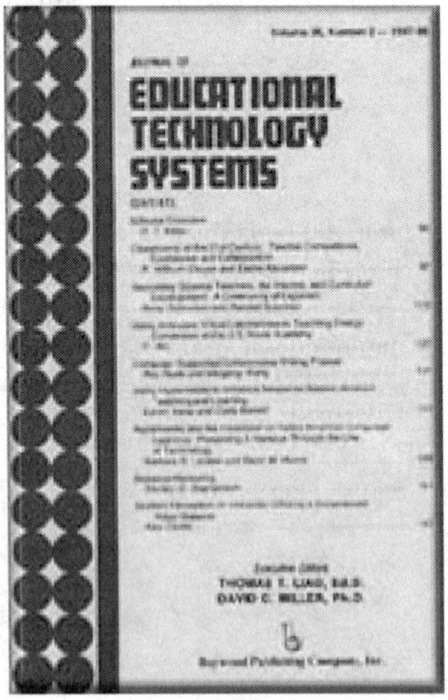

★ *Naturalistic approach*: organises evaluations around the participants' key concerns and issues. Uses qualitative data collection such as journals (Figure 20-1), observations and interview. The advantages are that it acknowledges context and can be used to benefit those being studied, but participants may identify criteria with little educational worth.

Using this classification scheme, Alexander and Hedberg compiled a macro analysis of the current role of evaluation by surveying papers submitted to two major practitioner conferences.[1] Of the 29 papers concerning technology-based learning projects: 9 undertook no proper evaluation, 5 were objectives based, 10 decisions based, 2 values based, and 3 were naturalistic. The classification scheme provided a useful basis for comparing and contrasting approaches, but the analysis

Figure 20-1 An example of journal as a qualitative data collection

---

① http://www2.wmin.ac.uk/hearnsh1/Thesis/ch4.htm

serves to demonstrate the lack of coherence in educational evaluation.

**Issues with Objective-based Research**

Objective positivist research has validity by its historical credentials within traditional science, but it has many critics within the world of educational research. There is much uncertainty about the educational environment: cognitive models, appropriate teaching methods, and learning in general. When so many factors cannot be readily measured, quantified, controlled, or regulated, there can be a tendency to de-contextualise the investigation. Laurillard states that it would be wrong to assume that objective de-contextualised results will transfer reliably back into the learning context. Additionally, objective evaluation often requires large control groups. The Open University is fortunate in having large numbers of students in a similar situation, and so their trials can be more objective, but findings cannot be assumed to transfer directly to a local environment.

Many have also seen positivist methods as being reductionist in the way it appears to explain life but is only based on a very narrow sub-set of mechanistic issues. [2] Parlett and Dearden warn against using "*botany*" suited objective evaluation as it is "*a paradigm for plants not people*". They say that because of some success in other areas it has established itself as "the model to be striven for", but that in educational environments "...the paradigm gives rise to research that cannot be done in practice." Because it is concerned with generalisations through aggregate data, it is insensitive to important individual variations, and in its attempt to control the mass of variables the tendency is to do away with useful factors for the reason that they cannot be controlled. "The natural tendency, then, is to make the best of it, to take and use the best available list of objectives as a sort of lowest common denominator." Evaluation is restricted by preconceived ideas of outcomes, which stifle formative change and cannot harness unintended outcomes. Because it tries to impose quantitative order "...the paradigm forces people to oversimplify almost to the point of rendering the data meaningless." Alexander and Hedberg observed similar outcomes from their study: "Evaluations of technology-based programs have tended to adopt the more simplistic and deterministic models."

Because of the difficulties in defending the use of objective methods, educational research has traditionally "borrowed" methods from social science and made use of subjective empirical analysis where a clear outline of the context and its implications are given. [3]

## Text B

## Evaluating Web-based Learning①
### —A Clustered Study of Two Online Projects

**Project Overview**

In this study, we investigated the interrelationship of implementation, pedagogical

---

① http://www.edu.yorku.ca/~rowston/aera99.html

perspectives and practices, and perceived outcomes in the case of two Canadian national telelearning projects based on different pedagogical models and delivery systems, one of which was judged by participating teachers to be more successfully implemented than the other.[4] By means of a comparative analysis of the two programs, we sought to determine what teacher and practice factors beyond training and support contributed to the relative success and failure of the two programs and to describe how these factors interacted with traditional implementation concerns.[5] Grounded in this analysis, a theoretical model of project implementation was then articulated and contrasted with other views of implementation.

Figure 20-2  An example of digital satellite and an example of digital satellite receiver

The two projects we studied were Writers in Electronic Residence (WIER) and the Satellite Networked Schools (SNS) project. WIER uses a Web-based conferencing system to link writing and language arts students to Canadian authors, teachers, and each other for the exchange and discussion of original work. WIER is a relatively large telelearning network by Canadian standards, involving the participation of up to 120 classes in any given year from all areas of the country and including students ranging from the junior elementary to the senior high school levels. It is also one of the few projects at a mature stage of development, having been in operation for over ten years now. The SNS project links three Canadian schools via digital satellite (Figure 20-2) to a commercial curriculum content provider headquartered in the United States. Although the SNS service was well established in many schools in the US at the time of the research, only three Canadian schools had been connected. We studied all three of these sites during their first and second years of implementing the service.

WIER has three primary learning objectives: 1) making use of computer and network media to enhance students' creative autonomy and to broaden the scope and shape of classroom experience; 2) helping students to (re)consider the value of revision in the writing process and the students' role in using language to interpret and understand as well as be understood; and 3) prompting these novice writers to revisit their creative efforts in the light of the ideas that they receive and generate in their conferencing interactions with both author-mentors and their peers. Students "post" drafts of creative works into forums which the assigned author reads and then responds to, posting back comments and suggestions for revision to the student (which others accessing the conference are free to read). Students also read and respond to work posted by other schools. WIER strongly encourages participating teachers to require every student who submits a composition to provide a written response to two other student works.

SNS is a curriculum resource delivery service that was purchased by the schools primarily with the goal of enhancing mathematics and science teaching and learning. The service provided teachers in these schools unlimited access to their collection of over 12000 videos indexed to the K-12 curriculum. Teachers interacted with company personnel via a two-way television channel to search out and select relevant videos. In addition, the company would develop "custom curriculum" upon a teacher's request, incorporating new or existing videos and live interaction with a subject specialist if desired. As part of its service, the company also provided a Web site, printed curriculum resources via a faxback service, and a selection of interactive software in CDI (Compact Disk Interactive) (Figure 20-3) format. To ensure that all elements of the service interoperated, the company sells a complete turnkey installation to schools, including a file server (Figure 20-4), networked computers with Internet connections, fax machines, digital satellite receivers and an antenna, TV monitors (Figure 20-5), and VCRs. (Figure 20-6)

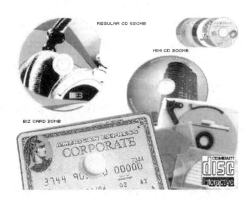

Figure 20-3   Examples of compact Disk Interactive for storing valuable data

Figure 20-4   An example of a file server. You don't only store files on it, but also share files throughout the network.

Figure 20-5   An example of TV Monitor to show videos

Figure 20-6   An example of Camcorder

## Methodology

In order to investigate teachers' experiences in the WIER and SNS programs and to collect their reflections on program implementation and its effects, interviews were conducted with staff directly participating in the programs. For WIER, we interviewed teachers using the program in eleven participating schools across Canada. These teachers had recently completed or were completing twelve weeks of WIER activities with at least one class in either Creative Writing or Language Arts. (The normal duration of a WIER project is twelve weeks, however schools may elect to participate in many projects.) In the case of the SNS program, we conducted preliminary interviews at each of the three schools at the beginning of the project and returned a year later to interview the teachers on their experiences during the intervening period. A total of 38 partially structured interviews were conducted. All interviews for both programs were audiotaped and transcribed.

A qualitative coding and analysis of the transcripts suggested that at the end of two years the SNS project was perceived by most teachers to be only a very limited success. This was especially true at the two high school sites. On the other hand, WIER was roundly praised by teachers as being a very successful online experience. The apparent success or failure of a program is a function of many factors; however, this study focused on the teacher-related dimensions that determine the success of an online program. We found that the SNS and WIER programs could be differentiated on two factors related to teachers beyond training and support. These factors were (1) the teachers' perceptions of the value of the program, and (2) the congruence between the pedagogy implicit in the program and the teachers' own practices. Our conclusion was that these two aspects, together with training and support, played a significant role in determining the ultimate success and sustainability of the program.

**Discussion**

We began this research as two separate studies of teacher practices at approximately the same time. Each study was multisite study as we looked at implementation of the projects at several schools. Originally there was no connection between the WIER and SNS projects other than the fact that the same researchers were working on both projects. It became apparent fairly early on that SNS was not proceeding particularly well in its implementation. Therefore, we felt that more could be learned by comparing SNS to WIER, as this project was proceeding well, rather than continuing to study SNS on its own. Now that the project is completed, I am convinced of the wisdom of that decision as we would not have been able to otherwise develop our understanding of the interaction between teacher training and support, perceptions of value, and pedagogical congruence.

Our experience with the WIER/SNS project supports Kozma and Quellmalz's position on the value of clustering network-based project for evaluation. By clustering projects with generally similar goals, the evaluator can make use of common instruments and data collection procedures, and can aggregate the projects for most analyses and interpretations. Kozma and Quellmalz see "cluster evaluation," not only as a cost-effective method of evaluating several projects simultaneous, but as a way to promote sharing of information among the projects' stakeholders to improve performance and effectiveness. A further advantage he suggests is that clustering will encourage the development of communities of practice "that can share effective project strategies and lessons learned."

## Text C

### Computer-assisted Assessment (CAA)[①]

**What is CAA?**

Computer-assisted assessment (CAA) refers to the use of computers in assessment. The term encompasses the use of computers to deliver, mark and analyze assignments or examinations. It also includes the collation and analysis of data gathered from optical mark readers (OMRs). (Figure 20-7)

Figure 20-7  Optical mark readers(OMR) can realize the reading of the presence or absence of a pencil or similar mark at various locations on a sheet of paper.

**What is the difference between CAA and CAL?**

CAL stands for Computer Aided Learning and refers to teaching and learning content material delivered by computers. CAA refers specifically to assessment, but elements of CAA may be included within CAL packages.

**How is CAA used?**

The following are the three main types of assessments for which CAA is used:

★ *Diagnostic*—tests which are taken to determine a student's prior knowledge of a subject.

★ *Self-assessment*—tests which are taken by students to check their understanding of particular concepts and terminology.

★ *Formative*—assessments which assist learning by giving feedback which indicates how the student is progressing in terms of knowledge, skills and understanding of a subject.[6] In CAA, this often takes the form of objective questions with feedback given to the student either during or immediately after the assessment. Formative assessment may be monitored by the tutor, used purely for self-assessment or used to contribute marks to a module grade.

★ *Summative*—assessments where the primary purpose is to give a quantitative grading and make a judgment about the student's achievement in a particular area. Summative assessment can include marked coursework as well as end of module examinations and can incorpo-

---

① http://www.caacentre.ac.uk/resources/faqs/fqgen.shtml

rate feedback to the student.

**What are some of the advantages of CAA?**

☆ **Pedagogic advantages**:

- Lecturers can monitor the progress of students through more frequent assessments.
- Students can monitor their own progress; self-assessment can be promoted.
- Detailed, specific feedback is available to students during and immediately after a test.
- A wide range of topics within a body of knowledge can be tested very quickly.
- Students acquire information technology (IT) (Figure 20-8) skills (CBA only).
- More frequent assessment of students is made possible by the automatic marking of scripts.
- Potential to introduce graphics and multimedia allows for inclusion of questions not possible with paper assessments. (CBA only)
- Quality can be monitored by looking at the facility and discrimination of questions and tests.

Figure 20-8  Information technology is "the study, design, development, implementation, support or management of computer-based information systems, particularly software applications and computer hardware."

- Formative assessments can be repeated as frequently as desired to aid student learning.
- Adaptive testing can be used to match the test to the student's ability.
- Students can be provided with clues and marked accordingly.

☆ **Administrative advantages**:

- Marking is not prone to human error.
- Computerized marking of tests saves staff time.
- Large groups can be assessed quickly.
- Diagnostic reports and analyses can be generated.
- Aids with the transmission and administration of marks which can be automatically entered into information management systems and student records databases.
- Can reduce cheating through the randomization of questions.
- Eliminates the need for double marking.

**What are some of the limitations of CAA?**

a) Construction of good objective tests requires skill and practice and so is initially time-consuming.

b) Because of the above, testing of higher order skills is difficult.

c) Implementation of a CAA system can be costly and time-consuming.

d) Hardware and software must be carefully monitored to avoid failure during examinations.

e) Students require adequate IT skills and experience of the assessment type.

f) Assessors and invigilators need training in assessment design, IT skills and examinations management.

g) A high level of organization is required across all parties involved in assessment (academics, support staff, computer services, quality assurance unit, and administrators.)

**What subjects are suitable for CAA?**

The 1999 CAA Centre survey into the use of CAA has compiled statistics on the number of CAA tests found in different subject areas. The results show that nearly every academic discipline registered some CAA activity.

Those subject areas with the highest numbers of CAA tests were computing/IT, biomedical science (Figure 20-9), geological science, mathematics, engineering (Figure 20-10), other sciences (chemistry, physics), modern languages, business and accountancy.

Figure 20-9  Biomedical Informatics is the scientific field that deals with the storage, retrieval, sharing, and optimal use of biomedical information, data, and knowledge for problem solving and decision making.

Figure 20-10  Engineering, manufacturing and construction of large industrial gas plants

These results are consistent with the findings of the 1995 national study of CAA conducted by Derek Stephens and Janine Mascia of Loughborough University. Although there is a bias towards science and technology subjects, there are increasing examples of the use of CAA in other disciplines. These include the following recent CAA work in humanities:

• Poetica is a project which delivers CAA to students taking a first year poetry module at the University of Sunderland.

• "Web + Qmark + Humanities" by Chris Hopkins is a case study published in *Computers and Texts* 16 which details the introduction of CAA into a first year module called "Modernity and Modernisation" offered by the Cultural Studies department at Sheffield Hallam University.

## New Words

paradigm   *n.* 1. (一词的)词形变化表 2. 范例;样式;模范

unintended   *adj.* 非故意的,无意识的

classification scheme　分类表
practitioner　*n.* 1. 习艺者,实习者 2. 从业者(尤指医师)
positivist　*n.* 实证哲学家,实证主义者
credential　*n.* 外交使节所递的国书,信任状
contextualise　*vt.* 将(词语等)置于上下文中研究
reductionist　*n.* 还原论者,化约主义,化约论者,化约主义者 *adj.* 化约主义的
sub-set　*n.* 子集
botany　*n.* 植物学
generalisation　*n.* 一般化,普通化,归纳,概论
aggregate　*n.*〈正〉数,总计 *vt.* 总计达…… *vt. & vi.* (使)聚集
lowest common denominator　*n.* 最小公分母
preconceived idea　先入之见,成见
stifle　*vt. & vi.* (使)窒息;(使)窒闷 *vt.* 镇压;遏制
render　*vt.* 1. 报答;归还;给予 2. 呈递;提供;开出 3. 演出;扮演;演奏 4. 翻译 5. 使;致使
deterministic　*adj.* 确定性的
empirical　*adj.* 以观察或实验为依据的
clustered　*adj.* 1. 丛生的;群集的 2. (柱子、圆柱、门柱等)簇柱
implementation　*n.* 执行
autonomy　*n.* 自治,自治权
mentor　*n.* (无经验之人的)有经验可信赖的顾问
faxback　自动传真回复,回函传真
turnkey　*adj.* 可立即投入使用的
congruence　*n.* 适合,一致,叠合,全等,相合性
sustainability　*n.* 可持续性,永续性,持续能力
cost-effective　*adj.* 有成本效益的,划算的
module　*n.* 1. 单元,单位 2. (宇宙飞船上各个独立的)舱
Qmark　产品标志
modernisation　*n.* 现代化

## Notes

[1] Using this classification scheme, Alexander and Hedberg compiled a macro analysis of the current role of evaluation by surveying papers submitted to two major practitioner conferences.

**译文**:借助这种分类方法,Alexander 和 Hedberg 通过对投递到两大重要从业者会议的论文进行调查,从而对总体性地分析评价之当今角色的论文加以了编辑。

- Using this classification scheme 是现在分词引导的方式状语从句。

◆ submitted to two major practitioner conferences 是过去分词做后置定语,用来修饰限定 papers。
◆ macro analysis 总体分析
◆ submit to 向……呈交(递送)……

[2] Many have also seen positivist methods as being reductionist in the way it appears to explain life but is only based on a very narrow sub-set of mechanistic issues.

**译文:**许多人也认为实证主义方法是一种简约主义,从某种程度上来说,它似乎是在解释生活,但它只是建立在机械论的一个狭小的子集之上的。

◆ see...as 看作,把什么看作,在这里,as 后面引导的是方式状语从句。
◆ in a way 在某种程度上
◆ it appears to explain life but is only based on a very narrow sub-set of mechanistic issues 是定语从句,用来修饰限定先行词 way。
◆ but is only based on a very narrow sub-set of mechanistic issues 这里 but 后面省略了主语 it,与前一个 it 一样,都是指代 positivist method。

[3] Because of the difficulties in defending the use of objective methods, educational research has traditionally "borrowed" methods from social science and made use of subjective empirical analysis where a clear outline of the context and its implications are given.

**译文:**由于很难为使用客观方法这一做法进行辩护,因此教育研究按惯例向社会科学借鉴了一些方法,并且使用了主观经验分析,即给出了语境的清晰轮廓及含义。

◆ difficulty in doing sth. 是固定搭配,表示做某事有困难。
◆ where a clear outline of the context and its implications are given 是由 where 引导的地点状语从句。
◆ subjective empirical analysis 主观经验分析

[4] In this study, we investigated the interrelationship of implementation, pedagogical perspectives and practices, and perceived outcomes in the case of two Canadian national telelearning projects based on different pedagogical models and delivery systems, one of which was judged by participating teachers to be more successfully implemented than the other.

**译文:**在此研究中,我们探寻了实施、教育学视角与实践这三者间的相互关系,并就两个加拿大国家远程学习项目这个例子来观察所探寻的结果,这两个项目立基于不同的教学模型和传输系统,其中一个项目由参与的老师来判断,因此比另一个项目更能被成功地实施。

◆ in the case of 至于……,就……来说
◆ based on different pedagogical models and delivery systems 是过去分词作后置定语,用来修饰先行词 projects。
◆ one of which was judged by participating teachers to be more successfully implemented than the other 是由 which 引导的非限制性定语从句,也是用来修饰先行词 projects。

[5] By means of a comparative analysis of the two programs, we sought to determine what teacher and practice factors beyond training and support contributed to the relative success

and failure of the two programs and to describe how these factors interacted with traditional implementation concerns.

**译文**：通过对两个项目的比较分析，我们试图去确定在没有培训和支持的情况下，什么样的教师和实施因素能够促进两个项目的相对成功和失败，并且能够描述这些因素是怎样与传统方式执行时所关注事物相互作用的。

- by means of 用，依靠
- seek to *vt.* 请求，征求；求教 *vi.* 企图；试图
- what teacher and practice factors beyond training and support contributed to the relative success and failure of the two programs 作为 determine 的宾语从句，其中，contributed to the relative success and failure of the two programs 是过去分词引导的定语从句，用来解释说明 factors。
- how these factors interacted with traditional implementation concerns 作为先行词 describe 的宾语从句。

[6] *Formative*—assessments which assist learning by giving feedback which indicates how the student is progressing in terms of knowledge, skills and understanding of a subject.

**译文**：形成性评价通过给予反馈来帮助学习，其中这些反馈表明学生在知识、技能和对课题的理解这些方面取得了多大的进展。

- which assist learning by giving feedback 是定语从句，用来修饰限定先行词 *Formative*—assessments。
- which indicates how the student is progressing in terms of knowledge, skills and understanding of a subject. 是定语从句，用来修饰限定先行词 feedback，其中，how 后面引导的从句是宾语从句。
- in terms of 就……而言，从……方面说来

## Selected Translation

## Text A

### 教育评价

**教育评价的模型**

Alexander 和 Hedberg 在 1994 年总结了过去 50 年里教育研究的代表性方法，并且给出了如下四种关键模型，并且他们认为，每种模型都有其优点和缺点：

★基于目标的模型：评价是决定教育目标被实现程度的进程。它遵循科学传统，并且能被直接运用，但是它并没有考虑这种模型会产生的意想不到的后果，也没有考虑学生作为个体有许多不同之处。

★基于决策的模型：致力于在发展和改进的过程中做出决策。这对于大规模或多层次的项目是有用的，但需要决策者的合作。另外，这种模型很难实施，维护起来也昂贵。

★基于价值的模型：评价并不只关心目标，还关心这些目标是否值得实现。评估员不仅使用形成性评价和总结性评价，还考虑项目的主要影响、成就和后果。这种模型承

认这种意想不到的后果的重要性和学习者对于学习经验的认知,而且不需要知道目标就能做出评价。不过这种模型的缺点是它可能会遗漏重要的问题。

★自然主义方法:它围绕参与者的主要关注点和重要问题来组织评价。它使用定性资料,例如期刊、观察数据和采访。优点就是它承认学习的环境并可以使那些被研究的人获益,但是参与者几乎不可能将这种标准与教育价值相等同。

借助这种分类方法,Alexander 和 Hedberg 通过对投递到两大重要从业者会议的论文进行调查,从而对总体性地分析评价之当今角色的论文加以了编辑。其中的 29 篇是关于基于技术的学习课题:9 篇没有采取合适的评价,5 篇是基于目标的评价,10 篇是基于决策的评价,2 篇是基于价值的评价,还有 3 篇是基于自然主义方法。这种分类为比较评价方法提供了有用的基础,但是其分析却显示出了教育评价缺乏一致性。

**与基于目标的研究相关的问题**

目标实证主义研究在传统科学里有着历史的证据,因此它是有效的,但在教育研究领域里它受到很多批评。教育环境中有很多不确定因素,总的来说,有认知模型、适当的教学方法还有学习。当这么多的因素不能被迅速地测量、确定其数量、控制或管理时,那么就有可能使科学研究去语境化。Laurillard 声明,想当然地认为目标去语境化的结果将可靠地转移到学习环境的做法是错误的。而且,目标性评价通常需要大规模的控制组。开放大学有幸拥有处在相似环境下的大批学生,因此他们的试验可以更客观,但是我们不能假定试验结果可以直接转移到本地环境下。

许多人也认为实证主义方法是一种简约主义,从某种程度上来说,它似乎是在解释生活,但它只是建立在机械论的一个狭小的子集之上的。Parlett 和 Dearden 告诫说,不要使用适应植物学的目标性评价,因为这种评价是"为植物而不是为人设计的模型"。他们认为,由于在其他领域的一些成功,适应植物学的目标性评价将自己确定为"有待人们奋斗的模型",但在教育环境,"……这种模型引起了一些不能在实践中实现的研究"。由于这种研究关心的是通过综合数据来进行归纳,因此它对重要的个别变化并不敏感,而且为了控制变数的数量,通常是去掉一些有用的因素,原因在于,它们不能够被控制。"那么,自然趋势就是充分利用数据,采用最容易得到的目标清单作为某种最小的公分母。"评价被结果的先入之见所限制,阻碍了形成性变化,并且不能利用这种意想不到的结果。因为它试图强加数量上的顺序,"……这种模型强迫人们过分简化数据以至达到毫无意义地解释数据的地步"。Alexander 和 Hedberg 从他们的研究中发现了相似的结果:"基于技术的项目的评价趋向于采取更简化的和更确定的模型。"

由于很难为使用客观方法这一做法进行辩护,因此教育研究按惯例向社会科学借鉴了一些方法,并且使用了主观经验分析,即给出了语境的清晰轮廓与含义。

## Exercises

**1. Please Explain the Following Professional Terms:**

a) naturalistic approach

b) macro analysis

c) cognitive model

d）subjective empirical analysis

e）computer-assisted assessment

f）information technology

**2. Short Answers：**

（1）What are the four key paradigms given by Alexander and Hedberg?

（2）What are the two online projects studied in Text B and what two factors could differentiate them related to teachers beyond training and support?

（3）What is the difference between CAA and CAL? And what are the limitations of CAA?

# 应用文写作之二——简历和求职信

## 一、简历

简历是我们打开人生之门的钥匙，现在社会的竞争日益激烈，在求职的过程中，简历的重要性不言而喻。

1. 英文简历的组成及常见的类型

（1）简历的组成部分和内容

简历是针对自己想应聘的工作来简要地列举求职意向、经验、个人情况等内容，以达到向雇主推销自己的目的，所以在简历中，应该突出自己的强项。一般来说，简历可以由以下几部分组成：

- 姓名、地址、电话（Name, Address, Telephone Number）
- 个人资料（Personal data）
- 求职目标和资格（Objective and Qualifications）
- 经历（Work Experience）
- 学历（Education）
- 著作/专利（Publications or Patents）
- 外语技能（Foreign Languages Skills）
- 特别技能（Special Skills）
- 课外活动/社会活动（Extracurricular Activities or Social Activities）
- 业余爱好/兴趣（Hobbies or interests）
- 证明材料（References）

以上各项不需要全部列举。一般而言，各项内容根据个人的具体情况或应聘的职位而定。

（2）常见的英文简历类型

个人简历没有固定的格式，应聘者可以根据个人情况，对简历的某些方面有所侧重。例如，对于即将毕业的学生或工作经验很短的人而言，简历可以以学历为主；对于工作经历丰富的人来说，工作经历和工作成绩是简历的亮点。按照简历的不同侧重点，我们把简历分为四类。

① 以学历为主的简历

以学历为主的简历的重点是学习经历,适合于即将毕业的学生或有很短工作经历的人。它一般包括以下几项内容:

- 个人资料
- 学历(Education):一般从最高学历写起,写出就读学校的名称、所获学位、所学专业、各阶段学习的起止时间、与应聘职位相关的课程以及成绩、所获得的奖励如奖学金、优秀学生称号等。
- 兼职
- 特别技能
- 兴趣爱好

② 以经历为主的简历

有工作经验的应聘人写简历时可以侧重自己的工作经历,把和应聘工作有关的经历和业绩写出来。此类简历主要包括以下几项内容:

- 个人资料
- 求职目标
- 工作经历(Work Experience):按照时间顺序列出所工作单位的名称、所负责的工作、工作业绩等,其中,工作的创新点和收获是可以重点写的内容。
- 特别技能

③ 以技能、业绩或工作性质为中心的简历

此类简历主要是强调应聘人的技能和工作业绩,即以所取得的成绩或所具备的技能等来概括工作经历,也就是说,把成绩和技能先行列出,不再是将工作经历按照时间顺序一一列出,工作经历在最后可简单地提及。

④ 综合性简历

这是以上第三种和第四种简历的综合,既要突出技能与业绩,也要把工作经历列出。

总之,简历的书写不能一概而论,可以根据自身的情况做出选择。

2. 英文简历常用词汇与句型

(1) 常用词汇

① 个人情况

Name 姓名  Sex 性别  Male 男  Female 女  height 身高  Birth 出生  Birth date 出生日期  Born 生于  Province 省  City 市  Street 街  Road 路  District 区  Citizenship 国籍  Address 地址  postal code 邮政编码  home phone 住宅电话

② 学历

Education 学历  Curriculum 课程  Major 主修,主课,专业  Minor 选修,辅修  Courses Taken 所学课程  Part-Time Job 业余工作、兼职  Professor 教授  Summer Jobs 暑期工作  Vacation 假期工作  Social Activities 社会活动  Rewards 奖励  Scholarship 奖学金  Semester 学期(美)  Term 学期(英)  President 校长  Vice-president 副校长  Abroad Student 留学生  Master 硕士  Department Chairman 系主任

Guest Professor 客座教授　Teaching Assistant 助教　Doctor 博士　Bachelor 学士

③ 经历

Achievements 业绩　Earn 获得，赚取　Cost 成本，费用　Effect 效果，作用　Direct 指导　Assist 辅助　Guide 指导，操纵　Accomplish 完成（任务等）　Create 创造　Launch 开办（新企业）　Lead 领导　Manage 管理，经营　Analyze 分析　Profit 利润　Manufacture 制造　Reinforce 加强　Spread 传播，扩大　Motivate 促动　Mastered 精通　Negotiate 谈判

④ 其他

Hobbies 业余爱好　Fishing 钓鱼　Boating 划船　Golf 高尔夫球　Oil painting 油画　Skiing 滑雪　Interests 兴趣、爱好　Skating 滑冰　Boxing 拳击　Writing 写作　Jogging 慢跑　Traveling 旅游　Dancing 跳舞　Cooking 烹饪　Collecting Stamps 集邮　Swimming 游泳

（2）实用句型举例

① 求职目标

• A responsible administrative position that will provide challenge where I can use my creativity and initiative.

负责行政事务的、具有挑战性的职位，能发挥创造力与开拓精神

• A position as an editor that will enable me to use my knowledge of editing.

能发挥所学编辑知识的编辑之职

• A position as a Chinese language instructor at college or university level.

大学汉语讲师之职

• Editor of a publishing company.

出版公司的编辑

• To apply my accounting experience in a position offering variety of assignments and challenges with opportunity of advance.

申请能提供各种机遇、挑战、提升机会以及能发挥本人在财会方面经验的职位

• Seeking a teaching position where my expertise in American literature will be employed.

能运用我在美国文学方面专业知识的教师职位

• To offer my training in business administration in a job leading to a position of senior executive.

能运用我在商业管理方面知识的职位，最终目标是高级主管

• To devote my talent in computer science as a computer engineer to a position with growth potential to a computer systems manager.

发挥我在电脑方面才能的电脑工程师之职，并有晋升为电脑系统部经理的机会

• To employ my professional training in the area of electronics engineering.

能运用我在电子方面专业知识的职位

• To begin as a system analyst and eventually become a technical controller.

## Part 7  The Evaluation of Educational Technology

从系统分析员开始,最终成为技术管理人员
- An administrative secretarial position where communication skills and a pleasant attitude toward people will be assets

寻求行政秘书之职位,它能让我用上交际技巧和与人为善这两种优势

② 学历及所学课程
- Major courses contributing to management qualifications:

对管理资格有帮助的主要课程:
- Among the pertinent courses I have taken are…

所学的有关课程是……
- Courses taken that will be useful for secretarial work:

所学的对秘书工作有用的课程:
- Academic preparation for electronics engineering:

电子工程方面的专业课程:
- Completed four years of technical training courses at college:

完成大学 4 年的技术培训课程:
- Specialized courses pertaining to foreign trade:

与外贸有关的专业课程:
- To fulfill the plan for continued study in the field of computer science, I have completed the following courses:

为完成在计算机方面的继续深造的计划,已完成以下课程:
- Following college graduation, I have taken courses in English at Beijing University as part of self-improvement program:

大学毕业后,作为进修计划的一部分,已完成北京大学的以下英语课程:

③ 经历
- Engineering sales specialist, responsible for petroleum sales and technical support to the industrial and commercial industries of the Boston metropolitan area.

工程销售专家,负责推销石油并向波士顿市区内工业及商业性工业提供技术援助。
- Sales manager. In addition to ordinary sales activities and management of department, responsible for recruiting and training of sales staff members.

销售部经理。除正常销售活动和部门管理之外,还负责招聘与训练销售人员。
- As a mechanical engineer, responsible for developing mechanical specifications, engineering analysis and design for selecting rotating equipment.

机械工程师,负责开发机械使用说明、工程分析,以及进行设计来选择旋转设备。
- Computer Programmer. Operate flow-charts, collect business information for management, update methods of operation.

电脑程序员。管理流程表,收集管理商务信息,掌握最新的操作方法。
- As a senior market researcher, responsible for collection and analysis of business information of interest to foreign business offices stationed in the Building.

高级市场研究员,负责收集和分析住在大厦内的外国商务办事处的商业信息。

3. 英文简历范例

已经有工作经验的人可以参考以下的范例:

(1) 电子工程师

BACKGROUND:

Over Eight years of extensive electronics experience. Versed in both digital and analog electronics with specific emphasis on computer hardware/software. Special expertise in designing embedded system. Proficient in VHDL and C# programming languages. Excellent in PCB.

WORK EXPERIENCE:

51-singlechip Systems, Shanghai, China, 1997—1999

Sales Engineer, 1999—2000

Responsible for the characterization and evaluation of, and approved vendors list for: Power supplies, oscillators, crystals, and programmable logic used in desktop and laptop computers. Evaluated and recommended quality components that increased product profitability. Interacted with vendors to resolve problems associated with components qualification. Technical advisor for Purchasing.

Design Evaluation Engineer, 2000—2003

Evaluated new computer product designs, solving environmental problems on prototype computers. Conducted systems analysis on new computer products to ensure hardware, software and mechanical design integrity.

Assistant Engineer, 2003—2005

Performed extensive hardware evaluation ion prototype computers, tested prototype units for timing violation using the latest state-of-the-art test equipment, digital oscilloscopes and logic analyzers. Performed environmental, ESD and acoustic testing. Designed and built a power-up test used to test prototype computers during cold boot.

EDUCATION:

Bachelor of Science in Electrical Engineering

—Peking University, 1997

Job descriptions:

Work that is related to the analyzing, designing and evaluation of the embedded system.

下面再来看一个应届毕业生的简历:

(2) 市场营销员

Chinese Name: Wei Zhang

English Name: Andy

Sex: Male

Born: 7/18/82

University: Tsinghua University

Major: Marketing

Address: 110#, Tsinghua University

Telephone: 1356＊＊＊＊321

Email: ＊＊＊＊@yahoo.com.cn

Job Objective:

A Position offering challenge and responsibility in the realm of consumer affairs or marketing.

Education:

2002—2006　Tsinghua University, College Of Commerce

Graduating in July with a B.S. degree in Marketing.

Fields of study include: psychology, economics, marketing, business law, statistics, calculus, sociology, product policy, social and managerial concepts in marketing, marketing strategies, consumer behavior, sales force management, marketing research and forecast.

1999—2002　The No.2 Middle School of Beijing.

Social Activities:

2000—2002　Class monitor.

2003—2005　Chairman of the Student Union.

Summer Jobs:

2004 Administrative Assistant in Sales Department of Beijing Samsung Company. Responsible for selling, correspondence, expense reports, record keeping, inventory catalog.

Hobbies:

Swimming, Internet-surfing, music, travel.

English Proficiency:

College English Test-Band Six.

Computer Skills:

Dream weaver, Flash, Adobe Photoshop, AutoCAD, Microsoft office, etc.

References will be furnished upon request.

## 二、求职信

### 1. 求职信的特点

求职信(application letter)属于商业信件,因此文体及格式要正式;语言要简洁、客观、明了;表达要准确;语气要客气。

(1) 正式的文体及格式

求职信的文体及格式要正式,这样才能表现出求职者的尊重和礼貌,也才能反映出求职者的性格和办事作风。如果求职信写得很随便,会让读信人认为求职者不重视此事或给人马马虎虎的感觉。

(2) 简洁、客观、明了的语言

求职人要以客观、实事求是的态度,运用简练的语言把事情表达清楚;要做到主题突出、层次分明、言简意赅。表达要直接,不可绕圈子。此外,不要提与主题不相关的事;在说明个人经历或能力时,要说出具体的业绩,不可笼统概括。

（3）准确的表达

表达不要模棱两可,不可过多使用形容词和副词。要避免生僻的词。对有疑问的词语,要多请教他人或词典。

（4）客气的语气

话语要礼貌,充满自信。既要表现出对对方的尊重,又不要表现出过分的热情或恭维。

2. 求职信的内容

一般来说,求职信包括以下四个方面的内容：(1)你得知这份工作的渠道。(2)学历及经历的概要。(3)你的个性以及能力。(4)联络地点、联络方式,以及最后的感谢语等。求职信可以发挥创意的空间非常大。求职信在于延续履历表的内容,更清楚地表现工作意向、个性、特质等。

3. 写英文求职信要点

（1）篇幅不宜过长,简短为好；态度诚恳,不需华丽词汇；让对方感觉亲切、自信、实在即可；不要误看其他错误的写作方法,以免耽误了你的求职机会。

（2）纸张的选用：建议你用灰色、黄褐色或米色纸作最终打印信纸,象牙色也是可以接受的；灰色或任何其他颜色的信纸因缺乏对比度最好不用。当然还应该注意配合信封的颜色。

（3）书写：字体要写得整洁可辨,使用打字机把信打出来。98%的求职信和简历都是用黑墨打印在白纸上的。

（4）附邮票：英语求职信内需附加邮票或回执信封。这会给别人的回信带来方便,而且也会让别人感受到你的真心。

（5）语法：准确无误的语法和拼写使读信人感到舒畅。错误的语法或拼写则十分明显,一目了然。且不可把收信人的姓名或公司地址拼错了。

（6）标点：正确地使用标点符号可以更好地表达自己的意愿。这里也有一些要注意的：

- 标题中除冠词(a, an, the)外每一个字都要大写,4个字母以下的介词(of, in)等不大写,第一个字始终要大写。

I have read *Gone With the Wind*.

- 书籍和杂志用斜体或下划线表示：

The Business Women

- 所有商标一律大写：

Coca-Cola  Wahaha

- 家庭成员的称呼在不用名字时大写：

When I have problems with my homework, I always turn to Brother.

I cried, "Father, help me!"

- 带名字称呼其他亲属时要大写：

My Aunt Kate had promised, but she didn't make it.

My aunt and cousin had promised, but they didn't make it.

（7）数字：数字的使用也有一定的规则，正确使用它们也是非常重要的。

- 从 1 到 10 的数字需拼出；11 以上都是多音节词，需用阿拉伯数字。如果把 120 写成 one hundred and twenty,读起来就不方便。
- 数字出现在句子开头时必须拼出：Twenty years is the term contained in the contract.
- 数字组合以及数字和词组合在一起使用时需用连字符。

150-ton goods/56-miles from the harbor/thirty-two years ago

- 如果一句中有一个数字在 10 以下，另一个大于 10，按规则都用数字。

I asked for 6 Yuan, but Father gave me 16.

（8）引号

引号成对使用，一半在引语之前，一半在引号之后。至于在使用引语时逗号和句号的位置，只要掌握下面的规则即可：所有的逗号和句号都在引号内（注意逗号和其他标点符号在引语前的用法）；而冒号和分号始终在引号之外。

He said in a low voice,"How much time left to us?" and was told,"Don't worry! We still have plenty of time."

"We will call you back"; this phrase is popular with interviewers.

（9）问号根据句子的结构可以放在引号之内或引号之外。

Where can we find the "real romance"?

My teacher asked me,"Have you finished your homework?"

（10）缩写词

缩写词是几个词的缩写，使用缩写词能节约篇幅和代替一个完整的词。省略的规则是在被省略的词后面加下圆点。例如：Dr. , A. M. , P. M. 等等。

有些省略语是我们熟知的，我们已经不再用他们的全称了，而更多的是使用缩略语，例如：我们常说 B. A. 而不说 Bachelor of Arts, 常说 M. B. A. 而不说 Master of Business Administration。

4. 求职信常用句型

（1）开头句型

- My interest in the position of Sales Manager has prompted me to forward my resume for your review and consideration.
- The sales Manager position advertised in *China Daily* on July 12 intrigues me. I believe you will find me well-qualified.
- With my thorough educational training in accounting, I wish to apply for an entry-level accounting position.
- Your advertisement for a network support engineer in *China Daily* has interested me very much. I think I can fill the vacancy.
- Attention of Human Resource Manager: Like many other young men, I am looking for a position. I want to get started. At the bottom, perhaps, but started.

- I am very glad that you are recruiting a programmer! I hope to offer my services.
- I am very delighted to know that you have an opening for an English teacher in Beijing Evening News.
- I am forwarding my resume in regard to the opening we discussed in your Marketing Department.
- I want a job. Not any job with any company, but a particular job with your company. Here are my reasons: Your organization is more than just a company. It is an institution in the minds of the Chinese public.

（2）说明经历的句型
- Since my graduation from Beijing Foreign Studies University 6 years ago, I have been employed as an interpreter in a foreign trade company.
- My three years of continuous experience in electrical engineering has taught me how to deal with all the phases of the business I am in right now.
- As the executive manager assistant of LingDa(China) Investment Co., Ltd, I have had a very extensive training in my field.

（3）说明教育程度的句型
- I have a PhD from Beijing University of Aeronautics and Astronautics in electronics engineering and was employed by Samsung Computer for 4 years.
- I received my Mater's degree in Chinese literature from Huazhong Normal University in 2000.
- I am a graduate student in the Chemistry Department of Beijing Normal University and will receive my Mater's degree in March this year.
- My studies have given me the foundation of knowledge from which to learn the practical side of international trade.
- My outstanding record at school and some experience in business have prepared me for the tasks in the work you are calling for.
- I have a good command of two foreign languages: English and Japanese.
- I am quite proficient in three computer languages: BASIC, C#, .Net.
- I can speak and write English very well and have worked as an interpreter for two years.

（4）说明薪金待遇的句型
- I should require that your factory provide me with an apartment.
- With regard to salary, I leave it to you to decide after experience of performance in the job.
- I should require a commencing salary of 5000 Yuan per month.
- My hope for welfare is to enjoy free medical care.
- The yearly salary I should ask for would be 100000 Yuan, with a bed in the school's dormitory.

- The monthly salary of 3800 Yuan will be acceptable if your company houses me.

（5）推荐自己的句型

- I am presently looking for a position where my experience will make a positive contribution to the start-up or continuing profitable operation of a business in which I am so well experienced.

- I am an innovative achiever. I feel that in nowadays society where competition is fierce, there is a need for a representative who can meet and beat the competition. I feel that I have all the necessary ingredients to contribute to the success of Any Corporation. All I need is a starting point.

- Your advertisement in the June 20th issue of *Lawyers Monthly* appeals to me. I feel that I have the qualifications necessary to effectively handle the responsibilities of Administrative Judge.

- My ten years employment at the LIDOO Company provides a wide range of administrative, financial and research support to the Chief Executive Officer. I have a strong aptitude for working with numbers and extensive experience with computer software applications.

- As you will note, I have twelve years of educational and media experience. I am proficient in the operation of a wide variety of photographic, video, and audio equipment. I am regularly responsible for processing, duplicating, and setting up slide presentations, as well as synchronized slide and audio presentations.

（6）结束语句型

- I should appreciate the privilege of an interview. I may be reached by letter at the address given above, or by telephone at 98675213.

- I feel that a personal meeting would give us the opportunity to discuss your short-and long-term objectives and my ability to direct your organization towards successfully achieving those goals.

- I should be glad to have a personal interview, and can present references if desired.

- Thank you for your consideration.

- I have enclosed a resume as well as a brief sample of my writing for your review. I look forward to meeting with you to discuss further how I could contribute to your organization.

- Thank you for your attention to this matter. I look forward to speaking with you.

- The enclosed resume describes my qualifications for the position advertised. I would welcome the opportunity to personally discuss my qualifications with you at your convenience.

- I would welcome the opportunity for a personal interview with you at your convenience.

5. 求职信范例

（1）软件工程师

Reading *Beijing Youth Daily* on the web yesterday, I was very impressed by an article on your company's contribution to the development of China's IT industry. I would like to offer my experience in computer science and am writing to inquire whether your company has any position available.

I will graduate in June from Tsinghua University of Science and Technology with a Bachelor's degree in computer's science. Courses taken include Programming, System Design and Analysis, Operating System, .NET, etc. In addition, I have experience with programming as I have worked as a part-time programmer for almost two years in a software company. I have passed College English Test Band 6 and got a score of 650 in TOFEL.

Working in a company like yours would be a great way to expand my skills and contribute something to the development of computer science. If there is a position available in your company, I do hope that you will consider me. Enclosed is a copy of my resume. I will appreciate if you could give me an opportunity of a personal interview at your convenience. In any event, thank you very much for your time.

Yours sincerely,<br>Wang Lei

(2) 电脑工程师

Dear Sir or Madam,

In reply to your advertisement in today's 51 Job, I am respectfully offering my service as an engineer for your company. My college educational background and work experience in the field of IT industry have prepared me for the task in the work you are calling for.

I have worked as a computer programmer in HuaWei Company for three years, during which I become more and more expert in programming. I developed a sales and management software and won a prize for The Administration of Hotel system software. I am diligent worker and a fast learner and really interested in coping with difficulties in computer science.

However, in order to get a more challenging opportunity, I'd like to fill the opening offered in your company, which I am sure will fully utilize my capability. With regard to salary, I leave it to you to decide after experience of my performance in the job.

I would appreciate it if we could set an appointment so you can get to know me better. Thank you for your kind attention. I hope to hear from you.

Yours sincerely,<br>Zhang Wei

# 北京大学出版社
## 教育出版中心 精品图书

### 21世纪教育技术学精品教材（张景中 主编）
| 书名 | 作者 | 价格 |
|---|---|---|
| 教育技术学导论 | 李芒 金林 编著 | 26元 |
| 远程教育原理与技术 | 王继新 张屹 编著 | 41元 |
| 教学系统设计理论与实践 | 杨九民 梁林梅 编著 | 29元 |
| 信息技术教学论 | 雷体南 叶良明 主编 | 29元 |
| 网络教育资源设计与开发 | 刘清堂 王忠华 李书明 主编 | 30元 |

### 21世纪教育科学系列教材
| 书名 | 作者 | 价格 |
|---|---|---|
| 教育心理学 | 李晓东 主编 | 34元 |
| 心理与教育测量 | 顾海根 主编 | 28元 |
| 教育计量学 | 岳昌君 主编 | 26元 |
| 现代教育评价教程 | 吴钢 著 | 32元 |
| 现代教学论基础 | 徐继存 赵昌木 主编 | 35元 |
| 教育技术定义与评析 | [美] 艾伦·贾纳斯泽乌斯基 迈克尔·莫伦达 主编 | 39元 |

### 21世纪信息传播专业英语系列教材
| 书名 | 作者 | 价格 |
|---|---|---|
| 教育技术学专业英语 | 吴军其 严莉 主编 | 32元 |

### 21世纪教师教育系列教材
| 书名 | 作者 | 价格 |
|---|---|---|
| 课堂教学艺术 | 孙菊如 等 | 22元 |
| 新时期教师职业道德与专业化发展 | 孙菊如 等 | 19元 |
| 教师教育技术一级培训教材（配光盘） | 刑磊 主编 | 20元 |

### 21世纪教师教育系列教材·教师教育金钥匙丛书
| 书名 | 作者 | 价格 |
|---|---|---|
| 教研活动概论 | 雷树福 主编 | 45元 |
| 教学研究概论 | 冷泽兵 著 | |
| 高校辅导员工作理论与实践 | 王小红 著 | |
| 中小学班主任培训理论与实践 | 罗琼英 主编 | |
| 班级教育与班级管理 | 杜学元 主编 | |
| 教育心理学的经典理论及运用 | 洪显利 主编 | |

### 21世纪引进版精品教材·学术道德与学术规范系列
| 书名 | 作者 | 价格 |
|---|---|---|
| 如何为学术刊物撰稿：写作技能与规范（英文影印版） | [英] 罗薇娜·莫 编著 | 26元 |
| 如何撰写和发表科技论文（英文影印版） | [美] 罗伯特·戴 等著 | 28元 |
| 如何撰写与发表社会科学论文：国际刊物指南 | 蔡今忠 | 25元 |
| 如何查找文献 | [英] 萨莉拉·姆齐 | 25元 |
| 给研究生的学术建议 | [英] 戈登·鲁格 等著 | 26元 |
| 学术道德学生读本 | [英] 保罗·奥利弗 著 | 17元 |
| 科技论文写作快速入门 | [瑞典] 比约·古斯塔维 著 | 20元 |
| 社会科学研究的基本规则 | [英] 朱迪斯·贝尔 著 | 18元 |
| 做好社会研究的10个关键 | [英] 马丁·丹斯考姆 著 | 20元 |
| 阅读、写作和推理：学生指导手册 | [英] 加文·费尔贝恩 著 | 25元 |
| 如何写好科研项目申请书 | [美] 安德鲁·弗里德兰德 等著 | 25元 |

### 21世纪引进版精品教材·研究方法系列
| 书名 | 作者 | 价格 |
|---|---|---|
| 教育研究方法：实用指南 | [美] 乔伊斯·高尔 等 | 78元 |
| 高等教育研究：进展与方法 | [英] 马尔科姆·泰特 | 25元 |
| 社会研究：问题方法与过程（第三版） | [英] 迪姆·梅 | 32元 |

### 大学教师通识教育读本（教学之道丛书）
| 书名 | 作者 | 价格 |
|---|---|---|
| 如何成为卓越的大学教师 | 肯·贝恩 | 24元 |
| 给大学新教员的建议 | 罗伯特·博伊斯 | 28元 |
| 理解教与学：高校教学策略 | [英] 迈克尔·普洛瑟 等著 | 26元 |
| 规则与潜规则：学术界的生存智慧 | [美] 约翰·达利 等主编 | 28元 |
| 给研究生导师的建议 | [英] 萨拉·德拉蒙特 等著 | 26元 |

### 科学素养文库·科学元典丛书（国家"十一五"重点图书出版规划）
| 书名 | 作者 | 价格 |
|---|---|---|
| 天体运行论 | [波兰] 哥白尼 著 | 39元 |
| 化学哲学新体系 | [英] 道尔顿 著 | 39元 |
| 自然哲学之数学原理 | [英] 牛顿 著 | 39元 |
| 化学基础论 | [法] 拉瓦锡 著 | 39元 |
| 笛卡儿几何 | [法] 笛卡儿 著 | 38元 |
| 心血运动论 | [英] 哈维 著 | 30元 |
| 热的解析理论 | [法] 傅立叶 著 | 39元 |
| 怀疑的化学家 | [英] 波义耳 著 | 36元 |
| 光学 | [英] 牛顿 著 | 35元 |
| 光论 | [荷兰] 惠更斯 著 | 35元 |
| 关于托勒密和哥白尼两大世界体系的对话 | [意] 伽利略 著 | 38元 |
| 基因论 | [美] 摩尔根 著 | 39元 |
| 海陆的起源 | [德] 魏格纳 著 | 34元 |
| 狭义与广义相对论浅说 | [美] 爱因斯坦 著 | 36元 |
| 薛定谔讲演录 | [奥地利] 薛定谔 著 | 34元 |
| 地质学原理 | [英] 莱伊尔 著 | 79元 |
| 物种起源 | [英] 达尔文 著 | 39元 |
| 从存在到演化 | [比利时] 普里戈金 著 | 32元 |
| 进化论与伦理学 | [英] 赫胥黎 著 | 38元 |
| 人类的由来及性选择 | [英] 达尔文 著 | 49元 |
| 人类和动物的表情 | [英] 达尔文 著 | 39元 |
| 希尔伯特几何基础 | [德] 希尔伯特 著 | 34元 |
| 条件反射 | [俄] 巴甫洛夫 著 | 46元 |
| 居里夫人文选 | [法] 玛丽·居里 著 | 36元 |

### 特别推荐（一）
| 书名 | 作者 | 价格 |
|---|---|---|
| 科学的旅程 | [美] 雷·斯潘根贝格 等著 | 69元 |
| 地理学思想史（第三版） | [法] 保罗·克拉瓦尔 著 | 39元 |
| 科研道德：倡导负责行为 | 美国科学院 | 28元 |
| 教育究竟是什么？100位思想家论教育 | [英] 乔伊·帕尔默 | 45元 |
| 小论文写作7堂必修课 | [美] 贝弗莉·安·秦 著 | 26元 |

| | | |
|---|---|---|
| 基因与人性 | 孔宪铎、王登峰 著 | 28元 |

高级迷信——学术左派及其关于科学的争论

    [美]格罗斯 等著　42元

| | | |
|---|---|---|
| 科学人文高级读本 | 任定成 主编 | 35元 |
| 科学·人文·社会 | 北京大学科学与社会研究中心编 | 35元 |

苏格拉底之道——最充分地运用你智慧的7把万能钥匙

    [美]罗纳德·格罗斯　26元

技术撬动战略——21世纪产业升级之路

    [澳]约翰·马修斯，[韩]赵东成 著　45元

## 科学与中国丛书（路甬祥主编）

| | |
|---|---|
| 科学与中国·院士专家巡讲团报告集（第一辑） | 29元 |
| 科学与中国·院士专家巡讲团报告集（第二辑） | 29元 |
| 科学与中国·院士专家巡讲团报告集（第三辑） | 29元 |
| 科学与中国·院士专家巡讲团报告集（第四辑） | 29元 |
| 科学与中国·院士专家巡讲团报告集（第五辑） | 29元 |
| 科学与中国·院士专家巡讲团报告集（第六辑） | 29元 |

## 新科学读本（珍藏版）（刘兵主编）

| | |
|---|---|
| 世上没有傻问题 | 25元 |
| 生命的颜色 | 25元 |
| 智慧的种子 | 25元 |
| 地球还会转多久 | 25元 |
| 绝妙的错误 | 25元 |
| 科学家不能做什么 | 25元 |
| 聆听大自然的呼吸 | 25元 |
| 科学是美丽的 | 25元 |

## 生命之旅丛书

| | | |
|---|---|---|
| 人心与人生 | 高新民 著 | 49元 |
| 西方死亡哲学 | 段德智 著 | 35元 |
| 死亡美学 | 陆扬 著 | 32元 |
| 死亡的尊严与生命的尊严 | 傅伟勋 著 | 25元 |

## 家庭教育丛书

| | | |
|---|---|---|
| 帮助孩子度过青春期 | [英]希拉·戴恩 著 | 19元 |
| 成为优秀父母的十大法则 | [美]劳伦斯·斯坦伯格 著 | 20元 |

## 后现代交锋丛书

| | | |
|---|---|---|
| 达尔文与主要主义 | [英]麦瑞尔·戴维斯 | 12.8元 |
| 爱因斯坦与大科学的诞生 | [英]彼得·科尔斯 | 12.8元 |
| 鲍德里亚与千禧年 | 克里斯托夫·霍洛克斯 | 12.8元 |
| 哈拉维与基因改良食品 | [英]乔治·迈尔逊 | 12.8元 |
| 麦克卢汉与虚拟实在 | [英]克里斯托夫·霍洛克斯 | 12.8元 |
| 库恩与科学战 | [英]蔡丁·沙达 | 12.8元 |

## 教育之思丛书

| | | |
|---|---|---|
| 文化传统与数学教育现代化 | 张维忠、王晓琴 | 20元 |

建设卓越学校：领导层·管理层·教师的职业发展（第2版）

    张延明 著　98元

| | | |
|---|---|---|
| 基础教育的战略思考 | 王炎斌 著 | 22元 |
| 教育凝眸 | 郭志明 | 16元 |
| 教育的痛和痒 | 赵宪宇 著 | 20元 |
| 教育思想的革命 | 张先华 著 | 15元 |
| 教育印痕 | 王淮龙等 主编 | 22元 |
| 教育印迹 | 王淮龙等 主编 | 18元 |

## 职业规划丛书

| | | |
|---|---|---|
| 全球高端行业求职案例 | 方伟 主编 | 28元 |
| 大学生职业生涯规划咨询案例教程 | 方伟 主编 | 28元 |

## 特别推荐（二）

| | | |
|---|---|---|
| 中国教育与人力资源发展报告 | 闵维方 主编 | 38元 |
| 透视美国教育 | 王定华 主编 | 42元 |
| 中小学管理文件选编 | 教育部基础教育一司 编 | 48元 |
| 大学情感教育读本 | 田玲 | 28元 |
| 大学科学教育改革与发展 | 王义首 | 32元 |
| 公务文件写作规范与文例分析 | 杨霞 | 40元 |
| 北大清华名师演讲录 | 两校名师讲堂编委会 | 36元 |
| 小学数学知识树 | 刘开云 等 | 28元 |
| 昆虫的故事 | [法]法布尔 著 | 16元 |
| 海底两万里 | [法]儒勒·凡尔纳 | 19元 |
| 环游世界80天 | [法]儒勒·凡尔纳 | 12.8元 |
| 爱的教育 | [意]德·亚米契斯 | 17.5元 |
| 化身博士·金银岛 | [英]史蒂文森 | 16.5元 |